ROBIN HOOD

THE UNKNOWN TEMPLAR

ROBIN HOOD

THE UNKNOWN TEMPLAR

John Paul Davis

Peter Owen
London and Chester Springs, PA, USA

PETER OWEN PUBLISHERS
73 Kenway Road, London SW5 oRE

Peter Owen books are distributed in the USA by
Dufour Editions Inc., Chester Springs, PA 19425-0007

This collection first published in Great Britain 2009 by
Peter Owen Publishers

Unless stated otherwise, all photographs are
from the author's collection.

ISBN 978-07206-1339-1

A catalogue record for this book is available
from the British Library

Printed and bound in Great Britain by
CPI Antony Rowe

ACKNOWLEDGEMENTS

When researching the ballads, I relied heavily on the collection compiled by Francis Child and to a lesser extent the earlier work by Joseph Ritson. Together, their superb collections provide some of the most important sources for this book. In addition, Thomas Ohlgren's *Medieval Outlaws* and *Robin Hood and Other Outlaw Tales,* edited by Ohlgren and Stephen Knight, provide an excellent guide to the ballads. When considering the earliest sources I am particularly indebted to the late D.E.R. Watt for his fantastic translation of *Scotichronicon*, Archibald Constable for his *Historia Majoris Britanniae* and many other authors now deceased for their useful translations of the Latin chronicles. Of the more modern sources, I would particularly like to acknowledge the work of Evelyn Lord and Malcolm Barber for their excellent books on the Knights Templar and also Karen Ralls, whose encyclopaedia has made available a wealth of historical information, some of which is not easy for the average historian to gain access to. While I am grateful to the authors of every book mentioned in the bibliography, the research and conclusions are my own.

When visiting various locations, such as those mentioned in the ballads, I have been fortunate to come across many helpful people who have gladly offered me information and support. In connection with these visits I am grateful to the local historians and clergy at the Church of St Mary Magdalene in Campsall, Yorkshire, for sharing their insights and making information available so readily. Similarly, at the Church of St Michael's and All Angels in Hathersage, Derbyshire, I would like to thank the clergy for making their local history available and for sharing their knowledge of Little John's grave. I should mention many helpful people associated with a number of locations that I have visited across the country that are connected with the Robin Hood legend, Simon de Montfort's rebellion and the Knights Templar. For their insights and, in some cases, permission to take photographs, I am indebted. In addition, I would like to thank the various librarians and institutions, including the Robin Hood Project, for answering numerous queries over the course of my research.

I extend my gratitude to all at Peter Owen Publishers and offer my heartfelt thanks to my copy-editor, James Ryan, for the sterling job he did in editing the book. My sincerest thanks go to Peter Owen himself for his enthusiasm and for agreeing to contract the book in its early stages.

On a personal note, I would like to thank my family and friends for their continuous support, particularly my brother and uncle, whose enthusiasm for the book has been strong throughout. Most importantly, I would like to thank my parents, whose encouragement and unfailing support has been invaluable – in particular my dad, Mike, whose excellent work on the images and constructive feedback has helped make the book what it is. For accompanying me on each of my journeys to take photographs and for contributing many of his own, I am truly grateful.

CONTENTS

List of Illustrations   9

Foreword   11

1   A Proud Outlaw   17

2   A Major History of Britain   31

3   Disinherited   47

4   Waichmen Were Commendit Gude   61

5   A Fellowship of Outlaws or
    an Outlawed Fellowship?   71

6   The Templars Versus the Bull   87

7   Into the Greenwood   101

8   To Rob from the Rich to Give to the Poor   117

9   A Hidden Divinity   135

10   Sir Robin of Locksley's Birth, Breeding,
    Valour and Marriage   151

11   Here Lies Bold Robin Hood?   173

12   True Tales of Robin Hood   193

Postscript   215

Notes and References   219

Bibliography   251

Index   263

ILLUSTRATIONS BETWEEN PAGES
144 AND 145

'Merry Robin Stops a Sorrowful Knight', 'Sir Richard
   Pleadeth Before the Prior of Emmet' and 'The Mighty Fight
   Betwixt Little John and the Cook' (from Howard Pyle's *The
   Merry Adventures of Robin Hood of Great Renown, in
   Nottinghamshire*, 1883)
Robin Hood (from Louis Rhead's *Bold Robin Hood and His
   Outlaw Band: Their Famous Exploits in Sherwood Forest*,
   1912)
Woodcut of John Major (from the title page of *In Petri Hyspani
   Summulas Commentaria*, 1505)
David, Earl of Huntingdon (from Sir Walter Scott's *The
   Talisman*, 1863)
King John signing the Magna Carta, Henry III and Edward I
   (from *Cassell's Illustrated History of England*, 1902)
Kenilworth Castle
A gathering of Knights Templar; Knights Templar on the battle-
   field (from nineteenth-century book illustrations)
The Church of St Mary Magdalene at Campsall, South Yorkshire
Map of West Yorkshire and North Yorkshire showing Knights
   Templar preceptories in the old West Riding
The Church of St Mary's at Temple Balsall, property of the
   Knights Templar until 1324
The Church of St Mary's at Edwinstowe, Nottinghamshire
The Church of St Mary's in Nottingham
Sherwood Forest in summertime
The Major Oak at Sherwood Forest, often celebrated as the
   former meeting place of the Merry Men

Barnsdale in summertime

Robin Hood's Well at Skellow, Yorkshire

Wentbridge, near the Sayles Plantation

'The Merry Friar Carrieth Robin Across the Water' (from Pyle)

Map of royal hunting forests (from Rhead)

Fountains Abbey

'Robin Hood Meeteth the Tall Stranger on the Bridge' and
    'Merry Robin Stops a Stranger in Scarlet' (from Pyle)

'Ye Sheriff of Nottingham' and 'Ye Proud Bishop of Hereford'
    (from Rhead)

Kirklees Priory gatehouse, where, according to *The Ballad of
    Robin Hood's Death*, Robin Hood was murdered (from
    Joseph Ritson's *Robin Hood*, 1887)

'Robin Shoots His Last Shaft' (from Rhead)

Robin Hood's grave, drawn by Nathaniel Johnston, 1665

Robin Hood relics at St Anne's Well (from R. Thoroton's
    Antiquities of Nottingham, 1797)

Drawing of a slab, bearing the letters L I, that supposedly once
    covered Little John's grave, now in the Church of St Michael's
    in Hathersage, Derbyshire

Little John's cottage at Hathersage

Presumed grave of Little John at the Church of St Michael's in
    Hathersage

Close-up of Little John's headstone

Supposed grave of Will Scarlock in the graveyard of St Mary's
    Church in Blidworth, Nottinghamshire

A collection of Templar crosses

Graves at the Church of St Mary's at Temple Balsall

Nottingham Castle gatehouse

Wall plaques and statues beneath Nottingham Castle by James
    Woodford, 1951, depicting Robin Hood and other characters

FOREWORD

Almost everyone believes they are familiar with the stories of Robin Hood. Celebrated throughout the world as a famous Saxon nobleman who roamed the forests of northern England with his band of Merry Men, robbing from the rich to give to the poor, living on the king's deer in defiance of his being outlawed by the tyrannical Prince John for displaying loyalty to the true king, he is held by many as a man of noble intention and a yearned-for ideal set against oppressive and unjust authority. Sentimentally this is a fair assessment of one of the greatest heroes of English legend. For over six centuries people have enjoyed the tales of this 'good' outlaw, and even in the twenty-first century his stories are continuing to evolve. Affection for his courageous and upright character, demonstrated in every ballad ever told of Robin Hood, remains as great now as it ever has been.

Although he is commonly viewed as a man who possessed integrity and generosity out of keeping with his time, history has been somewhat less revealing of his true identity. Over the centuries what began as a collection of ballads and rhymes about a group of outlaws in the forests of England has developed into something far greater. Years of retelling the stories have led to their being distorted, as traces of history have become merged with creations of the late Middle Ages and the modern era. The past century in particular has seen a noticeable change in the way Robin Hood appears to the world. Although his story lacks consistency, repetition and wide-scale exposure through television and other media have developed enormous awareness and interest. He has become a highly marketable and familiar cult figure, even though the character that is presented to the children and adults of the modern day would have seemed completely out of place to those in the Middle Ages.

The main aspects of the story are known to almost everyone. As it usually begins, the famous nobleman Sir Robert of Locksley, often referred to as the Earl of Huntingdon, returns home from fighting alongside Richard the Lionheart in the Crusades to find that his lands have been confiscated. As a Saxon of noble birth, Locksley finds himself in opposition to the king's brother, Prince John, who is seeking to establish his position as ruler in Richard's absence. The corrupt rule of the Norman usurper gives rise to an epic feud between Robin's Saxon rebels and the prince, supported by Sir Guy of Gisborne and the Sheriff of Nottingham.

With his lands confiscated and his loyalty to King Richard made clear, Robin takes to Sherwood Forest where he comes across a group of 'merry' outlaws whom he moulds into a band of formidable soldiers intent on providing stiff opposition to the Norman authority. Robin's role as a leader of peasant revolt becomes legendary as he opposes the corrupt rule of the Normans in protection of the common people. By killing the supporters of the prince and stealing from them to give to the poor, he becomes celebrated as a noble outlaw as well as an outlawed noble. In these stories he embarks on numerous adventures, fighting Normans, winning archery competitions, sparring with other outlaws such as Little John, who later join his band of Merry Men, and, of course, in defeating the Normans he rescues the heroine of the tales, the lovely Maid Marian.

This all seems very familiar. Yet even since the mid-1980s new facets of the legend have arisen, and historically this poses a problem. It is difficult enough searching for a possible historical origin for someone who has remained elusive for over six hundred years, but in the case of Robin Hood any historical validity has become inextricably intertwined with legend, and fact has been overwhelmed by fiction. As time has passed, new stories have been created, various characters have been added and parts of the legend have become largely unrecognizable. What remains constant is the enduring legend of the 'good' outlaw. And what also linger are the questions about who he was, where he operated and when he existed – if, indeed, he existed at all.

The legend of Robin Hood has become a hotchpotch. Like the equally legendary King Arthur, he is viewed as an iconic metaphor rather than a historical person. Various attempts have been made over the years to uncover a historical figure who fits the legend, but the results have been somewhat mixed. As a result, many people have doubted his existence, choosing instead to explain his creation as a work of fiction loosely based on real-life outlaws such as Eustache the Monk, Hereward the Wake and Fulk FitzWarin or on ancient woodland mythology. Every theory about Robin Hood's identity has its advocates, yet its authenticity is still disputed. Over the past two centuries there has also been a tendency to link his identity to men with similar names. This has also provoked criticism, not least because some of the links have proved to be based on unsubstantiated assumptions or, in the case of the famous Robert Fitz Ooth, a complete forgery.

This book is primarily about history. Legend has undoubtedly manipulated history and produced mutilated and often comical results, yet the early ballads insisted that Robin Hood was real. The famous ballad *A Gest of Robyn Hode* begins by asserting that Robin was a historical figure who 'walked on ground', and proof of his existence is offered in many important historical chronicles from the Middle Ages, although they often contradict one another. In a sense every Robin Hood book contradicts those that have gone before it, and the tales of the outlaws are themselves quite ambiguous. In keeping with its historical purpose, the content of this book focuses largely on the early ballads and chronicles rather than popular tradition. It concentrates on the rough-and-ready outlaw of the early ballads. However, it is not intended for historians alone, nor is it a rigorous investigation of the ballads, as carried out by Knight and Ohlgren; rather, it examines them for clues to a possible history. The question remains whether the ballads are fictitious or historical, and a definitive answer for this will probably never be found. The ballads cannot be regarded unquestionably as fact, but if Robin Hood did exist it seems most likely that they were based on events in his life. The various chapters of this book also examine the historical references to Robin Hood's life as depicted in the chronicles, including claims that he lived during the reign of either Richard I or Henry III. In addition, other possibilities relevant to the ballads are investigated, including the suggestions that Robin Hood existed during the reigns of Edward I or Edward II and the equally ignored premise linking him with the fugitive Knights Templar who roamed the countryside after 1307.

Although my research concentrates on the early sources, the work of various authors in the last forty years or so has not been completely overlooked. This book would be superfluous if it simply endorsed the outcomes of previous investigations, which are themselves rather inconsistent, but that work has provided considerable insight and help in taking me forward on my journey to unearth the truth about Robin Hood and the legends that surround him. Thanks largely to the efforts of Joseph Ritson and Francis Child in the eighteenth and nineteenth centuries, there exists a collection of all the known ancient poems, songs and ballads of Robin Hood. Maurice Keen's book *Outlaws of Medieval Legend* is, I believe, an extremely important work, as is J.C. Holt's *Robin Hood*, written in 1982 and revised in 1989, which was a groundbreaking study that has facilitated greater insight and understanding of the legend. The investigations by Dobson and Taylor, and more recently Knight, Ohlgren and Pollard on the ballads, have also opened up the possibility of greater understanding by returning the focus of attention to the accounts of the Robin Hood who was familiar to the audiences of the fifteenth century and away from the more fanciful elaborations and embellishments of more recent times.

I

A PROUD OUTLAW

Attend and listen, gentlemen,
Who are of freeborn blood;
I shall tell you about a good yeoman,
Whose name was Robin Hood.

Robin was a proud outlaw,
While he walked on ground:
So courteous an outlaw as he was
Otherwise was never found.[1]

So begins the famous ballad regarding that beloved outlaw commonly known as Robin Hood. Titled *A Gest of Robyn Hode*, this 456-stanza poem is the longest and one of the earliest surviving ballads known to provide insight into the life of the elusive outlaw. What existed during the fifteenth century as one of several orally recited rhymes, all similar in content and format, telling of a 'proud outlaw who walked on ground' and providing a source of cheap and exciting entertainment for audiences during the Middle Ages, now stands as a rare tangible reminder of Robin Hood's medieval legend and a prelude to several later ballads, countless plays, novels, Hollywood films and television series, some of which are still being produced.[2] What little is known of the early legend can largely be credited to these early ballads. The origin of the legend itself cannot be accurately determined. As a result, the information that exists, dating back over five hundred years, has become all the more important, often acting as a starting point for any serious investigation into the subject of Robin Hood.

In total, five of these early ballads have survived in their original form. Written in Middle English by an anonymous prose writer, or writers, and without a definitive historical setting, the ballads of *Robin Hood and the Monk, Robin Hood and the Potter, Robin Hood and Guy of Gisborne, Robin Hood's Death* and *A Gest of Robyn Hode* are a limited and damaged collection of the medieval legend based on the style of the early rhymes. Generally dated between 1450 and 1520, their stories appear strange and unfamiliar when viewed against the perception of Robin Hood in the twenty-first century but provide the reader with a realistic view of an outlaw at the time. Despite only surviving in fragmentary form, the material successfully introduces the lives of the outlaws and has become the basis for the later legend.[3]

Surviving in poor condition in the library of Cambridge University, the ballad of *Robin Hood and the Monk* is generally agreed to be the oldest of the known ballads, dated to some time after 1450, although its survival in printed form is attributed to a collection belonging to Robert Jamieson from 1806.[4] Initially entitled *Talkyng of the Munke and Robyn Hode*, the ballad was later retitled by Jamieson and included in the work of Francis Child, who compiled a significant collection of ballads in the nineteenth century.[5] The ballad begins with a description of an appealing setting in Sherwood Forest where Little John speaks happily of the May morning but the devoutly pious Robin Hood bemoans that he has been unable to attend mass or matins for over a fortnight. Frustrated, Robin decides to risk going to St Mary's in Nottingham, inspired by his devotion to the Virgin Mary, despite the possibility that he may be caught by the Sheriff of Nottingham. With concern for his safety, Much the Miller's son suggests he takes with him at least twelve men, but Robin refuses, taking only Little John.[6]

The outlaws depart for Nottingham and during the journey wager their archery skills by shooting arrows at a tree. Little John wins, but Robin Hood fails to honour the bet and a fight ensues. Robin Hood strikes Little John, who then leaves Robin to travel on unprotected. Undeterred, Robin continues to Nottingham, where he prays in the church, unaware that he has been recognized as an outlaw by a monk whom he had once robbed of £100 and has been reported to the sheriff. Robin is captured, and the Merry Men are shocked to learn of their master's fate.[7] Little John is the only man alert to the significance of the danger and leads the Merry Men as they set out to rescue Robin. On the way they find and capture the monk, who is carrying letters from the sheriff to the king about Robin Hood's capture, and his page. Little John murders the monk for treachery, and Much the Miller's son kills the page to keep it a secret, following which he and Little John go to the king.[8] They present the king with the letters the monk had been bringing and tell him that the monk had died on the journey. The king in return appoints them Yeomen of the Crown and commands them to bring Robin before him.[9] The Merry Men then appear before the sheriff with the king's orders, informing him that the monk has not come himself as he has been made the Abbot of Westminster. Much and Little John are granted permission by the sheriff to enter the prison, where they kill the gaoler and escape with Robin. The sheriff is furious that he has been tricked by the outlaws and fears the wrath of the king should he find out. When the king learns what has happened he curses their being fooled but praises Little John's loyalty and lets the incident go unpunished. Robin Hood admits Little John has done him a good turn, and they are reconciled.[10]

Violence is a recurring theme in the ballad of *Robin Hood and Guy of Gisborne*. Surviving only in a manuscript owned by Bishop Thomas Percy dated to the seventeenth century, commonly referred to as the *Percy Folio*, the ballad is generally accepted as being older in origin than the seventeenth century, largely because its plot and style are similar to that of a play, *Robin Hood and the Knight*, from 1475 which is also consistent with the Middle English used in the other early ballads.[11] Set in Barnsdale in Yorkshire rather than Sherwood, this ballad begins when Robin Hood awakens from a dream in which two unknown strangers capture him. Determined to track the men down, he dismisses the advice of Little John that the dream was meaningless, and the pair set off into the forest. They soon encounter a stranger, and Little John and Robin quarrel when Little John suggests that Robin remain out of sight while he investigates the stranger. Robin refuses, and Little John returns to the Merry Men to find them engaged in a fierce fight with the sheriff and his men. Little John kills one but is subsequently captured.

In the meantime, Robin exchanges greetings with the stranger and offers to be his guide through the forest. As they travel he learns that the stranger is a bounty hunter named Guy of Gisborne who has been instructed by the Sheriff of Nottingham to come to Barnsdale to capture an outlaw known as Robin Hood. Gisborne is unaware of Robin Hood's identity, and they engage in a friendly archery competition. After Robin Hood wins he reveals his identity, and a sword fight commences. Robin kills Gisborne and then returns, disguised in Gisborne's cloak, to rescue his men, and Little John kills the sheriff.[12]

The ballad of *Robin Hood and the Potter* differs slightly in style to the other four as it emphasizes Robin Hood's art of trickery and cunning when embarrassing the Sheriff of Nottingham. Described by Child as 'an unheard of old piece', the ballad survives in a single manuscript dated around 1503 and refers to a chance meeting between the Merry Men and a potter.[13] After attempting to charge the potter a levy for venturing into the forest, Robin spars with the stranger and loses. Despite the defeat, Robin shows good nature towards the potter and offers to go into Nottingham and sell his pots for him. Robin changes into the potter's clothes and carries out his promise but sells his goods at rock-bottom prices. Among his customers is the wife of the sheriff, who takes to Robin and invites him to dinner.[14] While at dinner, Robin informs the sheriff he knows Robin Hood and tricks the sheriff into the greenwood the next day. Although surrounded by his Merry Men, Robin shows courtesy towards him because of the kindness of his wife.[15]

Surviving in at least five similar editions, the *Gest* is perhaps the most famous of the ballads, dated some time between 1450 and 1520.[16] In style and structure this ballad is an epic poem, of which some text appears to be missing. It comprises several Robin Hood stories, some of which follow on directly from one another, collected together in eight fyttes.[17] According to the ballad, Robin Hood and his Merry Men are outlaws in Barnsdale. It begins at evening time in the forest when Robin declares that he will not dine unless he has a guest with whom to share his food. He instructs the Merry Men to find him a guest, and they waylay a knight named Sir Richard at the Lee who is travelling towards Doncaster.[18] Robin invites the knight to dine with him, although insisting he pay for his own meal. When dinner is over Robin learns that Sir Richard has fallen on hard times, owing £400 to the monastery of St Mary's in York for mortgaging his land to pay bail for his son who had killed two men. Recognizing that the knight is true to his word, Robin, inspired by his own generosity and their mutual devotion to the Virgin Mary, agrees to lend him £400. Before they part, Robin also provides the knight with horses and clothing befitting his station and arranges for Little John to guide him on his journey.[19]

The following day sees the knight travel to St Mary's Abbey in York where the abbot and a monk, the villains of the story, are more interested in repayment of the loan than in the possibility that the knight may lose his lands and son. Despite having the money available to pay off the debt, the knight pleads for further time but is refused. Bemoaning the greed of the holy men, Sir Richard reluctantly repays the money, and with his debt paid he sets about raising money to repay his debt to Robin Hood.[20] The ballad continues with Little John shooting in an archery competition in Nottingham where he impresses the Sheriff of Nottingham. The sheriff declares he has never seen such fine shooting and decides to employ Little John as his servant.[21] Little John later steals £303 and many silver vessels from the sheriff and then returns to Robin Hood accompanied by the sheriff's cook, who later joins the Merry Men. The sheriff himself is also tempted out into the greenwood by Little John, where he is captured by Robin Hood and forced to spend the night in Robin's custody. The sheriff swears an oath of friendship to Robin and is released but soon sets about plotting revenge.

The ballad continues with Robin Hood again refusing to eat dinner unless he has a guest. His men set out once more to find one and waylay a monk from St Mary's Abbey passing through the forest. They dine, and Robin insists the monk pay for his meal. The monk claims he is poor, but Robin discovers £800 among his possessions, including the money repaid by Sir Richard, which Robin steals. As a result, when Sir Richard at the

Lee returns to repay the loan Robin refuses to accept it, stating that the Virgin Mary has been good to him.[22]

Later on, the Sheriff of Nottingham arranges an archery contest in an attempt to capture Robin Hood. Although they recognize that the contest is a trap, Robin and a number of the Merry Men decide to take part. They all shoot to a very high standard, with Robin eventually winning. Thereupon the sheriff ambushes the Merry Men, but they manage to escape and accept refuge at the knight's castle, which is later attacked by the sheriff and a countryside militia.[23] Battle commences, and the Merry Men successfully repel the attack. Soon after, the sheriff goes to London to inform the king about what has happened. The king angrily insists that the outlaws and the knight must be caught. The sheriff arrests Sir Richard for his part in assisting the outlaws, but Robin later rescues him. The king is outraged at the knight's escape and comes to Nottingham himself to capture him and Robin Hood. The king journeys across Lancashire and is outraged by the loss of deer in the royal forests. He resorts to dressing up as an abbot to enter the greenwood and find the elusive outlaws. He encounters Robin in the forest, where they engage in discussion, and the king takes kindly to him. After the king has dined with Robin Hood and watched the Merry Men shoot arrows, they all walk on together to Nottingham, with Robin having no idea of the abbot's true identity. Robin's loyalty to the king, now identified as one of the King Edwards, is never in doubt and the king pardons the Merry Men, taking Robin Hood into his service. After fifteen months Robin returns to live in the greenwood until his death at Kirklees Priory – also described in the ballad of *Robin Hood's Death*.[24]

The events recorded in each of the ballads are generally consistent. While they portray a Robin Hood who is different from the hero of the modern-day legend, they nevertheless provide the reader with several similarities that seemingly stem from early tradition. They are set in the forests of Barnsdale and Sherwood in the month of May, and life as an outlaw is described in an appealing way, with descriptions of the foliage on the trees and the singing of the birds providing an early insight into the forest life which many associate with Robin Hood. Conditions in the forest were undoubtedly hard, but poetic licence provides a romantic and somewhat idealistic picture of Robin Hood roaming the forests of England with his band of Merry Men enjoying a life free from responsibility and oppression. The Merry Men are present at the beginning of each ballad, and Robin has already established a reputation as being the greatest of archers. His tendency to rob from the rich is demonstrated in the *Gest* and *Monk* ballads, but with only limited explanation of what he does with the proceeds. His generosity to the knight in not forcing him to pay back the loan goes some way to demonstrate his charitable nature, which is also acknowledged at the end of the *Gest*:

> Cryst have mercy on his soule.
> That dyded on the Rode!
> For he was a good outlawe
> And dyde pore men moch god.[25]

Exactly how much of the early tradition has been lost over the centuries is difficult to assess. Equally, much of twenty-first-century tradition differs considerably from the medieval ballads. Modern tradition firmly establishes Robin Hood as being of noble status, but this is inconsistent with early ballads, which open with a clear description of Robin Hood and his Merry Men as yeomen. Also absent at this stage is a definitive historical setting. Popular legend refers to Robin Hood's allegiance to

Richard I, yet the ballads refer to the king as an Edward. Historically this also poses a problem, particularly as none of the contemporary chroniclers recorded the existence of Robin Hood during the reign of Richard I. Yet the search for a historical Robin Hood is not completely without foundation. In the year 1377 the poet William Langland made reference to the popularity of the legend in his epic poem *The Vision of William Concerning Piers Plowman*. In this there is a passage criticizing negligent priests in which the priest Sloth claims: 'I can noughte perfitly fit my pater-noster, as the priest singeth, but I can rymes of Robin Hood and Randolf Earl of Chester.'[26] In modern English this translates as: 'Nor am I perfect in my paternoster – not as a priest should sing it – though I do know *ryme*s of Robin Hood and Randolph Earl of Chester.'[27] The rhymes Langland talks about could include some of the early ballads as they appeared in oral form. The *Monk, Gest, Gisborne, Death* and *Potter* ballads may have been widely recited by this time despite not being recorded in text before 1450. While it cannot be clearly identified when the rhymes of Robin Hood were first recited, evidence of the tradition is in place before the time of Langland.

Another early reference to Robin comes around 1400. Captured in a poem located in the library of Lincoln Cathedral are the lines

> Robyn hod in sherewod stod
> hodud and hathud and gosu and schod
> four and thuynti arrows
> he bar in his hondus

which may be translated as

Robin Hood in Sherwood stood
hooded and hatted and hosed and shod.
Four and twenty arrows
he bore in his hands.[28]

This poem does not provide any significant insight into the activities of a possible historical figure, but it does at least confirm that a connection between Robin Hood and Sherwood Forest existed by the fifteenth century. The poem provides a further reference to archery, and describes the outlaw as wearing a hat, hood, stockings and shoes. Unfortunately still missing is a time period.

The first attempt to determine one comes in a similarly vague mention some twenty years later when Robin Hood and Little John are recorded as outlaws in the *Orygynale Cronykil of Scotland*, written around 1420 by the Scottish chronicler Andrew of Wyntoun. Here Robin Hood and Little John are said to be outlaws in Inglewood and Barnsdale in the years 1283–5.[29] The passage refers to outlaws, but Wyntoun offers no explanation as to why they were outlawed. The year 1283 is nearly a hundred years after the time of Richard I and places Robin at a time when King Edward I ('Longshanks') was preparing for war with Scotland. In the chronicle Wyntoun is very critical of Edward I, accusing him of a multitude of war crimes against Scotland.[30]

Later in the fifteenth century Robin Hood is chronicled again, this time in a more precise historical context. Entitled *Scotichronicon*, this chronicle was composed in Latin by John Fordun, a Scottish chronicler from Mearns, between 1377 and 1384, and revised by his pupil Walter Bower, also a Scottish chronicler from East Lothian, in about 1440. Regarded by the National Library of Scotland as a very important medieval account of early Scottish history, *Scotichronicon* consists of sixteen completed books providing a thorough insight into the history of Scotland. The first five of these books were written by Fordun as an attempt to provide a reliable history of Scotland dating from the Dark Ages up to the death of King David I in 1153. In addition, Fordun started work on a sixth book, later updated by Bower. Among Bower's additions to Fordun's work was a reference to a real-life Robin Hood and Little John, who fought for the barons in their rebellion against King Henry III. Following their defeat at the Battle of Evesham, in the year 1266, Robin is described in Latin as a *famosus siccarius,* meaning a well-known murderer.[31] Interestingly, Bower is quite critical of fans of Robin Hood and states that 'the foolish populace are so inordinately fond of celebrating him in both tragedies and comedies, and about whom they are delighted to hear the jesters and minstrels sing above all other ballads'.[32]

Those who are familiar with the stories and ballads of Robin Hood will not be surprised by the word 'comedy'. The tales of Robin are frequently associated with humour. The ballad *Robin Hood and the Potter* could perhaps be described as a 'comedy' as it demonstrates Robin's art of trickery and the gullibility of his enemies in a light-hearted and humorous manner, not normally a characteristic associated with a common criminal. The amusing scenes where Little John tricks the king and sheriff in the *Monk* ballad were also enjoyable occasions for the reader. In contrast, other events that occur in the *Monk* ballad, documented very soon after Bower's revision of *Scotichronicon*, are far more violent than those in many of the other ballads and may account for what he means by 'tragedy'. It is likely that the tradition of Robin Hood's death was well known to Bower.[33]

If Bower was correct, the period in England's history when Robin lived is later than modern tradition suggests. By placing a historical Robin Hood in the context of Simon de Montfort's rebellion against Henry III, Bower implies Robin was active around 1265–6. The date differs from the 1283 in the *Orygynale Cronykil*, but Bower does build on his claim that Robin was an outlaw in Barnsdale. In addition, by suggesting he was involved in the rebellion he has effectively connected Robin with an event that would later result in the formation of Parliament.[34]

It is fascinating that Robin Hood, about whom the foolish populace 'are delighted to hear the jesters and minstrels sing above all other ballads', is described as a famous murderer. The modern perception of the heroic freedom fighter is out of place when viewed against *Scotichronicon*, as Bower's outlaw is little more than a highwayman. Even so, reference to him as a murderer may not be too surprising given his reputation in popular culture for killing Normans and indeed the sheriff and Guy of Gisborne in the ballads. His tendency to steal from the sheriff, among others, in the ballads is also clearly known to Bower. Nevertheless, as with the poem by William Langland and the chronicle by Andrew of Wyntoun, Bower testifies to the widespread popularity of the rhymes and also provides a different account of Robin – one to which most people today will readily relate. Bower illustrates Robin's more religious side, describing a scene where Robin celebrates mass in the forest and refuses to be disturbed by the prowling sheriff, waiting until mass is over before he kills the enemy.[35]

The early ballads and chronicles make no reference to Robin Hood's ethnicity. There is no indication that he is a Saxon, and there is definitely no reference to him as a nobleman at this stage. The ballads and chronicles were written at a time of violence, and the ballads glamorize it. His loyalty to the king is made clear, but there is still a question mark over just who the king was.[36]

The first attempt to identify Robin Hood as a historical character living during the reign of Richard I came when he was chronicled in *Historia Majoris Britanniae*, a history of Great Britain written by the respected John Major in 1521.[37] This relates the story of Hood in a more objective manner than the pro-Scottish descriptions of Bower and Wyntoun, but, in addition to cutting the ties to Scotland, Major moves the period from the reign of a King Edward to that of Richard the 'Lion-heart'.[38] Major's eulogy of Hood presents him in a form not dissimilar to the modern-day portrayal. He is a bold hero with values and principles. He kills but only in self-defence, and those he does kill are often killers themselves. He is also a protector of women and the poor. The story of the *Gest* certainly existed by Major's time, as did the other early ballads. The *Gest* identifies Robin as a leader and so does Major. *Historia Majoris Britanniae* was written in Latin, and in it reference is made to Robin with the word 'dux', Latin for leader but also meaning general, commander, guide or duke. Depending on interpretation, the word can be taken to ascribe to Robin an aristocratic title and even a blood link to the king.[39]

From his humble beginnings as a hardened soldier and religious woodsman in the ballads, Robin Hood now has a possible title and is portrayed as a formidable fighter, but there is no mention of his devotion to the Virgin Mary. He is acknowledged to be a thief, but he seems to share his wealth. As in the *Gest*, Major refers to his dislike of the abbots, and he clearly steals from them. Otherwise, similarities between this Robin Hood and the character from the early chronicles and ballads are already beginning to diminish.

2

A Major History of Britain

By the time Major wrote *Historia Majoris Britanniae* the legend
of Robin Hood had already developed considerably. The humble
soldier featured in the early ballads, and referred to as a well-
known murderer by Walter Bower, is now portrayed as a man of
superior social principles who may have links with the aristocracy. Despite his tendency to lose one-to-one fights, as revealed
in ballads such as *Robin Hood and the Potter*, his reputation as
a leader of fighting men and as an archer was already established,[1] but in Major's version Robin's accomplishments are on
a grander scale. Bower's *famosus siccarius* is now capable of
taking on 400 men with the support of only 100 archers, and,
although Major condemns his robbing of abbots, he excuses him
because of his virtuous qualities. The most intriguing development is the change of date from 1266 to 1193–4, of which Major
wrote:

> About this time it was, as I conceive, that there flour-
> ished those most famous robbers Robert Hood, an
> Englishman, and Little John, who lay in wait in the
> woods, but spoiled of their goods those only that were
> wealthy. They took the life of no man, unless he either

attacked them or offered resistance in defence of his property. Robert supported by his plundering one hundred bowmen, ready fighters every one, with whom four hundred of the strongest would not dare to engage in combat. The feats of this Robert are told in song all over Britain. He would allow no woman to suffer injustice, nor would he spoil the poor, but rather enriched them from the plunder taken from the abbots. The robberies of this man I condemn, but of all robbers he was the humanest and the chief.[2]

By mentioning that the 'feats of this Robert are told in song all over Britain', he identifies this man clearly as the hero of the ballads.[3] At this stage Robin Hood has the support of his Merry Men, yet there are some notable absentees from the popular legend. Robin's followers are mentioned in the ballads, but they have not yet acquired the name of Merry Men in the Latin chronicles.[4] Emphasis in the ballads and chronicles is on Barnsdale more than Sherwood Forest as his home, and perhaps most interesting of all there is no Maid Marian.[5]

Although Major's eulogy of Robin Hood exaggerated some of the events described in the ballads and other chronicles, and despite his failure to provide definitive proof of his claims, his work has been largely accepted since the late sixteenth century. Nevertheless, intense curiosity and speculation regarding the true identity of Robin Hood continue to this day. It is clear that his character has gained in nobility and stature, but even by the time of Major he was a long way from the Saxon lord and defender of the people that popular tradition now describes.[6] To have any hope of understanding a historical Robin Hood, it is important to appreciate how his character has been manipulated by myth, legend and, in many cases, fiction. If we are to go on the early information alone, then Robin's character becomes clearer. Although the Latin chronicles written by Wyntoun, Bower and Major have a tendency to contradict one another, their content was intended to be factually accurate. While it is unfortunate that all the chroniclers wrote of Robin Hood at least a hundred years after the time at which they claim he existed, for Major the time lag is more significant. By the time Major penned his work, 144 years had passed since Langland's mention of the rhymes and a century since Andrew of Wyntoun recorded a reference to Robin Hood and Little John. By the sixteenth century plays starring Robin Hood were a popular source of entertainment, and the *Monk*, *Potter*, *Gisborne* and *Gest* ballads were all available in print with no indication of Major's additions being present.[7] Bearing this in mind, the changes he makes are even more surprising. It is unfortunate that Major did not refer to Robin Hood in more detail. His summary is intriguing but gives little insight into the life of the character other than placing him clearly during the early years of the reign of King Richard I.

The role of King Richard in the stories is as legendary in the twenty-first century as the hero himself. As he was the third son of King Henry II, Richard was not expected to become a king. Following the death of Henry's first son, William, in infancy, it was his second son, Henry, who became his heir. Known as 'the Young King', Henry was crowned as joint king alongside his father but never inherited the full title. In 1173 he rebelled against his father, largely owing to his frustration at not being given any realm to govern, and this continued until his death in 1183. Following the death of Henry the Young, Richard should have been in line to replace his father, but Henry had instead promised the throne to his youngest, and favourite, son Prince John. This was hardly surprising. Tension between King Henry and Richard had been running high for several years. Richard's decision to join

Henry the Young in a rebellion against him had left the pair at loggerheads, a rift exacerbated by Richard's loyalty to his mother, Eleanor of Aquitaine, whom King Henry had earlier imprisoned owing to her encouragement of her sons' rebellions.[8] Richard was his mother's favourite and was due to inherit her possessions. This prompted Henry II to support an invasion of Aquitaine by Henry the Young and his other son, Geoffrey, in 1183. Richard's resilience in withstanding this invasion proved to be a major and lasting obstacle for Henry. Despite Henry's initial intention to name John, rather than Richard, as his successor to the English throne, he relented when Richard joined forces with Philip of France to wage war on England. Following defeat by Richard in 1189 Henry agreed to name Richard, his oldest surviving son, as his successor, and following his father's death later that year Richard ascended to the throne of England.[9]

Living most of his life in France, Richard never really developed an affinity with England. A good-looking and capable warrior, he had earned the epithet 'Coeur-de-lion' for his reputation as a formidable fighter in the earlier rebellions.[10] Following an uneasy truce between Philip and Henry II, Richard inherited a humiliated kingdom. His father had suffered the shame of all his sons revolting against him, and his truce with Philip was a major embarrassment as Philip was his biggest enemy. Since the Norman invasion of 1066 the French territories under the suzerainty of the Norman monarchs of England had been under constant attack by ambitious kings, including Philip Augustus of France, seeking an opportunity to extend their power. Now, however, Philip's aims changed, since both he and Richard desired to embark on a further Crusade.[11] When Richard ascended to the throne the Crusades had been raging for ninety years. Much of the Holy Land was back under Saladin's control, but a third Crusade was in preparation.[12] An agreement between Richard and Philip to continue the peace and mount a joint attack on the Holy Land did not take long to conclude.

The cessation of hostilities between the English and French brought an end to the taxation imposed to fund the war, but it was replaced by a new tax, known as the 'Saladin Tithe', levied to fund the assault on the Muslims.[13] The incessant taxation was a heavy burden on the people of England, who had little interest in the fate of the Holy Land. By the year 1192, Richard was a prisoner at the hands of Duke Leopold after being captured when passing through Austria.[14] In Richard's absence, his ageing mother ruled England from France, with the help of William Longchamp, Bishop of Ely, who acted as regent. She attempted to raise the ransom of 150,000 marks demanded for Richard's release, which was another severe burden on the English tax-payer, particularly as the earlier Saladin Tithe had been extremely unpopular. Meanwhile, Richard's bitter relationship with his brother John had left the latter isolated. At the time John had control of six English counties and Ireland, which had been given to him by Richard.[15] As the brother of the king, John believed it was his right to rule as Regent. When he heard that Richard had been imprisoned he sought to bargain with the King of France by offering territory in exchange for the French King's support for his claim to the throne of England. Unfortunately for John this treasonable act was unsuccessful, and eventually the ransom for Richard's release was paid.[16]

Despite Richard's release and triumphant return to England, only a few months elapsed before he left to spend the remaining years of his reign reclaiming lost lands and defending the Duchy of Normandy.[17] During his entire reign Richard spent only seven months in England, and he never learned to speak the language.[18] Further taxation after his return increased the burden on the people of England, but none of this was John's fault; most of the money raised in tax during Richard's reign went either to pay his ransom or to aid his campaigns in the Holy Land.

In popular culture the role of Robin Hood in support of the absent King Richard is legendary, but the historical evidence is not strong. Major's somewhat ambiguous reference to Robin Hood as a 'dux' in *Historia Majoris Britanniae* upgraded his status from that of a yeoman to a possible nobleman, a promotion later further developed by the printer and scholar Richard Grafton, who referred to Robin as an earl. Grafton, a follower of Major, was the first chronicler to provide detail of the life of Robin Hood, building on the work of his predecessors and noticeably highlighting events from the ballads as history.[19] In his *Chronicle at Large*, written in 1569, Grafton re-emphasized the new dating by Major and referred to old records that he claimed verified the existence of Robin Hood as a historical figure. He wrote:

> But in an olde and auncient Pamphlet I finde this written of the sayd Robert Hood. This man (sayth he) discended of a nobel parentage: or rather beyng of a base stocke and linage, was for his manhoode and chivalry advaunced to the noble dignité of an Erle. Excellyng principally in Archery, or shootyng, his manly courage agreeyng therunto: But afterwardes he so prodigally exceeded in charges and expences, that he fell into great debt, by reason wherof, so many actions and sutes were commenced against him, wherunto he aunswered not, that by order of lawe he was outlawed, and then for a lewde shift, as his last refuge, gathered together a companye of Roysters and Cutters, and practised robberyes and spoylyng of the kynges subjects, and occupied and frequentede

the Forestes or wilde Countries. The which beyng
certefyed to the King, and he beyng greatly offended
therewith, caused his proclamation to be made that
whosoever would bryng him quicke or dead, the king
would geve him a great summe of money, as by the
recordes in the Exchequer is to be seene: But of this
promise, no man enjoyed any benefite. For the sayd
Robert Hood, beyng afterwardes troubled with sick-
nesse, came to a certein Nonry in Yorkshire called
Bircklies, where desirying to be let blood, he was
betrayed and bled to deth. After whose death the
Prioresse of the same place caused him to be buried by
the high way side, where he had used to rob and
spoyle those that passed that way. And upon his grave
the sayde Prioresse did lay a very fayre stone wherin
the names of Robert Hood, William of Goldes-
borough and others were graven. And the cause why she
buryed him there was for that the common passengers
and travailers knowyng and seeyng him there buryed,
might more safely and without feare take their jorneys
that way, which they durst not do in the life of the sayd
outlawes. And at eyther end of the sayde Tombe was
erected a crosse of stone, which is to be seene there at
this present.[20]

Grafton's testimony was not entirely original, but as well as
reiterating the information provided by Major he made additions
of his own. Although most scholars credit Major as the origi-
nator of the claim that Robin Hood was from a noble family, by
the end of the century Grafton's depiction of him as an earl had
caught the imagination of the famous playwright Anthony
Munday. Munday, a friend of Grafton, later developed the theme

in two plays, depicting Robin Hood as the Earl of Huntingdon. The historically unverified Sloane Manuscript, written by an anonymous prose writer around 1600, was less informative about Robin's lineage but agreed with Major's dating by claiming he was born around 1160.[21] In time the chroniclers' claims became accepted as fact, culminating in the eighteenth century when the scholar Dr William Stukeley endeavoured to authenticate Robin Hood as a historical Earl of Huntingdon by seeking to pass on his own fictional creations as a genuine pedigree for the earl.[22] Nevertheless, Grafton's description of an earl disgraced through profligacy does have historical foundation. Although Grafton did not specify that Robin was the Earl of Huntingdon, a later addition by Munday, his story may link to the genuine earl.

David, brother of the King of Scotland, William the Lion, was Earl of Huntingdon during the reign of King Henry II. A nephew of the king, David endured a strained relationship with his uncle, eventually resulting in his decision to assist Henry the Young in his unsuccessful rebellion in 1174. As a consequence, David lost his earldom for a decade. Although he later made his peace with Henry II, it was Richard I to whom he offered his allegiance. In 1189 David is recorded as having attended Richard's coronation and having carried one of the three ceremonial swords. His whereabouts during the next few years, however, have been the subject of conjecture. Following his marriage to Maud of Chester in 1190 the earl is not mentioned in any records for over three years. According to the chronicler John Fordun, he joined Richard in the Crusades, but no contemporary chronicler noted this. In later legends Robin Hood is said to have fought alongside Richard, a suggestion that may have been inspired by Fordun's claim. Officially the earl does not reappear in the history books until he is recorded as having fought alongside King Richard I in

1194 when they besieged Nottingham Castle to reclaim the throne for Richard.[23]

On Richard's death in 1199, John ascended to the throne and the earl was disinherited of much of his possessions. Suffering financially, David was later accused of being party to a plot against John in 1212. Officially this was never proven; however, he did support the barons in their rebellion against John in 1215 .[24] In many ways that event may have helped pave the way for the signing of the Magna Carta in 1215, but the financially stricken earl was no longer in a position to influence matters.[25]

For the first time the testimony of a chronicler had a direct link to an authentic historical person. In common with Grafton's Robin Hood, David was an earl who fell from grace. Like the Robin Hood of later legend, David himself was charged with forest offences, notably in 1207 when he was fined £200. In 1211 he was severely in debt to the Exchequer and was forced to sell much of his land.[26] Whether Grafton's references to 'ancient pamphlets' and Exchequer records are relevant to David is impossible to determine due to the vagueness of Grafton's statements. David's opposition to Prince John, despite supporting his claim to the throne following Richard's death in 1199, was apparent in 1194, and he was in favour of the Magna Carta.

In addition to David's connection with King Richard and Nottingham, further evidence highlighting his significance comes when we consider William Langland's reference to the rhymes of Robin Hood and Ranulf, Earl of Chester. Historically, there were three Ranulfs, Earl of Chester. Following the death of Richard d'Avranches in 1120 without leaving an heir, the earldom passed to Ranulf le Meschin, nephew of the 1st Earl, Hugh d'Avranches. Le Meschin became the 3rd Earl in 1121 and held the title until his death in 1129. His son, Ranulf de Gernon, replaced him until he died in 1153.[27] Following the death of his son, Hugh de Kevelioc, the 5th Earl, the title passed to de Gernon's grandson, Ranulf de Blondeville (1172–1232), brother-in-law of David, Earl of Huntingdon.[28] Of the three historical Ranulfs, Earl of Chester, de Blondeville is the most likely candidate for Langland's Ranulf owing to his strong links to Earl David. There is no reference to the Merry Men, Sherwood Forest or Barnsdale Forest at this stage, but there is a Barnsdale in Rutland which was associated with the Earls of Huntingdon.[29]

Although similarities exist between Robin Hood and Earl David, they give rise to a number of questions. Perhaps the most interesting concerns Ranulf, Earl of Chester. Langland refers to the rhymes of Robin Hood and Ranulf, Earl of Chester, but he may not be referring to them in the same context. Perhaps rhymes concerning the activities of Robin Hood and the Earl of Chester did exist in oral form but no longer survive. Certainly the Earl of Chester does not feature in any of the ballads we know. Yet, considering that the man of the ballads is a yeoman, it is conceivable that the character from the early ballads might not be the same man referred to by Langland. Equally, none of the chroniclers specifies Robin Hood as the Earl of Huntingdon. Grafton builds on the popular tradition of Robin Hood, referring to him keeping the company of roysters and cutters before meeting his death at Kirklees where he was bled.[30] Grafton's description of Robin's death is in keeping with that in the *Death* ballad and the end of the *Gest* but noticeably different from Earl David's death in 1219 at Yardley in Northamptonshire.[31]

Norman–Saxon rivalry has been a recurring theme of the Robin Hood legend since the nineteenth century, and his status as an Anglo-Saxon is a key element in emphasizing the unjust oppression of the Norman autocracy, often referred to as the 'Norman Yoke'. Historically this is a grey area whose significance has been exaggerated, in part through its becoming intertwined with the Robin Hood legend. The term 'Norman Yoke' was first mentioned in a paper from 1642 entitled the *Mirror of Justices*, a translation of a thirteenth-century French work which identified the gentry and nobility of England as descendants of 'foreign usurpers' who destroyed a Saxon golden age.[32] Many historians dismiss the notion of such an age, but its adherents extol the reigns of Saxon kings such as Alfred the Great and Edward the Confessor. This period came to an end when William the Conqueror appointed Norman officials in the Church and replaced English earls and thegns with Norman nobility.[33] The significance of the principles of individual freedom and the rights of citizenship that were suppressed by the Norman Yoke became central to later debates about reform. In the seventeenth century the English jurist Sir Edward Coke penned many important writings on English Common Law, emphasizing that its foundations had existed prior to the Conquest.

The Norman–Saxon conflict flared up in the Peasants' Revolt of 1381, but earlier examples are less obvious.[34] Prince John's lust for power may have led to the seizing of some Saxon lands, but the extent of his oppression of the Saxons, as popularly portrayed in the Robin Hood tales, cannot be determined. Moreover, the ballads make no reference to ethnicity. Bearing in mind that Richard's taxation of the poor to fund the Crusades was highly oppressive, the suggestion that he returned to England to free its people from unjust authority and corruption is little short of ludicrous. Richard I was, of course, himself a Norman.

Another further recurring theme in the legend is the feud with the Sheriff of Nottingham. Popular tradition now emphasizes excessive corruption on the part of the sheriff, whose treatment of the Saxons is tyrannical, but the ballads do not suggest this. During the reign of Richard I the job of sheriff changed hands almost annually. If the Sheriff of Nottingham of the Robin Hood legend was in office during the early 1190s, it is likely that it was the powerful Norman Lord William de Wendenal.[35] At the time the High Sheriff of Nottingham was not appointed as such, but the role was allocated on the strict condition that the incumbent was to pay a retainer every year to the king. How the sheriffs raised the money was their business. This system was inevitably open to abuse, and de Wendenal may well have been tyrannical and autocratic in the manner in which he chose to discharge his responsibilities, free from any constraint of higher authority or supervision. In a period when record keeping was inconsistent and unreliable, all trace of de Wendenal disappears from history in 1194 when William de Ferrers replaced him as sheriff. The fact that de Wendenal's disappearance coincided with the return of Richard I may be significant and tie in with the timing of Earl David and de Blondeville's return, but reliable information about his final days is not available.

In addition to Earl David, some commentators have suggested that the lives of historical outlaws Eustache the Monk and Hereward the Wake had an impact on the development of the Robin Hood legend. Although similarities exist, a French text dating from 1325–40 – a version of which also exists in Middle English – may provide a more direct influence. This tells the story of the historical life of outlawed nobleman Fulk FitzWarin.

According to the text, Fulk FitzWarin was born in the latter half of the twelfth century into a noble family from Shropshire as one of five sons of his father, also named Fulk, and his mother, Hawyse. During the reign of King Henry II, Fulk's parents stayed for a considerable time at the court of the king, and the younger Fulk grew up in the company of the princes. While most of the princes befriended Fulk, a quarrel with Prince John resulted in a grudge that lasted into adulthood.[36] Following Richard I's death in 1199, John's quest for power had a direct impact on Fulk, who was stripped of his title and land and outlawed in retribution for the quarrel of earlier years.

Once he was outlawed, Fulk's anger at his former friend developed into a thirst for revenge, and from this point on there are similarities between the tales of Robin Hood and Fulk FitzWarin. On one occasion Fulk's brother, John, ambushes a caravan of ten merchants carrying expensive cloths, furs and spices to the king and queen. In the *Gest* Little John and Much stop a caravan of monks and yeomen. In both cases the groups are abducted into the forest where they dine with the outlaws and are then relieved of their goods before being allowed to leave and continue their journey. Fulk, like Robin Hood, is clearly gifted in the art of trickery and deception. On one occasion, disguised in the clothes of a collier, he finds King John hunting deer in Windsor Forest. After greeting the king, Fulk lures him into a trap and his men capture the monarch. Fearing for his life, John offers Fulk a full pardon in exchange for his life. Fulk agrees to his request, but it is not long before the king sets about plotting revenge on his childhood foe. In the *Gest* it is interesting that a similar story is recounted, this time involving the Sheriff of Nottingham. During the battle after the archery tournament in the *Gest*, Little John is wounded as the sheriff tries to capture Robin. Little John fears he will die and begs Robin to kill him rather than allow him to be captured, but Robin carries him away and he survives.[37] In the story of Fulk FitzWarin a similar situation occurs when a Norman soldier wounds Fulk's brother.[38]

Despite credible evidence of his existence, the story of Fulk may not be based entirely on fact. As may be the case with Robin Hood, it is one thing to confirm that he lived but another to clarify the events of his life with accuracy rather than exaggerated romantic portrayals. The text refers to him smiting giants, for example. Fulk existed at the correct time, if Major's assertion about the timing of Robin Hood's life is to be accepted, but the Fulk FitzWarin story takes place in Windsor Park rather than Barnsdale and Sherwood, ruling out any chance that Fulk and Robin Hood were the same person.

Whether the stories of Earl David or Fulk influenced the views of the chroniclers is unclear. There is scope to acknowledge the contributions of Major and Grafton, but their account of a Robin Hood living during the reign of King Richard the Lionheart cannot be reconciled with the life of the yeoman described in the *Gest*. Major's eulogy of Robin Hood also raises questions about the man he was describing. Neither Fulk nor Earl David is a yeoman, nor is the Robin Hood described by Major and Grafton. The time period is also a significant change from the early ballads, which consistently place Robin's lifetime during the reign of one of the King Edwards, something Major undoubtedly knew about. Depending on which King Edward the ballads referred to, Major's work suggests that he lived at least eighty years earlier. The change needs to be clarified. Was Major referring to Earl David? Did he make the change to coincide with Fulk?[39] Did he misunderstand Robin's friendship with Sir Richard at the Lee as a friendship with King Richard I?[40] To determine when a historical Robin Hood might have lived seems to be dependent on a judgement about which chronicler is correct. To cast doubt on the belief that Robin Hood lived during the reign of King Richard would be to doubt the integrity, or at least the historical capabilities, of Grafton and especially Major.

Details of Major's life are drawn primarily from his own works. Without question his reputation was celebrated during the fifteenth and sixteenth centuries as an innovative thinker and a capable teacher. He was known as a scholar of theology, and as a philosopher his views would have had an influence on many scholars of the time.[41] The title of his work, which contains reference to Robin Hood, *Historia Majoris Britanniae*, means 'A History of Greater Britain' but could translate to 'Major's History of Britain'.[42] Teaching at Paris and Glasgow universities developed his reputation, and throughout his life he was admired as a historian, an enquiring and observant individual who had a particular influence in works on logic, science, politics and the Church, as well as the relationship between will and faith, unity of the human mind and will versus intellect.[43]

In his writings on international law he displayed a particular interest in human rights; he was notably concerned with the invasion of South America by the Conquistadors, during which the native Aztecs and Incas were slaughtered and their cities plundered. His legal views were influential, playing a pioneering role in the eventual acceptance in Spanish law that the native populations of South and Central America were free human beings worthy of the same rights as the Spanish people themselves. Although the Spanish Crown never enforced the law officially, this was a significant breakthrough in human rights law as the Conquistadors' slaying of the 'savages' of South America was condemned.[44]

While Major was almost certainly aware that Fulk FitzWarin had been outlawed at the time of King John, in placing Robin in the era of King Richard the Lionheart he portrayed him not so much as a rebel against authority as a man concerned with the rights and freedoms of the common people. In the other chronicles Robin Hood was regarded as a criminal, but in the adaptation by Major his crimes were not portrayed as immoral. In this new role he displayed an unexpected appreciation of human rights, particularly for an outlaw and even more surprising for the twelfth century. The principles and practices of the changes in Spain in the early sixteenth century appear to have been championed by Robin Hood some three hundred years earlier.

As a historian, Major was quick to dismiss much of the work of Andrew of Wyntoun and John Fordun as inconsequential, particularly Fordun's telling of various fables. Fordun had earlier put into writing a Scottish version of the Greek myth *Gathelus of Greece*, known as *Goídel Glas*, which Major viewed as an invention by Fordun to outdo the English myth that Brutus of Troy was Britain's first king.[45] Major was renowned for his logical approach, and most of his arguments can be regarded as sound common sense, particularly when viewed with the hindsight of the present day. In his work *De Gestis Scotorum*, also dated 1521, he concentrated on presenting a patriotic view of Scotland, free of myth and legend, intended for a European audience rather than the Scottish one to whom the *Orygynale Cronykil* and, to a degree, *Scotichronicon* was directed. This in turn supported his view that England's and Scotland's future lay in unification.[46] In style the paper *De Gestis Scotorum* appeared less pro-Scottish than earlier works by Wyntoun, Fordun and Bower and was seemingly based on fact, notwithstanding that the historical sources available were limited. Major's sources for *Historia Majoris Britanniae* have similarly never been verified and may also have been limited.[47] Despite the respect accorded to his approach, some of his content seems curious. His reference to Robin Hood living during the time of King Richard the Lionheart is difficult to accept, particularly as the ballads refer to the king as an Edward. Did Major have sound evidence for his portrayal, or did he use Robin Hood as a vehicle to highlight his views on human rights? Regardless of the reason, evidence supporting the view that Robin Hood, the yeoman, was the ally of Richard the Lionheart is absent.

3

DISINHERITED

Following the death of Richard I in 1199, Prince John finally ascended to the throne. Unlike Richard he did not embark on any Crusades; instead he spent much of his time strengthening England's fleet and consolidating peace with Ireland, Scotland and Wales.[1] His efforts won him the respect of many commoners as a fair judge, and he travelled extensively throughout his kingdom until his death. However, although his reign was not as turbulent as the Robin Hood legend has come to suggest, by 1213 he had alienated many of the nobles.[2] His inability to keep the barons on side led to England's third civil war, eventually resulting in the signing of the Magna Carta.[3] This was a significant moment in English history, but in fact the document offered fewer freedoms than is commonly supposed. It ensured the rights and liberties of the nobility and the Church, but in many cases they were not implemented in practice, nor were they extended to the average Englishman.[4] The king was no longer above the law, but the extension of the barons' power did not amount to the establishment of democracy.

Although he had agreed to the terms of the Magna Carta, it was not long before King John sought to renounce it. The pope, a supporter of John's, was persuaded to annul the Magna Carta, which in turn led to further pressure from the barons. When John resorted to force to impose his will, the barons enlisted the help of King Philip of France. John died of dysentery and fever in 1216, and the kingdom was left to his nine-year-old son, who was crowned King Henry III.[5] The barons might have anticipated that they would be able to influence and direct the actions of the young king, but things turned out somewhat differently as the new king seemed more open to the views of his mother and her close allies.[6] The barons' hesitancy in deciding what action they would take following John's death almost certainly contributed to the turmoil that ensued throughout the new king's reign.[7]

Earl David made peace with Henry III and lived uneventfully until his death in 1219. David's death saw the Earldom of Huntingdon pass to his son, John, who also replaced de Blondeville as Earl of Chester in 1232. Although there was nothing at the time to suggest that the deceased earls were associated with a Robin Hood legend, within six years of David's death the use of the term 'Robin Hood' was becoming increasingly common. From 1225 onwards the names Robbinhod, Robinhood, Robehod, Rabunhod and Hobbehod are frequently found written on the rolls of many English justices. Between 1260 and 1300 there are at least eight accounts of Robinhood in England, found between Hampshire and the city of York.[8] Reference to Robin Hood in this form was not meant as a name but, rather, a label. The term refers to an outlaw or fugitive. The first known example, mentioned in the York assizes – the sessions of the principal court exercising civil and criminal jurisdiction – in 1225 explains that a sheriff was made responsible for the personal belongings of outlaw Robert Hod, later to be labelled Hobbehod. A similar reference to a fugitive thus labelled comes from the year 1260 when legal records show that a man named William Son of Robert Le

Fevere was reprimanded for the creation of a band of armed men and two women. He then reappears on the rolls a year later under the name William Robehod.[9]

Therefore, while it is difficult to accept that the Robin Hood of the ballads existed during the reign of King Richard, it is clear that many outlaws were labelled as 'Robin Hoods'. It is less obvious whether a historical figure inspired the term or whether it was simply an invention of the authorities to describe any law-breaker. Robert was a common name, yet the term 'robin' could quite easily describe a robber. Equally, Hood was a common sur-name that could also apply to a cloaked figure. A robber in a hood or a hoodlum seems to go hand in hand with both the description of a criminal and Robin Hood's robbing from the rich, which may indicate that the individuals labelled in this way had no physical connection with the man from the ballads.[10] Major confirms that Robin Hood is a thief but, in common with Wyntoun and Bower, refers to him by the name Robert. Refer-ences to Little John as an alias were also increasingly common by the late thirteenth century.[11] The timing here is intriguing as it comes less than thirty years after the period when Robin Hood and Little John were said, by Bower, to have been fighting along-side Simon de Montfort.

Strengthened by his marriage to the king's sister, Eleanor, in 1238, Simon de Montfort emerged as the most powerful baron of his time.[12] He was a royal favourite for a long period, acting as an ambassador for the king between 1248 and 1252, but none the less remained firmly of the view that the king must comply with the restrictions placed on him by the Magna Carta.[13] As the barons' patience with the recalcitrant king wore thin, they began to meet in groups to discuss matters of policy. Representatives from county and city were allowed to attend, and the first steps towards the establishment of a parliament were taken. In 1258 a council was summoned by the barons in Oxford with the intention that it should act as an advisory body to the king, to meet with him and aid his rule.[14] The new developments were viewed with displeasure by the king, who sought the support of the pope to oppose them. Henry's links with the papacy, formed at his coronation years earlier, were to be of great value throughout his reign, and with the pope's approval he dismissed all plans for reform, continuing instead to rule as he wished.[15] Under the leadership of de Montfort, the barons resolved to impose restrictions on the authority of the king by force, thus leading the country into the second Barons' War.[16]

The king's position was favourable. In addition to enjoying a numerical advantage, his army was better organized than the rebels'. Despite this, the barons achieved a significant victory at the Battle of Lewes in 1264.[17] For the royalists this was a calamity. Not only did the king's army suffer a serious defeat but the barons succeeded in capturing the king and his son Edward.[18] Shortly after the barons' victory, de Montfort called a parliament which included nobility, gentry from the shires and burgesses from the towns. This, the first event of its kind in English history, marked the start of de Montfort's fifteen-month rule of England.[19]

Despite their success, the barons were dissatisfied. Continuation of the conflict and acts of brutality by supporters of de Montfort led to claims from some barons that they were acting too brutally towards the royalists. It was commonly believed that wherever the royalists went plunder, killing and the burning of villages by supporters of de Montfort followed.[20] However, it was not just the rebels who were responsible for the widespread violence. During the reign of Henry III the role of sheriff was amended and the old system was replaced with one in which four knights were appointed to every county and charged with keeping the peace.[21] Despite the change, rather than conserving the peace, many of the knights were accused of abusing the system and promoting disorder.[22]

In addition to accusing de Montfort's men of brutality, many of the barons were also becoming uneasy about his increasing power. History does not indicate that he abused his power, but it was clearly too much for the majority of the barons, who had lost authority themselves after briefly enjoying extended powers under the new laws of the Magna Carta during the early years of King Henry's reign. However, things were about to change. In 1265 Prince Edward escaped from captivity and brought an army against de Montfort at Evesham.[23] The 1st Baron of the Marches, Roger de Mortimer, was one of many noblemen who fought for the king. His gallantry had almost resulted in his death at the Battle of Lewes, but he returned triumphantly at the Battle of Evesham where he successfully blocked the only escape route for de Montfort's forces, at Bengeworth Bridge. As de Montfort fled from the battlefield he was caught and brutally murdered by Mortimer, following which his head was placed on a pike, and his limbs were torn and scattered around the towns that had favoured his cause.[24] In gratitude and recognition for his achievements Edward awarded Mortimer de Montfort's severed head, among other things.

De Montfort's death was a serious blow for his followers. Further full-scale rebellion was never likely; resistance continued, not in the hope or expectation of victory but as the only option available against royalist forces intent on revenge. A new parliament met in September 1265 and, prompted by greed rather than a desire to mete out appropriate punishment, decided that the rebels would be disinherited of all their titles.[25] John Fordun and Walter Bower detail the events of the time in their chronicle, *Scotichronicon*. In Bower's additions to Fordun's work, he included a curious passage making reference to Robin

Hood as a fighter for de Montfort's cause who had become outlawed as a result of the defeat:

> Then arose the famous murderer, Robert Hood, as well
> as Little John, together with their accomplices from
> among the disinherited, whom the foolish populace are
> so inordinately fond of celebrating both in tragedies
> and comedies, and about whom they are delighted to
> hear the jesters and minstrels sing above all other bal-
> lads. About whom also certain praiseworthy things are
> told, as appears in this – that when once in Barnsdale,
> avoiding the anger of the king and the threats of the
> prince, he was according to his custom most devoutly
> hearing Mass and had no wish on any account to inter-
> rupt the service – on a certain day, when he was hearing
> Mass, having been discovered in that very secluded
> place in the woods when the Mass was taking place by
> a certain sheriff and servant of the king, who had very
> often lain in wait for him previously, there came to him
> those who had found this out from their men to sug-
> gest that he should make every effort to flee. This, on
> account of his reverence for the sacrament in which he
> was then devoutly involved, he completely refused to
> do. But, the rest of his men trembling through fear of
> death, Robert, trusting in the one so great whom he
> worshipped, with the few who then bravely remained
> with him, confronted his enemies and easily overcame
> them, and enriched by the spoils he took from them and
> their ransom, ever afterward singled out the servants of
> the church and the Masses to be held in greater respect,
> bearing in mind what is commonly said: 'God harkens
> to him who hears Mass frequently.'[26]

The account given in *Scotichronicon* is generally in keeping with the historical events. The death of de Montfort may be regarded as the end of the rebellion, but the younger Simon de Montfort and Roger Leyburn continued to resist, as did John D'Eyville. Bower then again mentions Robert Hood in a reference to the rebels ending their hostilities and most of them taking refuge at Kenilworth Castle:

> In that year also the disinherited English barons and those loyal to the king clashed fiercely; amongst them Roger de Mortimer occupied the Welsh Marches and John-de-Eyville occupied the Isle of Ely; Robert Hood was an outlaw amongst the woodland briar's and thorns. Between them they inflicted a vast amount of slaughter on the common and ordinary folk, cities and merchants. King Henry, however, along with his son Prince Edward and a huge army also besieged the very well fortified castle of Kenilworth, where almost all the nobles who were rebelling against the king had taken refuge. There the remnant of Simon-de-Montfort's following, seeing that the castle with its towers and protecting walls was impregnable, defended themselves steadily with all their might. At length, worn out by lack of food and starvation, they handed over the castle on the condition that they keep life and limb.[27]

Bower's reference to Robin as a famous murderer is in keeping with the disorder of the time. It is given extra credibility here, particularly as he accurately describes the activities of Roger de Mortimer and John D'Eyville. The ballads themselves identify Robin Hood as a murderer – Gisborne and two sheriffs die at his hand – but there is no mention of his slaughter of the 'common and ordinary folk'. Equally, Bower's depiction is in stark contrast to Major's later testimony that Robin killed only in self-defence, yet some might sympathize with Bower's Robin Hood for supporting the man often celebrated in England as the founder of Parliament. The story of a man who refused to be denied mass is also consistent with the early ballads.[28]

The rhymes were widely recited by the time Bower was writing, and his reference to their popularity provides evidence of this. Since Bower claims that the activities of Robin Hood took place around the year 1266, his king and prince must be identified as King Henry III and Prince Edward, later to be crowned Edward I. If this was correct, then the ballads describe Robin after he was outlawed as a result of the rebellion. The reference is reminiscent of the ballads, but this rhyme of Robin in Barnsdale has not survived.[29] Bearing in mind that Bower mentioned Little John and Robin being joined by their accomplices from the 'disinherited', it is quite conceivable that he was referring to some of the 'Merry Men'. In the ballads, Robin and Little John's accomplices include Will Scarlock, Much the Miller's son, Reynold Greenleaf and Gilbert Whitehand.

Most people are familiar with Little John, Will Scarlock and Much the Miller's son, Robin Hood's three major lieutenants. Additionally, all the important chroniclers, except for Grafton, make some reference to Little John. Renowned for his size and strength, John is a seasoned fighter in the ballads. He is Robin's faithful companion and right-hand man. Second in command of the Merry Men, he appears in all the early ballads. Although it is unclear what his real name was, the ballads suggest he was a hardened warrior strong in strength and stature – sometimes portrayed as being over seven feet tall. His skills as a swordsman and archer are first rate and even rival Robin Hood's.[30]

Modern tradition depicts Little John as more of a brutish

woodsman and even a bumbling sidekick than a disciplined soldier, whereas the ballads suggest that he was experienced in war. In the *Gest* Little John is partly responsible for capturing Sir Richard and shows courtesy for his station by providing him with clothing and acting as his guide.[31] He is headstrong and cunning and often comes to blows with Robin. His trickery in the *Gest* and *Monk* ballads is particularly impressive, and he also demonstrates that he is a fine leader of men in Robin's absence. In the Middle Ages the term 'little' often meant tricky rather than being a jokey reference to a person's height.

Will Scarlock is another key member of the Merry Men whose reputation as a formidable fighter is in keeping with the rest of the outlaws. 'Scarlock' is not intended as a name but as a fitting alias.[32] He is portrayed as a fiery character with bright-red hair, Scarlett or Scar meaning red, lock meaning hair. Confusion over his name eventually resulted in both Will Scarlett and Will Scathelocke, but not Scarlock, appearing as Merry Men in Howard Pyle's novel from 1883, *The Merry Adventures of Robin Hood*. Scarlock's involvement with the Robin Hood legend dates back to the early ballads. Like the others, he is intelligent and a trusted henchman of Robin's. He is often portrayed as the youngest member of the band and also Robin's only kinsman.[33]

Much the Miller's son is also a seasoned fighter in the early ballads. His strength is demonstrated on countless occasions, and his merciless butchering of a page to hide Little John's murder of the treacherous monk reveals that he has a ruthless capacity for violence. In the *Gest* he demonstrates cunning, the equal of Little John's, to help capture the knight, and later displays an understanding of military insignia when he provides the knight with a horse. He is referred to as being strong enough to carry Little John and, despite being shorter than most, is a grown man with military experience.

Reynold Greenleaf and Gilbert of the White Hand are briefly mentioned in the *Gest*, where Gilbert is described as the only Merry Man capable of equalling Robin at archery.[34]

The idea that the outlaws were part of some sort of military organization is hardly surprising in view of the highly developed fighting skills they are shown to possess in the ballads, and such a suggestion is not entirely new. However, their intentions have been unclear. The indication from *Scotichronicon* is that Robin Hood was engaged in an ongoing guerrilla campaign against the king. This, in part, would make sense of theories linking Robin Hood with the exploits of Roger Godberd, who was outlawed after the Battle of Evesham where he fought with de Montfort. Between 1267 and 1272 Godberd was famed for his continued resistance against King Henry III, operating largely from Charnwood in Leicestershire where he caused widespread panic. The former Sheriff of Nottingham eventually captured him in 1272; he stood trial at Newgate prison in 1272 before disappearing from the historical records after 1276.[35]

There are a number of clear parallels between Godberd and Robin Hood. Earlier historians made reference to Godberd's close friendship with a knight named Sir Richard Foliot who granted Godberd and his men refuge in his castle – somewhat reminiscent of Sir Richard at the Lee, although Foliot in fact surrendered his castle, whereas in the ballads they survive.[36] During his time as an outlaw Godberd was reported as having a hundred men at his disposal, which can be compared with Robin's seven score yeomen. His activities in Derbyshire, Leicestershire and Nottinghamshire add to the possibility that he is Bower's Robin Hood, but its relevance has been exaggerated because of past misinterpretation of Charnwood as Sherwood.[37] Equally the ballads alone do nothing to strengthen the claim that Robin Hood was part of any continued rebellion.

Nevertheless, membership of an outlawed army is consistent with the personalities of the Merry Men. Their actions are in keeping with those of trained military, as are the cunning and intelligence shown by the key players in operations such as capturing the sheriff. The archery skills of the Merry Men and their expertise with swords go beyond the attainments of poachers, displaying instead characteristics associated with warfare. As for Robin Hood's status, the ballads clearly refer to him as a yeoman, but of exactly what type is unclear. The term 'yeoman' has often been the subject of debate; it covered a variety of social standings at different times during the Middle Ages,[38] and identifying the correct meaning depends in part on perception. The ballads originate from the mid fifteenth century, but the rhymes had been in existence since at least the mid fourteenth.

The term 'yeoman' could describe a rank in the royal household, not of noble blood and thus lower in status than the gentry, knights and squires, yet higher than a foot soldier.[39] Yeomen typically were capable swordsmen and archers and fought mounted or on foot. They often performed duties such as acting as bodyguards or protecting the sovereign or nobleman.[40] Yeoman status in this case applied to a paid soldier, which would be consistent with the view that Robin Hood and the Merry Men were fighting for the barons who opposed the king, although it is difficult to see how such a yeoman could be disinherited.

If Robin Hood had lived during the 1260s he could not have been a yeoman farmer, a social class only in existence between the late fourteenth and eighteenth centuries. A yeoman farmer owned a small amount of land and farmed it himself. A more likely use of the term when applied to Robin Hood would have been to describe his social status.[41] According to the Assizes of Arms of 1252, a yeoman was someone who owned land worth an average of between 40 and 80 shillings per annum, in size anything between 30 and 120 acres. In addition, as a mark of social standing, they were required to be trained with a bow.[42] Those at the higher end of the wealth scale must also have been trained with swords, and among them are likely to have been a number who became 'disinherited' when the king seized the lands of de Montfort's supporters. According to Bower, Robert Hood actively participated in the rebellion. After the defeat he would have lost his land – a clear and logical reason why he would resort to living the life of an outlaw. However, if Robert Hood was a member of the 'disinherited', what became of him? The year 1266 was a key one for the rebellion, as the 'disinherited' put up a final fight against the king, resulting in many issues in their dispute being resolved. John D'Eyville continued his resistance at Ely until the summer of 1267,[43] but the remainder of Henry's reign was spent settling differences with the rebels, leaving Edward free to embark on a two-year Crusade in the Holy Land. If Robert Hood was part of the rebellion, he may have been part of the garrison at Kenilworth Castle where, according to *Scotichronicon*, 'almost all of the Barons who were rebelling against the king had taken refuge', although Bower's reference to him being 'amongst the woodland briar's and thorns' suggests he was already active in the forests.[44] The Dictum of Kenilworth successfully secured the surrender of Kenilworth Castle but also involved some concessions from the Crown, including the right, initially, for the 'disinherited' to buy back their lands at seven times the annual value, although this was eventually reduced.[45]

If we read the ballads as a commentary on the lives of supporters of de Montfort who became disinherited as a result of participation in the rebellion, it seems that Robin Hood does not buy back his lands. It is unfortunate that Bower does not elaborate any further. It is equally disappointing that he did not provide more information about Robin's identity, but bearing in mind his criticisms of Robin's admirers it is clear that he did not like him. Godberd's arrest in 1272 fits with Bower's reference to Robin Hood being active in 1266, and the fact that Godberd was given refuge at Foliot's castle, Fenwick, placed him in close proximity to Barnsdale. Bower's suggestion that the king was Henry III and that both he and Prince Edward were seeking Robin is largely convincing, but unfortunately no other indication of this is given in the surviving ballads. If they are accepted as factually accurate, Robin Hood must have lived during the reign of an Edward. The first King Edward came to the throne only six years after the date Bower gives us.

4

WAICHMEN WERE
COMMENDIT GUDE

Following the death of Henry III in 1272, Edward I replaced his father as king and set to work consolidating England's position in Europe. Returning from the Holy Land for his coronation in 1274, he was determined to bring an end to any lingering threat of rebellion, with elements of dissent still present in Wales and Ireland. Although he agreed with the barons that he would honour the Magna Carta, his agenda was clear. Unlike the monarchs before him, his chief ambition was to become the undisputed ruler of the entire kingdom.[1]

Despite de Montfort's defeat resulting in the loss of the war for the barons, their aims were still partially met.[2] In 1295 the king summoned a parliament consisting of nobles, clergy and commoners, and subsequent experiments with the constitution continued throughout his reign. He appointed knights and burgesses to Parliament, but this was not intended as a boost for democracy: even after de Montfort the right to vote or nominate representatives in each borough was dependent on wealth. For Edward, raising money to finance his wars was an objective that he achieved through taxation and the ability of the country's merchants to raise money through trade.[3]

In Wales, many influential figures had supported Simon de

Montfort's rebellion, among them Prince Llewelyn ap Griffith. Since Edward's ascension to the throne of England, the Celtic lords had accepted the rule of the Princes of Gwynedd and, given their unanimous hatred of the Norman autocracy, Llewelyn refused to swear an oath of allegiance to the king.[4] Aiming to put an end to the discontent, Edward sought to conquer Wales and enforced his rule through the construction of an 'iron ring' of castles such as Conway, Caernarfon, Beaumaris and Harlech.[5] Many of the Welsh rebels were killed, while others sought refuge in the mountains where they were made to live in seclusion. By 1282 Llewelyn was defeated and Edward imposed his will, although the war in Wales continued until 1295.[6]

When Edward originally turned his attention to Scotland, he hoped to take the Scottish Crown without opposition. Since the death of Alexander III in 1286 there was no one in Scotland with a clear and rightful claim to the throne. Alexander's heiress was his granddaughter, Margaret the 'Maid of Norway', but owing to her youth her position was highly vulnerable. Despite her young age, Edward managed to secure her hand in marriage for his son, Edward, but she died before the wedding could take place.[7] The right of succession was then even less clear. Without an undisputed leader, the Scottish nobles turned to Edward to appoint an unbiased judge to act as steward for the kingdom. He appointed John Balliol.[8]

Not for the first time in Scotland's history there was unrest behind the scenes. The nobles' inability to agree to Longshanks's insistence on being the final judge in Scottish legal cases, in addition to Balliol's inability to control the ambitions of the nobles, forced him into a rebellion against England.[9] Edward 'Longshanks', 'the hammer of the Scots', invaded Scotland and defeated Balliol at Dunbar.[10] This may have been his plan all along. With Scotland taken, he could concentrate fully on the war with France.[11]

As Edward's attention turned to other areas, Scotland witnessed the emergence of the famous William Wallace – regarded by many as the Scottish Robin Hood. His early years are lost to history, but in Longshanks's absence he successfully gathered a force that expelled the king's representatives from Scotland, and in 1297 he went on to defeat the English army at the Battle of Stirling Bridge.[12] The setback was surprising, and Edward was so concerned that he ordered his armies to march north to deal with the threat. The Scots were defeated at Falkirk in 1298, and Scotland was back under Edward's control.[13] Wallace looked elsewhere for support, eventually resorting to guerrilla warfare. In 1305 he was captured and subsequently hanged, drawn and quartered.[14] When accused of treason he was said to have answered, 'I could not be a traitor to Edward, for I was never his subject.'

As with Robin Hood, folklore, legend and Hollywood have romanticized the life of Wallace. After returning from France in 1303 it is likely that he took to the forests until his capture, but for two years his whereabouts remained a mystery as he continued to elude the English forces. Andrew of Wyntoun was highly critical of Longshanks. In his *Orygynale Cronykil of Scotland*, written in 1420, he highlights Longshanks's treatment of William Wallace, accusing him of various war crimes against Scotland and heaping fulsome praise upon Wallace.[15] Wallace has long been regarded as a heroic figure in Scotland. His reputation has been enhanced by modern tradition, stemming perhaps in part from the *Orygynale Cronykil*. Robin Hood is also mentioned in the chronicle, appearing in four lines under the years 1283–5:

> Litill Iohne and Robyne Hude
> Waichmen were commendit gude
> In yngilwode and bernysdale
> And usit this tyme thar travale.

Translated into modern English, this becomes:

> Little John and Robin Hood
> As forest outlaws were well renown
> In Inglewood and Barnsdale
> All this time they plied their trade.[16]

The *Orygynale Cronykil* was very pro-Scottish. Rather than being intended as a serious history, it was a patriotic overview of Scotland written for a readership of patriots. This was in stark contrast to the work of Major, which was aimed at a wider European audience.[17] Wyntoun is full of praise for Wallace and Robin Hood and quick to condemn the actions of the English.[18] According to Wyntoun, Robin Hood and Little John operated in the border region of Inglewood in Cumbria. The *Cronykil* refers to them as 'Waichmen', meaning 'those who lie in wait'. This confirms they were outlaws, but it does not explain why. 'Plying their trade' makes reference to their thievery. The chronicle does not specifically suggest that Robin fought for Scotland, but given that Andrew of Wyntoun was quick to praise his efforts the possibility cannot be entirely ruled out.

If the *Orygynale Cronykil* is correct, Robin Hood and Little John were outlaws during the period 1283–5. The timing is coincidental in the sense that they appear at the height of England's war against Wales.[19] Wyntoun may, however, simply have been referring to the activities of Robin in a less accusing way than Bower's reference to a *famosus siccarius*. As outlaws Robin and his men were enemies of the Crown, and, bearing in mind that Longshanks's hostility towards rebels, notably Wallace, was fierce, Robin Hood may have been perceived as an ally of Scotland, even if only because of his status as an outlaw. Whether or not Robin participated in the war on behalf of Scotland, perhaps the old Scottish saying 'England's enemy is our friend' came to Wyntoun's mind.

Wyntoun makes reference to Barnsdale, demonstrating that Robin was already associated with Barnsdale in the rhymes at the time. More intriguing, though, is Wyntoun's placing of Robin Hood in Inglewood rather than Sherwood. Perhaps Robin Hood did operate in Inglewood and the rhymes describing this have not survived. The only possible reference to Inglewood in the ballads we know is a brief mention of Plompton Park, which has little or no relevance to Robin Hood.[20] Wyntoun was the only man to refer to Robin Hood and Inglewood. In doing so, by coincidence or intent, he connected Robin Hood with another famous outlaw, Adam Bell, who featured in the ballad *Adam Bell, Clym of the Cloughe and Wyllyam of Cloudeslee*, dated around 1505, around the same time as *Robin Hood and the Potter*. This ballad is the oldest surviving reference to Adam Bell and describes him in great detail. According to the ballad, Bell, Clough and Cloudesley were outlaws who sought refuge in Inglewood Forest, a large area that once existed in Cumbria. The content of the ballad is not dissimilar to that of *Robin Hood and the Monk*. Adam is an astute archer and swordsman, and William of Cloudesley in particular is an exceptional archer, capable of shooting an arrow directly through an apple placed on his son's head.[21]

Whether Adam Bell was a historical figure remains unclear, but there are many parallels between these outlaws and Robin Hood. In the early ballads Robin Hood is often portrayed as being single minded, as illustrated in the *Monk* ballad when he acts against the advice of Much the Miller's son, and William Cloudesley displays a similar trait when he ignores the advice of his close friend before making his way into the town of Carlisle.[22] Another similarity comes when a gaoler is harshly treated, not unlike the scene in the *Monk* ballad where Little John murders the gaoler to rescue Robin. A messenger is present in both stories, and, like Robin, Adam Bell demonstrates mastery of the art of trickery, which he puts to good effect when using a forged royal seal to gain entry into Carlisle.[23] In the ballad of *Robin Hood and the Monk* an almost identical event occurred, although the seal in that case was stolen rather than forged.

The reader understands from the start that Adam and his friends have been outlawed for poaching venison.[24] The Robin Hood ballads, however, do not provide any indication of why Robin should be an outlaw. Wyntoun's failure to explain this limits the conclusions that can be drawn from his narrative.

As the *Orygynale Cronykil* was completed in 1420, it is likely that Bower was aware of it when he revised *Scotichronicon* some twenty years later. The seventeen-year gap between Bower's date of 1266 and Wyntoun's of 1283–5 does not rule out the possibility that Bower and Wyntoun were writing about the same man.[25] If 1266 marked the beginning of the Robin Hood tales, and bearing in mind he is never permanently captured in the ballads, then it is quite conceivable that he and Little John were still at large in 1283. The time period in which the *Gest* is set is not stated, but it could have been any time after 1266. When Edward I ascended to the throne in 1272, just six years had elapsed since Robert Hood's alleged involvement in the rebellion against Henry III. Unless Robert died in those intervening six years, the chances are that Bower's 'disinherited' *famosus siccarius* was still an outlaw. The Dictum of Kenilworth may have removed some of the potential for a future war, but it was not altogether effective.[26] The terms of the agreement were amended in 1267 owing to their unfairness, and while many disinherited rebels did repurchase their lands this did not fully resolve the problem. Edward did not fight any further wars in England, but the supporters of de Montfort who did not repurchase their lands continued to demonstrate their commitment to the cause espoused by their late leader in many ways, short of further full-scale rebellion, causing constant unrest and problems for the new king well into his reign. It is known that at least some of de Montfort's supporters fled to the forests. In addition to Roger Godberd, there was the prominent Adam de Gurdon who, following de Montfort's defeat at the Battle of Evesham, fled to the pass of Alton where he lived the life of a highwayman, earning a living from robbery and plundering. In 1267 he was arrested by Prince Edward, later pardoned and granted lands.[27]

The first reference to Little John also comes in the *Orygynale Cronykil*; but, in common with that for Robin, the mention is brief. Wyntoun's choice of words is interesting and may even be ambiguous. He mentions that Little John and Robin Hood are outlaws in Inglewood and Barnsdale, perhaps indicating that they were outlawed together. Alternatively, he may have meant that Little John was an outlaw in Inglewood and Robin Hood in Barnsdale. This is the first time both characters are mentioned together in a historical source. By 1420 the ballads were probably not in print; if any were, they have not survived; but they would have existed in oral form. Wyntoun was undoubtedly familiar with the rhymes, and his reference to Little John and Robin Hood being outlaws in Barnsdale most likely stems from them.

Wider awareness of the work of John Major, made possible by its availability in printed form, may have helped reinforce the popular view that Robin lived during the reign of Richard I, yet the works of Wyntoun and Bower that preceded it were never accepted to the same extent. Major is celebrated as one of the greatest minds of his time. Wyntoun and Bower, on the other hand, were religious men. In addition to being a poet, Wyntoun was also a canon and prior of Loch Leven in the isolated Scottish highlands and later a canon of St Andrews.[28] He is remembered most famously for the *Orygynale Cronykil*, an eight-syllable metre describing the history of Scotland from the ancient times to the start of the reign of James I of Scotland in 1406. The chronicle was written at the request of his patron, Sir John of Wemyss, with the intention of providing a detailed account of the nation's history for the people of Scotland. Wyntoun was seventy years old when he wrote the chronicle, three years before his death.[29]

Walter Bower was an abbot in vocation at Inchcolm Abbey in the Firth of Forth from 1418 onwards.[30] Such a role may be viewed as ironic, bearing in mind that abbots were often victims of Robin Hood and his Merry Men in the ballads, and this probably influenced his criticism of the 'foolish populace'. Like Wyntoun, he was a patriot. In 1432 he appeared at the Council of Perth defending the rights of the Scots. His trustworthy reputation resulted in his being made a commissioner for the collection of the ransom of James I in 1424 following eighteen years as a prisoner in England.[31]

Bower is best remembered as a chronicler. Following on from *Chronica Gentis Scotorum*, the first five books of *Scotichronicon* penned by John Fordun, Bower wrote a further eleven books and developed the work of Fordun considerably. Fordun's first five books spanned the period from early history to the death of King David I. The beginning of a sixth book was more concerned with later history, and this was eventually a stepping-stone for Bower. *Scotichronicon* is well respected as a historical text. It was the first attempt at a continuous history of Scotland inspired by Fordun's patriotic fanaticism following the destruction of numerous records by King Edward III of England. Although the first three books are unverified, he was reputed to have travelled far and wide to gather a wealth of sources for his work, which he continued until his death in 1384. The fourth and fifth books are particularly respected. Bower's follow-up to the work of Fordun began in 1440 and continued until 1447, two years before his death at the age of sixty-four.[32]

It is seemingly coincidence that the chroniclers who acknowledge the existence of Robin Hood were mainly Scottish. Yet it is perhaps not totally surprising. The Scots appear to have an affinity with Robin Hood. This might be due simply to the many characteristics that he shares with Wallace but may also stem from deeper reasons. According to the poet William Motherwell, Robin Hood and Little John were as popular with the minstrels of Scotland as they were in England. Francis Child made the point that at the time of his indexing the ballads there were several 'fragments of songs regarding them' still to make their way into printed collections which would have made an 'interesting addition to Ritson'.[33] Perhaps in Scotland a different tradition existed which remains unknown. Alternatively, perhaps it was more acceptable for the Scots to enjoy ballads about English outlaws. Throughout the Middle Ages stories of outlaws were officially disapproved of. To be recorded in the chronicles would mean that the chronicler acknowledged the outlaws' existence, and in the case of the English chroniclers they did not. Equally, no chronicler from the twelfth or thirteenth century made reference to Robin Hood as living during 'their' time. Whether this means that Robin Hood did not exist, or that he was just not considered important, is not clear. Many references to Robin Hood in the chronicles can be construed as Scottish criticism of England, but this does not necessarily make them any less accurate. To establish Robin Hood's existence as an outlaw, it would be necessary to establish the reasons for which he was outlawed, and this was something on which no two chroniclers could ever agree.

5

A FELLOWSHIP OF OUTLAWS OR AN OUTLAWED FELLOWSHIP?

Despite the best efforts of the chroniclers to validate the existence of a historical Robin Hood, the differences and inconsistencies in their presentation and interpretation of information and events have succeeded only in stimulating a debate over his authenticity that has continued for more than five centuries. They all acknowledge the widespread popularity of the ballads and Robin Hood's status as an outlaw, but only Bower and Grafton attempted to explain why he was outlawed. The ballads are equally unforthcoming in this respect. We understand from the early ones that he was outlawed in the company of 140 yeomen – most of whom are never named – during the reign of one of the King Edwards. This contrasts with the stories of Adam Bell, Fulk FitzWarin, Eustache the Monk and Hereward the Wake, where the reader is made aware of the outlaw's situation from the outset.[1] The information provided in the early Robin Hood ballads is not much to go on, and theories put forward in later centuries are inconsistent.

Later ballads offer limited suggestions, such as *A True Tale of Robin Hood* by Martin Parker, although most of them lack credibility as they accept Robin Hood's status as an earl.[2] The Sloane Manuscript reinforces Grafton's claims that Robin Hood was a man of possible noble parentage outlawed for running up heavy debts, but despite the author's awareness of the *Gest* he is susceptible to Grafton's attempts to reinforce Major's view of Robin living during the reign of Richard I even though the *Gest* clearly refers to the king as Edward. The antiquary Roger Dodsworth offered an equally unfounded explanation claiming that Robin killed his stepfather with a plough before fleeing.[3] None of this was included in the early ballads.

The first ballad that attempts to explain why he was outlawed was *Robin Hood's Progress to Nottingham*. Printed in the seventeenth century, it was described by Child as a 'comparatively late ballad'.[4] Set in Nottingham, it tells of how a fifteen-year-old Robin Hood is harassed by some foresters whom, in fear for his life, he kills. The young Robin is then chased into the greenwood and becomes an outlaw.[5] The ballad is more in keeping with a yeoman's background and offers an alternative to suggestions by various antiquaries that he was an excessively generous nobleman or a rebel who became the enemy of Prince John or King Henry III. Nevertheless, its suggestion is unconvincing, considering that Robin Hood in the majority of the ballads is middle aged and possesses highly developed leadership skills and military expertise. This ballad is not widely accepted as offering an authentic historical origin for Robin Hood, although a more satisfactory one is still to be found.

Nor do the ballads offer a satisfactory explanation of how Robin Hood came to join his Merry Men. Logically there are two possibilities: they were outlawed either separately, or all together. Writers such as Dodsworth, and even some of the nobility theorists, suggest Robin Hood was outlawed on his own and sought shelter in the greenwood of Barnsdale or Sherwood; on his travels he then encounters various other outlaws, possibly alone or in small groups. He spars with them and gradually assembles a band of faithful followers.[6] In the later ballads Robin consistently meets new recruits, spars with them, loses, invites them to join the band and they accept. In ballads such as *Robin Hood and Little John*, for example, Robin meets Little John on a narrow bridge and they duel with quarterstaffs. In *Robin Hood and the Newly Revived*, and *The Bold Pedlar and Robin Hood*, both identified as literary origins for Will Scarlock, Robin waylays a stranger and insists that he hand over a certain amount of his belongings.[7] They fight, the stranger impresses, and ultimately the man joins the band. By such means Robin eventually gathers together a band of seven score yeomen, as identified in the *Gest*.

Over the years most people have come to accept the explanation that Robin drew together his band of supporters one by one, but the early ballads are unclear on the subject. While there are some accounts of attracting new members in these ballads, most references to the origins of the Merry Men are not found until the seventeenth century or later. In the *Gest* the sheriff's cook joins the Merry Men, and in the *Potter* ballad the potter is also invited to join them, but these men are not outlaws. Instead they choose to become honorary members of the band in return for certain gain.[8] Given the date of composition of the later ballads, it is difficult to accept them as more than inventions. The ballad of *Little John* is particularly strange as Little John fights with a quarterstaff whereas in the early ballads he is a formidable swordsman. The quarterstaff was not the weapon of a yeoman of the courts or of a soldier, which illustrates how the later tales take on a more rural form.[9]

The group could have been formed over a period of time, with Robin showing great skill in integrating seven score individual outlaws into an organized fraternity, but it seems unlikely. Why would 140 outlaws choose to follow a stranger and share the proceeds of their activities? That the structure of the fraternity is so deeply entrenched and resilient tends to suggest that it may have already been in place before its members were outlawed. In the *Gest* Will Scarlock, Little John and Much the Miller's son are all introduced early on. The *Monk* ballad also begins with Much and Little John outlawed together, and similarly in the *Potter* and *Gisborne* ballads the outlaws are already together. The fact that the ballads begin with the Merry Men already well established gives a strong indication that they had been outlawed for a significant period of time, and that they were probably all outlawed together. Evidence of a well-organized and formal group is presented from the very start. This raises further questions. What offences did these men commit? Did they all commit similar ones? That is possible, but the dynamic of the group suggests that they were not a fraternity of outlaws brought together by chance but, rather, a group who had been outlawed together.

Turning to the work of the chroniclers, Bower's reasoning is the most convincing. Nevertheless, it is unfortunate that the surviving ballads do not provide any supporting information to help determine whether the group might have comprised 'disinherited' rebels, Saxons or others with a common bond of allegiance. Bower suggests that there were rhymes in existence at the time he wrote *Scotichronicon* that positively identified Robin and his men as 'disinherited' rebels, but none of these has survived. The fact that no such rhymes are extant does not rule out the possibility that they did once exist, but they cannot be taken for granted. In the ballads that have survived the band are his 'Merry Men'. The first reference to the term 'Merry Men' comes in the *Monk* ballad. Little John refers to himself as a 'merry man', soon followed by Robin's description of his men when he asks Little John to bear his bow:

> A more mery man then I am one
> Lyves not in Cristianté.[10]

Shortly after this we hear:

> 'Of all my mery men,' seid Robyn,
> 'Be my feith I wil non have,
> But Litull John shall beyre my bow,
> Til that me list to drawe.'[11]

Twenty-first-century tradition may refer to the men as being merry, happy, tipsy on alcohol, etc., but the original term probably stems from an old Saxon word 'merry', meaning mighty, great and famous. Alternatively, early English use of the word suggests a follower or companion.[12] Having said this, the use of the words by Little John is ambiguous. In the *Monk* ballad he is a merry man on a merry morning in May. On other occasions Robin's 'Merry Men' are referred to as his 'Merry Meyne' or 'Mery Maney', suggesting they are men in arms.[13] The ballads refer to seven score of yeomen, which identifies the size of the group. However, they do not disclose what type of yeoman these are. The reference could be to a landowner or a servant in the court of the king or of the nobility, but there are other possibilities. The word 'yeoman' originates from the Saxon 'iunge' man or 'yonge' man. The latter form is used at least twice instead of 'yeoman' in the *Gest* ballad:

> It was upon a mery day
> That yonge men wolde go shete,
> Lytell Johnn fet his bowe anone,
> And sayde he wolde them mete

> 'Say me nowe, wight yonge man,
> What is nowe thy name?
> In what countré were thou borne,
> And where is thy wonynge wane?'[14]

The ages of the outlaws are never specifically mentioned, and the term 'yonge man' is often used to indicate a person's place in the fraternity.[15] This may be applicable to the Merry Men. Throughout the ballads Robin is described as a master, rather than a leader, a designation more in keeping with a fraternity or secret society than an army of the disinherited.

The term 'yeoman' also had another meaning in the fourteenth century, associated with being freeborn and of free tenure,[16] rather than a serf. As we have seen, yeomen who served in the royal courts were servants, that is, they were paid, and being freeborn was a necessity for them since they could not take up employment if they had a duty or obligation to another master. The term is also used in the *Gest*:

> Lythe and listin, gentilmen,
> That be of frebore blode;
> I shall you tel of a gode yeman,
> His name was Robyn Hode.[17]

In modern English the second line reads 'that be of freeborn blood'. This indicates that the target audience is anyone who is freeborn. Although it does not necessarily follow that the yeomen of the ballads are the same type of yeomen as the audience, the *Gest* begins by giving a clear indication that the audience are to identify with the outlaws who are of freeborn blood.[18]

In the ballads another possibility emerges when Robin declares himself a 'yeoman of the forest', an official term hardly applicable to an outlaw.[19] Foresters were employed during the Middle Ages to enforce the laws of the forest, and the Crown gave them this authority. Robin Hood, on the other hand, is not entitled to impose these rules; he has not been given authority by the Crown; so the term can only be describing his situation rather than his occupation.[20] Another alternative use of the term is given during the scene when Robin Hood allows Little John to join Sir Richard at the Lee to stand in the stead of a yeoman.[21] In addition to the other meanings previously discussed, 'yeoman' can also refer to a servant, assistant, deputy, loyal companion or even journeyman. The role of journeyman is particularly associated with the fifteenth-century guilds, which required that prospective members undergo an apprenticeship. In the first fytte of the *Gest*, when Robin assists Sir Richard, Little John acts as his servant, deputy and assistant, which is also appropriate to his social status below that of a knight. Robin could have been any of these types of yeoman. One consistent aspect in the use of the word is that it explains that the Merry Men are not of the nobility.[22]

Other than the fact that the Merry Men are all yeomen, regardless of which kind, the dynamic of their group has also been the subject of much examination. Throughout the early ballads there are constant skirmishes with the sheriff using swords or archery, demonstrating their proficiency in the skills and arts of war. The discipline shown by the men serving under Sir Richard at the Lee, including Robin, in fytte 6 of the *Gest* points to a level of understanding of military procedure and hierarchy that is not readily associated with someone who is not, or has not been, a soldier. References to the group of outlaws as a fraternity, or brotherhood, are not exclusively modern, but most discussion on the subject has centred on a fictitious society based on the medieval guilds rather than a historical army. The medieval guilds were associations of craftsmen rather than soldiers, and they were also wholly within the law. The Merry Men are not a guild, but as a fraternity their origin is unclear.

Meanings of the word 'fraternity' are various. During the Middle Ages and even in the present day it could mean different things. It involved a brotherly relationship to other members; it also incorporated the joining together of like-minded people for a common aim or purpose.[23] Types of fraternity include social clubs, benefit societies, secret societies and, at the time of the Crusades, chivalric orders. The Merry Men are a fraternity of yeomen who abide by the rules of the fraternity and are obedient to the master. Their organization allows entry to a cook and a potter, both of whom are yeomen. Rather than being portrayed as a group of thieves such as those led by de Gurdon and Godberd, one of the first things we learn of the Merry Men is that their code of conduct affirms that they are not to molest a knight or squire who would be a 'good fellow'.[24] In these respects the Merry Men go beyond the ordinary sphere of fraternity and even class. They are a fraternity of yeomen, but membership is not necessarily restricted to yeomen alone. Sir Richard at the Lee is a knight but is accepted by the group as a potentially 'good fellow', although he does not join the Merry Men formally.[25]

The term 'fellow' also requires clarification, as it, too, can have a number of meanings. In the case of the Merry Men, it refers to members of a fellowship. Robin uses the term 'fellowship' to describe the Merry Men in both the *Gest* and the *Potter* ballads. He offers the potter a 'fellowship' in the ballad of the same name.[26] This kind of fellowship implies that they are a band of people who share common interests or aims. The term can also mean good company, which is relevant here. In the case of these men, the purpose of their fellowship is to avoid detection and accept self-sacrifice and hardship while abiding by the rules of the fellowship for the greater good of all of its members.

The main difference between a fellowship and a fraternity lies in their respective structures. Whereas the structure of a fraternity consists of a formal hierarchy, a fellowship usually comprises a group of social equals. In the case of the Merry Men their yeoman status makes them social equals, but, as A.J. Pollard suggests in his book *Imagining Robin Hood*, a fellowship can be based on a fraternity and vice versa; indeed, many of the great livery companies of the fifteenth century were fraternities which came to model themselves as fellowships.[27] The Order of the Garter was similarly formed as a fellowship but was structured in the dynamic of a fraternity. In fact, all military orders established with statutes and dedicated to a patron saint were modelled as fellowships. The Merry Men are themselves equals whereas the 'disinherited', like other armies, were based on a strict hierarchical structure. Although Robin is the equal of his men as a yeoman, he frequently demonstrates characteristics in keeping with his role as master. In the *Gest* he refuses to eat unless he has a guest to dine with, whether it is a baron who can pay for the best food or a knight or squire who can also be entertained at his own expense:

> Here shal come a lord or sire
> That may pay for the best,
> Or som knight or squyer,
> That dwelleth here bi west.[28]

Robin's social status is interesting, particularly as he personally does not discriminate by class. The honour of dining with him is usually extended to those of higher social status, and when he instructs the Merry Men whom to waylay and whom to leave alone he is even-handed, telling them that they should not waylay any good yeoman, including foresters, or a knight or squire who would be a 'good fellow'.

> No more ye shall no gode yeman
> That walketh by grene wode shawe,
> Ne no knyght ne no squyer
> That wol be a gode felawe.[29]

Despite their outlawed status, the Merry Men abide by a code of conduct. The individual members are all bound by the rules of the fellowship. This again suggests that the fellowship may have once been law-abiding and that vows of obedience remain in force from an earlier period. This is more in keeping with a monastic order than an army, let alone a band of outlaws. Despite being a fellowship, there is a hierarchy in keeping with the structure of a fraternity or military group. In the scene at the knight's castle Robin and his men take up arms under the command of the knight. In the first fytte of the *Gest* Robin Hood is the knight's equal when they dine, but the knight has command over the fellowship in battle.[30] Without the knight Robin is well and truly the master of the Merry Men, yet his position as a master is not clear cut. In the *Monk* ballad, after Little John rescues Robin, proceedings take a further twist when Robin offers Little John the role of master. Little John rejects this, preferring to settle for being a 'good fellow'.

> 'Nay, be my trouth,' seid Robyn,
> 'So shall hit never be;
> I make the maister,' seid Robyn,
> 'Of alle my men and me.'

> 'Nay, be my trouth,' seid Litull John,
> 'So shalle hit never be;
> But lat me be a felow,' seid Litull John,
> 'No noder kepe I be.'[31]

For the only time in the ballads the reader understands that Robin's position as master is not an absolute right. There is no explanation for how this came about. Did he earn his position? Did he take it? Was it offered to him? Or was he elected? We cannot know, because the early ballads start with the group fully established. There is clearly a rule of obedience to the master, and when Robin returns to the forest at the end of the *Gest* the men all kneel before him as if he were a king; the king himself in the *Gest* refers to the men as being more at Robin's bidding than his own men are to him.[32]

When joining the Merry Men new members must undergo an initiation ceremony. In the *Potter* ballad the potter agrees to be a good fellow and swears allegiance to the master. In the *Monk* ballad Little John nearly comes to blows with Robin but restrains himself, even though later in the ballad he murders a monk:

> 'Were thou not my maister,' seid Litull John,
> 'Thou shouldis by hit ful sore;
> Get the a man where thou wilt,
> For thou getis me no more.'[33]

The men's willingness to serve under Robin suggests they are all willing to abide by the laws of a fraternity in which one pledges obedience to the master. He is appointed by all the members and exercises authority over what is otherwise a group of equals. We understand that seven score yeomen make up the band, yet only Much the Miller's son, Will Scarlock, Gilbert

Whitehand, Reynold Greenleaf and Little John are named. Much, Scarlock and Little John in particular are his main deputies. This suggests a pyramid of seniority, which was common in a fraternity and highly effective from the point of view of security as it ensured that only the most senior and trusted members would have full knowledge of the organization. If security were breached, as it nearly was at times, members of lesser importance would not be in a position to divulge vital information. In the case of the Merry Men the secrets of the fellowship may have been nothing more than where it was based. Nevertheless, it was vital that this information was not disclosed to anyone outside the group if the outlaws were to remain free and undetected. For an outlawed fraternity or fellowship to survive, trust would have been of paramount importance.

What is apparent in the early ballads, notably the *Gest* and *Potter* ballads, is that neither the Sheriff of Nottingham nor even the king has any idea who these men are. They are not categorized as wanted criminals and are not even well known. Bower describes Robin as a well-known murderer, but he may have been referring to Robin's reputation as a ballad hero at the time *Scotichronicon* was written. According to the ballads, the Merry Men are never captured despite the best attempts of the sheriff, which reflects their discipline and ability to preserve secrecy.

Throughout the ballads trickery is a recurring theme, and this may have helped make secrecy possible. If this group survived without detection, despite the fact that all 140 outlaws would sometimes meet up, they must have guarded their secrets vigilantly and operated an underground network that could not be breached. They would probably have used code or secret signs to make sure their communications were not understood by the wrong people. In order to ensure, for instance, in the case of the cook, that a new member was not a spy for the sheriff, hoping to infiltrate the band, a strenuous examination would have been needed. This fellowship would be very selective about taking on new members, whereas a more typical fraternity, operating within the law, was usually accessible to any person who met the membership criteria and paid the appropriate fee for the privilege. The sheriff would undoubtedly have relished an opportunity to infiltrate this band of outlaws with a rogue member, but the ballads suggest that this never happened. Only the king, posing as an abbot, managed to infiltrate the Merry Men.

The dynamic of the group is reminiscent of many societies of similar structure, but there is one strange aspect. If this fellowship, which incorporated many of the key characteristics of a fraternity, was a forest fraternity, comprised of many outlaws roaming the greenwood for one reason or another, later moulded into a virtuous group of men of noble intentions by Robin Hood, then they were unlike any other outlaws that ever existed. Was this really possible? Did 140 separate like-minded individuals who may or may not have been criminals really form a fellowship in the forest to do poor men much good? At the time it would have been very surprising for people living outside the law to be of noble intent. During the reign of King Edward II numerous gangs plagued the forests, making a living through stealing from the clergy and gentry, but what they stole they took for themselves. It is also curious that Robin Hood's band of outlaws is hospitable to its guests and frequently dines with them. The men do not steal from those truthful about their possessions or from the poor.[34] Other outlaws were frequently guilty of murder or rape, but the Merry Men kill only in self-defence or to exact retribution.[35]

As to the purpose or objectives of the group, the ballads are surprisingly neutral. They focus on the day-to-day lives of the outlaws and do not explain much about their political views or allegiances. The Merry Men are not identified as being part of any cause. Taking the ballads as sources in their own right, the Merry Men are enemies of the county authorities and thus the Crown because of their outlawed status, rather than the other way around. Especially curious is their vendetta against the clergy, which contradicts Bower's claim that Robin supported the Church.[36] Why followers of de Montfort should behave like this is unclear.[37] It could simply be that the clergy habitually carried large sums of money and were perceived as soft targets. Such an explanation is very much in keeping with the behaviour of Adam de Gurdon and Godberd but inadequate in the case of Robin Hood's band, which, with the notable exception of the monk killed for his treachery by Little John, invariably releases physically unharmed the clergy who fall into their hands. Nevertheless, hostility towards the Church is confirmed at the beginning of the *Gest* when Robin Hood says of bishops and archbishops that they are predetermined targets for his Merry Men. The rationale for this is not explained. The ballads are of course incomplete; much of Robin's life is omitted. Perhaps he did take part in a guerrilla campaign against Henry III, but, if so, why was this not known?[38] And if he did, it is hardly likely the populace would have been so fond of celebrating him. In the *Gest* Robin talks of his love for Edward, his comely king. For Robin to have been a rebel against the king would make him the king's enemy – a contradiction of his portrayal in popular culture as an outlaw who continued to fight in the cause of what he believed to be true kingship.

The vendetta with the clergy is perhaps the most interesting element of the ballads, particularly given Robin's devout piety. Although feuding with the Sheriff of Nottingham continues throughout the ballads, Robin is more of an enemy of the Church than of royal officials, as illustrated early in the *Gest*.[39] He is clearly intent on embarrassing the Church. Adam de Gurdon's experience fighting for de Montfort made him a formidable outlaw, yet he was quite different from Robin Hood in manner. De Gurdon's threatening and violent behaviour is far more akin to that of Godberd, which caused widespread panic and fear, in stark contrast to Robin's practice of not molesting a 'good fellow' or one who might make a 'good fellow', as indicated in the *Gest*.[40] Despite the military ethos, the dynamic of the fellowship is largely out of keeping with that of de Montfort's men but perhaps more characteristic of another band of outlaws who roamed the countryside almost thirty years after Wyntoun's praise of the waichmen.

6

THE TEMPLARS VERSUS THE BULL

Following the death of William Wallace, Robert the Bruce reappeared on the scene in 1307 and England once more entered into a bitter struggle against the Scottish rebels. The Bruce's re-emergence was unwelcome to Longshanks, who was again forced into action against Scotland. His hatred of the Scots never diminished, but by that time he was dying. One of his last commands to his son, later to be crowned Edward II, was that the war against the Scots was to continue until they were defeated for good.[1] Edward may not have regarded the threat from Scotland as a genuine danger to England, but the presence of Robert the Bruce and his raising an army to resist English dominion over the Scots ensured that peace would not come while Robert was still alive.[2]

Edward II was not like his father. Where the father was strong, the son was weak. Where Edward II had support, he often managed to upset the balance, and conflict frequently followed.[3] Despite his marriage in 1308 to Isabella, the 'she-wolf' of France, he seemed more attracted to his foster-brother Piers Gaveston.[4] Edward I had earlier banished Gaveston, fearing that he had a homosexual influence on the prince. Writing to her father, Philip IV of France, Isabella made reference to the rumours, describing herself as the 'most wretched of wives' and blaming Gaveston for all their problems.[5] Gaveston's return from exile after Long-shanks's death alarmed the barons, who feared for the security of the kingdom.[6] Maintaining that they were acting on behalf of the king and the country, they drew up a large number of reforms. For the first time in English history it was acknowledged that there was a distinction between the person of the king and the institution of the Crown.[7] The barons also had Gaveston executed at Kenilworth in 1312 and monitored the king closely.[8]

Despite the unrest in Scotland and the threat of rebellion against English rule, Edward was reluctant to act, and this allowed Robert the Bruce time to assemble an army. Finally, recognizing the danger, he sent a large army, consisting of around 20,000 men, to oppose Robert the Bruce's force of about 6,000. Under the efficient, determined and decisive command of Longshanks, an English army of such numerical superiority would almost certainly have been victorious, but that was not to be on this occasion. The English force became trapped in a bog at Bannockburn in 1314, and the Scots claimed victory in what would prove to be the decisive battle in the First Scottish War of Independence.[9]

Edward's lack of business acumen was notable. He preferred to spend his time indulging in entertainment rather than the duties of kingship, his reign was plagued by numerous blunders, and authority became largely decentralized. In some quarters the king's fairness had won him respect, but his indecisiveness in controlling his kingdom led to disorder. The barons' extended authority gave greedy landowners excessive power, and local authorities such as the Sheriff of Nottingham were granted autonomy in how they discharged their responsibilities, often leading to corruption and abuses of power.[10] Gangs of outlaws such as the Folvilles and Coterels plagued the forests of England, which quickly became notorious as places of extreme danger and lawlessness.[11] The records of the time do not give a clear indication of how many outlaws were at large, but it is estimated that there were more outlaws at this time than at any other period in England's history.

Much is made of Robin Hood's status as an outlaw. While the term often refers to a criminal, the true meaning is rather more specific: it refers to someone outside the protection of the law.[12] Being an outlaw was for some a matter of choice; they preferred outlawed status to escape the oppressive conditions of the time. Some would almost certainly have been criminals, choosing to become outlaws rather than face justice, but others may have been innocent people of lower class seeking to escape the oppressive burdens of the state imposed by greedy officials and landowners, who failed or deliberately chose not to discharge the duties of their office with integrity and impartiality.

The early years of Edward II's reign also witnessed a new and significant development. Within three months of his ascension, the King of France and the pope decreed the expulsion of the Knights Templar.

This group of knightly monks originated nearly two hundred years before the reign of Edward II. Following Pope Urban II's statement of intent at the Council of Clermont in 1095 to reclaim the Holy Land, which eventually led to the First Crusade, a French nobleman named Hugues de Payens founded the original Templars in 1118.[13] Comprising only himself and eight relatives of knightly class, the new Order approached King Baldwin II of Jerusalem to inform him of its existence and its mission to protect pilgrims on their journey to the Holy Land. Despite the capture of the Holy City of Jerusalem by the Christian forces in 1099, the Holy Land was in a state of disarray and the routes travelled by pilgrims were dangerous. Both King

Baldwin and Pope Gelasius II welcomed the Templars as an extra source of security.[14]

Initially, the Order was based at what is believed to have been the site of the Temple of Solomon.[15] In the early years it seems to have led an unremarkable existence, but this changed soon after the Council of Troyes officially sanctioned the Templars' mission in 1129.[16] Over the coming decades its reputation in Europe flourished and many Christian monarchs and noblemen endorsed the Order. From small beginnings as the Poor Knights of Christ, the Order developed significantly, and it received many large donations from noblemen throughout Europe. Able men of knightly descent were invited to join and, in doing so, swear an oath of allegiance to uphold the laws of the Templar 'Rule'[17] and abide by vows of poverty, pledging all their earthly possessions for the good of the Order.[18] Pope Urban II's early classification of fighting in the Crusades as a holy cause enticed many Christians to take up arms, and it was not difficult for the Order to attract members. The chance to fight for the Christian cause and put on the famous uniform adorned with the Red Cross on the Crusader soldier's mantle, which was used to represent martyrdom, became a romanticized ideal and developed the Templars' image in the eyes of the common folk as God's knights in shining armour.[19]

Following its initial success, by the time of the fall of Acre in 1291 the Order had an estimated 20,000 members choosing to forsake a freeman's lifestyle to abide by the strict rules of obedience, poverty, chastity and piety supporting the mission of the Church.[20] However, funding a 200-year Crusade was difficult. The initial authority given by the pope made the Order a charity, and under the Rule no member was allowed to own possessions. Two centuries of accumulating the possessions of its members resulted in the Order becoming immensely wealthy, yet even this was not enough to sustain military operations. To raise new funds, the Templars offered themselves as an early form of bank to nobles willing to take up the cross. To embark on a Crusade was a long-term commitment, and leaving lands and possessions unattended was to leave them at the mercy of the greedy, including some kings. Depositing funds or possessions with the Order ensured security for the Crusaders and provided additional funds for the cause.[21] The Templars benefited by receiving fees from depositors as an alternative to charging interest, since the Church officially forbade usury and from similar arrangements when offering loans to nobility and monarchs.[22]

The Templars had two purposes. First, they were to protect pilgrims journeying to the Holy Land, and, second, it was their job to raise money to support the war against the Muslim forces. Their success in the second of these tasks is readily apparent. The Order's influential political connections and ability to trade, which had become very well established by the late thirteenth century, had led to a position of power. Over a century of receiving generous donations and deposits – many from noblemen who died in battle and whose possessions then passed to the Templars – had secured for the Order significant landholdings throughout Europe.[23] Castles, churches, vineyards and farms were built and bought, and in time the Order's power and possessions grew to such an extent that it had more wealth than the King of France and became the largest independent army in Europe.

The precise cause and time of the downfall of the Templars is shrouded in controversy. Although some historians consider that it began as early as defeat in the Battle of the Horns of Hattin in 1187, it was not until the loss of Acre, the final loss of the Crusades, that the tide inexorably turned against them. Following this, the Templars went to Cyprus, and the inquest into the defeat began in earnest. Two centuries of accumulating wealth led to allegations by their critics of fraternizing and trading with the enemy and love of plunder, and bitter rivalries with other Christian orders such as the Teutonic Knights and the Knights Hospitallers had left them isolated. The Templars were founded for the Crusades, which were now over. An attempt in 1302 by the Templars' Grand Master, Jacques de Molay, and his armies to establish a presence in Palestine ended in failure, and the Order's long presence in the Holy Land came to an end.[24] It was estimated that an army 20,000 strong was needed to reclaim Palestine, but there was little to attract new members.

By the early years of the fourteenth century political considerations had replaced the religious ideals that had launched the Crusades, and this created further tensions. Bids by Philip IV of France to obtain a loan from the Templars to fund his war against Edward I had been rejected on a number of occasions, and the French monarch declared that he had a right to tax the French clergy, an action that in turn led to his being excommunicated by Pope Boniface VIII. The Templars' position was secure for a while, but Philip refused to give up. Seeking retribution, he sent an agent, Guillaume de Nogaret, to kidnap the pope, charging him with many offences including idolatry and heresy.[25]

The accusations took their toll. The pope survived the kidnapping but died in October 1303 from shock at the magnitude of the allegations.[26] As the credibility of the deceased pope was destroyed, the power of the king was enhanced. The new pope, Benedict XI, absolved Philip of any offence against the papacy but died after only eight months in office.[27] He was replaced by the weak and ailing Clement V, a childhood friend of Philip who fell under the influence of the French king. A posthumous trial, over which the king presided, heard the charges against the recently deceased Pope Boniface VIII, with the aim of exposing the corruptibility of the papacy, a goal achieved to Philip's satisfaction.

With France and the Church on a collision course, the Templars were deprived of their key ally. The Order had always depended on the support of the Vatican, but now a full inquiry into their dealings was sanctioned. Historians fail to agree on the exact circumstances of the trials that followed, whether the charges were genuine or invented by Philip for personal gain, but on Friday 13 October 1307 several of the Knights Templar, including Jacques de Molay, were arrested in Paris. The Order was charged with 104 articles – seventy-four relevant to the Order in Britain – varying from sodomy, simony, idolatry, blasphemy and deformation of the cross to actual heresy and many others intended to prove that the Templars were not an order of religious idealists but an organization pursuing high political ambitions.[28] The Templars had discussed the idea of forming their own state in the same way that the Teutonic Knights had formed Prussia or the Hospitallers had established themselves in Rhodes, and this was perhaps perceived by Philip as posing a major threat.[29]

The Templars remained under the protection of Rome, but with so many of their members based in France they were relatively exposed. After the arrests in Paris, Pope Clement V wrote to Philip questioning his grounds but took no further action to defend them. Those arrested were tortured, and many confessed to the crimes of which they were accused, although this was probably the result of the methods of interrogation and the intense pressures of the trial. The banking system established by the Templars was broken up and all monies owed to the Order were declared forfeit, an action from which King Philip certainly gained.[30] History records that very few Templar possessions were found at the Paris Temple, even though the Templars were taken completely off guard by the swiftness of the arrests and the measures taken against them. Equally surprising was that many key officials eluded capture and disappeared.

Although in France the Templars were in trouble, in the rest of Europe they fared better. Many monarchs were sympathetic to the Order. For this reason a Papal Bull, the *Pastoralis Prae-eminentiae*, issued in 1307 by the pope at the insistence of King Philip demanding full-scale Templar arrests across Europe and seizure of their assets, was not implemented immediately.[31] Many of the Christian monarchs had benefited from good business dealings with the Templars, and attacking the Order was not in their interests. In Germany, when a Templar preceptor stormed the council of the Archbishop of Mainz with twenty of his armoured knights and announced they were there to answer the charges, they were let off.[32]

In France the Order was slowly being dismantled, but in England things remained pretty normal.[33] On the whole the members in Britain served a different purpose to the rest of the Order. Although many English Templars fought in the Crusades, they were mainly farmers and moneylenders who posed no obvious threat to the Crown. Both King John and Henry III had done substantial business with them, and Edward I and Edward II confirmed the Templars' privileges when taking the throne. Edward I often used them as envoys to Scotland, and the Scottish Templars even fought alongside Edward I at the battles of Dunbar and Falkirk in 1296 and 1298.[34] In England the Templars had always enjoyed good relations with the Crown, and it may have been largely for this reason that Edward II was reluctant to act when the Papal Bull was issued. Despite a combination of threats and flattery from Philip IV, who later became his father-in-law, he resisted. He even wrote to the pope to express his concerns at the charges, which he believed were concocted and distorted by evil persons. However, he was faced with a choice: pursue the charges or risk excommunication. A Papal Inquisition was allowed into England and a new court was established with powers and jurisdiction outside English law.[35]

The Papal Bull was eventually implemented but without conviction. It had initially been sent to the monarchs of Christendom on 22 November, but it was not until 15 December that an order was sent out by Edward II to the county sheriffs of England. This informed them of a requirement to choose twenty-four men to attend them on the following Sunday when they would learn what was contained in a sealed mandate that was to be enforced with the aim of preserving the peace. The king then wrote to the pope on Boxing Day to inform him that he had carried out the instructions contained in the Papal Bull. Four days later the royal mandates were prepared and delivered to the sheriffs. The sheriffs themselves were forced to swear an oath before reading the mandates to ensure that their contents would not be revealed until they were put into effect. The arrests eventually took place on 9 and 10 January 1308.[36]

While Edward had done everything that was expected of him by the Vatican, he had carried out the instructions in the least effective way acceptable. The Templars who were arrested were treated well, particularly in comparison to their French counterparts; only a small number were arrested, and many of those subsequently escaped or were placed under open arrest. The Inquisition in England lacked authority. Although it is clear that many of the French Templars who confessed did so under torture, the Templars who were arrested in England were questioned but not tortured. As a result, their confessions were limited, and little of an incriminating nature was learned from the Templars themselves.[37]

The English Templars had probably known what was coming.

Despite being hated in some quarters because of their great wealth and exemption from taxes, the Order had many influential connections and had earlier thrived on its ability to identify with the feudal lords.[38] In England only a total of 153 arrests were made, fifteen of which were knights, and little evidence was found to validate Philip's claims. Many of the Templars who were questioned were ageing and did not resist arrest. Based on the possessions that were found, it was concluded that the Templars did not have any large hoards of money or treasure but led frugal lives under the strict codes and conditions befitting a monastic order.[39]

Philip's accusations were aimed primarily at the high-ranking French Templars, but the English were charged in the same way. They were criticized for holding their meetings in secret, and even lower-ranking Templars were vulnerable to some of the accusations, mostly arising from somewhat bizarre reports about their initiation rituals. None of the arrested English Templars was killed, but some, including Master William de la More, remained incarcerated in the Tower of London until their death.[40] This was not due to their being found guilty of any specific offences but, rather, to demonstrate a tough stance on their beliefs and their denial of any wrongdoing. In the eyes of the court, denying the charges could be viewed as a heresy as great as committing the crimes of which they were accused. The one consistent confession was the belief that the Templar Master was capable of absolving sins.[41] This was heresy but not in the sense that King Philip was implying. There were no confessions of devil worship or idolatry, spitting on the cross or any of the other bizarre crimes that the French trials claimed to have uncovered.

Those who were arrested were taken to the county sheriffs and questioned, but Edward did not show any urgency in the matter until 1309. In December that year, for instance, Edward sent instruction to Kent that all Templars at large must be apprehended. The instruction stated that the sheriff must 'arrest all Templars wandering about your bailiwick and send them to London as the king understands that divers Templars are wandering about in secular habits committing apostasy'.[42] This was a clear indication of Edward's lack of commitment and enthusiasm in complying with the papal edict. Whereas in France Philip IV forced the Templars to confess to the charges against them, in certain areas of England there appeared to be complete indifference to them.

In October 1309, two years after the arrest of de Molay, the Inquisition finally began in earnest. This was the beginning of the end for the English Templars. To placate the French king, Pope Clement eventually dispatched ten torturers from the continent to assist with the questioning of the Templars arrested in England, and he once again threatened Edward with excommunication if he refused to comply actively with the requirements of the Papal Bull.[43] Edward feared that his soul would be in jeopardy if he continued to disobey instructions from Rome. For the first time the arrested Templars, who had already been incarcerated for two years or more, were tortured, but only two further members of the Order were captured.[44] In 1312 Pope Clement V issued another Papal Bull, this time at the Council of Vienne, and the Templar Order was officially disbanded. In 1314 the remaining leaders, including Jacques de Molay, were executed and the last lingering elements were dissolved.[45]

Theories suggesting that the Order continued in secret have flourished over the centuries, but the evidence is unconvincing. Once the Crusades were over it no longer had a real reason to continue, and, in any case, by that time it was comprised largely of veterans.[46] The Crusades had lost much public support and credibility, and recruitment would have been very difficult.

For the existing members the situation was different. At its height the Order was thought to have comprised around 20,000 members, including as many as 3,000 in England.[47] According to the records of the time the number arrested was nowhere near that many. Even in Paris the number of depositions recorded did not exceed 138, of which only fourteen were knights.[48] As for the fate of those who were not arrested, in France the pope confiscated what was left of the Order's money, and nothing of value remained accessible to surviving members. The trials had taken their toll, and many key members of the Order had been murdered. The pope decreed that Templar property be passed to the Knights Hospitallers, and some Templars were welcomed into that order. In Spain the majority of the Templars' assets went to the Order of Montesa; the King of Aragon, a key benefactor of the Templars in the past, had opposed giving them to the Hospitallers. In Portugal the Order continued under the guise of the Knights of Christ and later journeyed across the Atlantic Ocean with Christopher Columbus.[49]

In England most of those arrested and questioned were eventually cleared and reconciled with the Church. They were free to join another order or become lay members of society. In total only 144 were questioned.[50] With so few arrests, the number of Templars remaining at large after the initial Papal Bull was considerable. Between the proclamation of the Bull in November of the previous year and the arrest orders being carried out, the Templars had plenty of time to plan their escape. Most of those who were questioned were sergeants and chaplains, and many of the knights who stayed behind were aged. Edward's soft stance certainly allowed many Templars the opportunity to flee, and, since the interrogation proceedings were conducted by a court under the direction of Rome, progress was slow, much to the annoyance of King Philip. Consequently, England would have had as many as 2,000 extra outlaws. Only two Templars were arrested in Scotland, and both were English.[51] Of the fifteen arrests recorded in Ireland they, too, appeared to be English.[52] This suggests that a number of Irish and Scottish Templars survived arrest and may indicate that some Templars from England successfully fled there from the Inquisition.

Thus hundreds, if not thousands, of men became fugitives practically overnight and disappeared from the records for ever, not only in England but throughout Europe. It seems very possible that, hunted by both Church and county officials, former Templars who had obeyed the strict code of the Order continued to do so, only now as outlaws, dwelling among the trees of England's forests.

7

INTO THE GREENWOOD

As the Christian kings of Europe implemented the Papal Bull, it
may have been impossible for large numbers of Templars to act
in unison, but it seems fairly likely that small organized
groups operated together, on at least a local basis, when they
fled from the Templar houses and preceptories. Edward II's
laxity in executing the pope's commands gave English members
of the Order ample opportunity to flee, and the lack of
recorded arrests demonstrates that many took advantage of the
delay. Two centuries of operating in secrecy may have been a
factor in their downfall, but it may also have helped them to
escape. The Order was renowned for its toughness and its
ability to survive in battle, and this was now tested. Because
members of the Order were required to take vows of chastity,
most had never been married and had no families to which to
turn. The bonds of brotherhood and fraternity that had always
been deeply entrenched, together with the disciplines of a religious military order, now assumed vital importance in enabling
large numbers of Templars to evade the inquisitors.

Avoiding detection may not have been difficult. Many Templars
were experienced in carrying out espionage and counter-espionage
in the Holy Land, and their inconspicuous appearance, often

wearing little more than a hooded attire befitting a monk, allowed them to move from place to place unhindered, as passers-by assumed they were nothing more than simple religious men.[1] Prior to 1307 they had carried out duties such as farming, and many of its members were used to living off the land.[2] The forests of northern England covered huge areas, in some cases spanning many counties, which provided a haven for gangs of outlaws resisting the authorities. Countless groups of outlaws were known to be roaming the forests at the time of the Inquisition. Taking into account the large number of Templars who managed to avoid arrest, it is likely that among the bands of outlaws were groups of fugitive Templars.

Whereas the typical criminal in the reign of Edward II preyed on the wealth of the religious and the gentry, it would be entirely out of character for these religious men to carry out the widescale robbery and murder associated with the ruthless Folville or Coterel gangs. Is it possible, then, that Robin Hood and his Merry Men were Knights Templar fleeing from persecution? The unique feature of the military orders of the Middle Ages was their ability to combine the military and religious ways of life. These qualities are demonstrated by the highly disciplined and trained military skills of the Merry Men and the manner in which they combine them with piety in their daily lives.

There are other similarities between the structure and ideals of the Christian military religious orders, such as the Templars, and the Merry Men. The latter were organized in a three-level hierarchy similar to the knights, lower-class sergeants and clergy in the Templar Order. For the Merry Men, Robin is the master, followed by Little John, Will Scarlock and Much the Miller's son, who act as Robin's closest advisers, and after them come the remaining unnamed yeomen. The fact that the men are yeomen confirms that there is no one of nobility or clergy in the initial group, which may explain why they are a fellowship operating as a fraternity rather than merely a fraternity. The Templars, too, had begun as a fellowship of nine knights with a common aim later developed into a hierarchically based fraternity. Throughout the ballads there is evidence of a tough and hardened organization at variance with the popular perception that the Merry Men were a frivolous and jovial gathering of characters, as portrayed in the writings of Pyle and Walter Scott.[3] Robin's tendency, as the master, not to eat with the other men and even fast until an equal is present is consistent with the Templar practice in which members would only eat with someone of equal status. Other traits mentioned in the ballads are strikingly similar to what we know of the Templars; for instance, Robin Hood's insistence in many of the ballads on taking Little John to bear his bow parallels the Templar custom that the Grand Master would be allocated a valet to carry his shield and lance.[4]

While in the early days knights made up the majority of the Templars, by the end the Order was comprised mostly of lower-class sergeants.[5] In battle the Templars were feared for their reputation as great fighters, and the Merry Men demonstrate similar characteristics throughout the ballads, notably in the battle with the sheriff's men in the *Gest*. Templar sergeants were accomplished fighters but also capable of performing skilled and unskilled tasks such as taking care of horses or trades like masonry or blacksmithing,[6] very like Will Scarlock, Much the Miller's son and Little John. Craftsmen such as drapers were highly esteemed in the Templar hierarchy, and emphasis was placed on the quality of members' mantles; Little John's role is draper-related, and he is responsible for providing Sir Richard at the Lee with clothing.[7] According to the *Gest*, the Merry Men all wore a common livery, initially scarlet and later Lincoln green, another consistent feature of every Christian military-religious order at the time.[8] The fact that every member wears the same mantle, even Robin Hood, is a sign of each member's equal status, a practice typical of Christian military societies; the policy of the Knights Templar, as stated in the Rule, was that a brother's mantle or clothing should not stand out in any way from that of his fellow brother.[9]

If Robin Hood and the Merry Men were indeed Knights Templar, it is likely that the ballads were set some time between 1307 and 1314 or possibly up until 1324.[10] Evidence from the early ballads suggests that Robin and his men may have been outlawed around this time. The reference to King Edward in the *Gest* opens the possibility that the king was Edward II, placing the timing of Robin Hood and his Merry Men somewhere between 1307 and 1327. The evidence in the ballads is hardly conclusive but it is not without foundation. The *Gest* refers to the king seeking out Robin Hood in Nottingham;[11] Edward II is recorded as having visited Nottingham in 1323, and then again in 1324, on his way to and from the north.[12] The *Gest* suggests that the king sought unsuccessfully for many months to find Robin, even disguising himself as an abbot in an attempt to infiltrate the Merry Men. The fact that the real king did pass through Nottingham at that time provides a possible historical link between Edward II and Robin Hood's Sherwood.[13]

Prior to their excommunication in 1307, the Templars had owned huge swathes of property across the country, most notably in Yorkshire, the setting of most of the Robin Hood ballads. Before the Papal Bull was issued, Yorkshire commanded the largest Templar presence and was the richest Templar region in England. Roger Mowbray, a major benefactor of the Order, had devoted much of his life to the defence of the Holy Land and had earlier given the Templars property on his estates in both Yorkshire and Lincolnshire, which remained in their possession until the trials.[14] In addition, there were ten Templar preceptories in Yorkshire: Foulbridge, Faxfleet, Penhill, Ribston, Wetherby, Temple Cowton, Temple Hirst, Temple Newsam, Westerdale and Copmanthorpe, five of which were located in the West Riding, close to Barnsdale.[15] Evidence emerging from the inquests on the Corrodians[16] and various Templar charters after the trial suggests that members of the Order travelled between the preceptories on a regular basis and that many of the brothers lived at more than one preceptory during the course of their careers.[17] Being well acquainted with the area would undoubtedly have given fugitive Templars an advantage when avoiding the inquisitors.

There is strong evidence that many fugitive Templars evaded arrest in Yorkshire. In addition to a direction to the Sheriff of Kent that fugitive Templars were to be arrested, over two years after the initial instructions to arrest the Templars in England Edward II wrote to the Sheriff of York on 12 March 1310 complaining that the sheriff was permitting Templars to wander about in contempt of the king's order and insisting that all fugitive Templars should be placed under the sheriff's supervision.[18] The king later wrote to the same sheriff on 4 January of the following year complaining that, despite his orders, this had still not been achieved. From this we can deduce either that the sheriff had not taken action or, perhaps more likely, that he had failed in his attempts to capture or recapture them.[19] The Templars who had evaded the attention of the authorities completely remained unaccounted for, and the pope complained to the Archbishop of Canterbury that a number of Templars were successfully integrating into everyday civilian life.

The Merry Men are also mentioned as being active in Yorkshire. The *Gest* and *Gisborne* ballads make clear reference to Robin Hood and the Merry Men being active in Barnsdale:

> Robyn stode in Bernesdale,
> And lenyd hym to a tre.[20]

The locations mentioned in the ballads are quite clear. Throughout the *Gest*, areas in close proximity to Barnsdale are described in some detail, suggesting, as pointed out by Dobson and Taylor, that if Robin existed he was a local figure.[21] Located in the West Riding area of South Yorkshire, the forest extended north-west of Doncaster, occupying the area between there and Pontefract.[22] It was once rich in game and, as with Sherwood, was visited by various monarchs on hunting trips. Joseph Hunter made reference to Barnsdale in his *Critical and Historical Tracts*, referring to a 'pretty extensive piece of country, which till recent inclosures was a woodland'.[23] The antiquary John Leland stated of Barnsdale that it was a 'Woody and Famous Forest' during the reign of Henry VIII.[24] This seems in keeping with evidence that Richard Rolle, a Bible interpreter, lived as a hermit within the borders of Barnsdale during the later years of his life.[25] Subsequent urban development has resulted in the forest shrinking into a small area at Barnsdale Bar, but in the Middle Ages it may have covered much of South Yorkshire.[26] At its peak, Sherwood Forest extended as far north as Doncaster, spanning 100,000 acres and encroaching into six counties, bringing it into close proximity to Barnsdale.[27] It is recorded that in 1194 Richard I roused a hart while hunting in Sherwood and pursued it all the way to Barnsdale.[28]

In addition to the forest, the reader is provided with several genuine place-names. In the first fytte of the *Gest* Robin refers to specific locations as he addresses his right-hand man, Little John:

> And walke up to the Saylis,
> And so to Watlinge Stret,

And wayte after some unkuth gest,
Up chaunce ye may them mete.[29]

As identified by Dobson and Taylor, the Saylis may be Sayles Plantation situated between Doncaster and Ferrybridge, close to Wentbridge, north of Barnsdale and near the fourteenth-century Watling Street.[30] In the Middle Ages this area could be used to observe traffic coming from Wentbridge – an ideal vantage point for outlaws intent on waylaying passers-by.[31] Another possible location, and perhaps more likely since Wentbridge is not specifically mentioned at this stage of the *Gest*, is Sayles Wood and Quarry, situated between Doncaster and Pontefract but further south of Wentbridge. This site, only a short distance from Barnsdale Bar, lies directly between the curiously named Robin Hood's Stone and Robin Hood's Well just off the modern A1.[32]

The Saylis and Watling Street are not the only areas of interest associated with the ballad. East of the villages of Wrangbrook and Skelbrooke a Templar-owned mill once stood in close proximity to the millpond, just one of a number of Templar properties in this area of Yorkshire. The Burghwallis Mill was situated close to Barnsdale Bar and would have been known to the Merry Men. Mills were rare at the time and potentially profitable for the Order.[33] The existence of the watermill, dating back to 1185, offers the most plausible explanation available for the presence of Much the Miller's son, as no other mills existed in such close proximity. The objective of the Templar Order as a whole was to fight in the Crusades, but this was of less significance for its members in England, whose chief purpose was to raise money to be transferred to the Holy Land. Many of the estates that the Templars obtained were farms that were later used to generate funds in support of the cause. Those who became members were often charged with managing the property. Many of the Templars worked on farms themselves, but they often employed additional labourers or even hired out the land to tenants, saving the Order considerable expense.[34] Many farms in Yorkshire were Templar owned, and in the ballads Robin, oddly, remarks that working on farms constitutes a good fellow. In addition to his instruction not to waylay any squire or knight who would be a good fellow, Robin says:

> 'Therof no force,' than sayde Robyn,
> 'We shall do well inowe;
> But loke ye do no husbonde harme,
> That tilleth with his ploughe.'[35]

In modern English this is an injunction not to harm any small farmer who tills with his plough.

It seems that many things can constitute a 'good fellow'. Being a yeoman appears to be quite significant, but squires and knights can also be good fellows. Honesty seems to be important, a quality Sir Richard at the Lee showed when he professed a lack of money, unlike the mendacious monk.[36] Obedience clearly constitutes being a good fellow, as displayed by the cook, the potter and Little John.[37] Poverty constitutes a good fellow, as revealed by Robin's appraisal of the pity shown to the wrestler by Sir Richard in the *Gest*. Piety certainly matters, as demonstrated by Sir Richard's devotion to the Virgin Mary (and of course Robin's own), and Robin also takes pity on two priests in the ballad of *Robin Hood's Golden Prize* for their piety.[38] Perhaps, too, working in support of the Crusades constituted being a good fellow. It would make sense for former members of a Christian military order to show loyalty to people who had once supported their cause and even farmed their estates.

The first fytte of the *Gest* provides an interesting insight into the assets of Robin Hood and the Merry Men. They own large amounts of clothing and have sufficient money to provide the knight with a loan from a common fund, together with a courser and a packhorse.[39]

> 'Ye must give the knight a hors,
> To lede home this gode.
> Take hym a gray coursar,' sayde Robyn,
> 'And a saydle newe.'[40]

Coursers were knights' horses, and it is clear that the Merry Men have experience in handling them. Yet their possession of a courser is rather mysterious. During the Middle Ages these horses were sometimes used for hunting, but primarily they were employed in battle or for delivering messages because they were famed for being light, strong and extremely fast. How might these outlaws have become familiar with coursers, and why did they have them in their possession? They must either have had some connections with the nobility, or they had previously been involved in military operations. The barons' armies undoubtedly had a large selection of horses which they used in their wars against the royals. Participation in those wars on the side of the barons would offer a clear explanation why Robin Hood and his men possessed a supply of horses. Equally, the Templars' regular requirement for horses was well documented. According to the Rule, a Templar could only miss prayers to attend to his horses. The Templar Masters were allocated one Turcoman[41] and had a further four horses at their command. Drapers were also allocated four horses, knights three and sergeants one,[42] despite the Templar emblem depicting two men and one horse.

In addition to the courser, the Merry Men owned at least one packhorse. These were commonly used in warfare in the Middle Ages as all-purpose horses. In the case of the Templars, palfreys or *roncins* were frequently used either in war or as packhorses to carry equipment.[43] The Merry Men use a palfrey to carry equipment.

> 'And a gode palfray,' sayde lytell Much,
> 'To mayntene hym in his right.'
> 'And a peyre of botes,' sayde Scarlock,
> 'For he is a gentyll knight.'[44]

The presence of the courser in the ballad is of great significance to the legend, yet its inclusion is invariably overlooked. In the ballads, Robin Hood frequently turns up in Nottingham and Barnsdale, in some cases very rapidly and without explanation. The great benefit of the courser was its speed which sometimes made it a preferred choice over other war-horses such as the destrier or the palfrey.[45] Covering the distance from Barnsdale to Sherwood, by certain routes as little as thirty-five miles, was no mean feat, but it could be done within hours on a courser.[46] The courser's speed made it a particularly popular choice for messengers. The Templars often acted as messengers for kings, nobles and popes.[47] The fact that the outlaws could provide horses of both kinds for the knight suggests that the Merry Men had a good supply of horses and highlights the capabilities of Will Scarlock and Much the Miller's son in dealing with horses for Robin.

Geography is of recurring importance towards the end of the *Gest*, when Robin Hood seeks to leave the service of the king after fifteen months at court. Having stated his intention to return to Barnsdale and pay homage to Mary Magdalene at a chapel dedicated to her, Robin comes before the king to seek temporary leave to return to the forest.

> Forth than went Robyn Hode
> Tyll he came to our Kynge:
> 'My lorde the kynge of Englonde,
> Grante me myn askyne.
>
> 'I made a chapel in Bernysdale,
> That seemly is to se,
> It is of Mary Magdaleyne,
> And thereto wolde I be.
>
> 'I myght never in this seven nyght
> No tyme to slepe ne wynke,
> Nother all these seven dayes
> Nother ete ne drynke.'[48]

The *Gest* tells us he never returns to the king's service, choosing instead to resume his life as an outlaw. Unfortunately, the ballad gives no indication whether Robin actually goes to his chapel or if it was merely an excuse to leave court. Positive identification of the chapel to which he referred is difficult. A number of churches in England are dedicated to St Mary Magdalene, but if the writer of the *Gest* was referring to a real church, which would be in keeping with his practice of mentioning genuine places, there is only one in Barnsdale: the church of St Mary Magdalene in Campsall. This ancient church was located within the forest during the Middle Ages. Constructed following the Norman Conquest, throughout the Middle Ages it served the local population, most of whom undertook agricultural and rural employment, many working on Templar land and properties.

Centuries of unauthenticated legend have developed the tradition that Robin Hood and Maid Marian married at this church. Although this is undoubtedly fiction, the geographical location, only two miles from Barnsdale, does appear to fit with that described in the *Gest*. Historically, Campsall had direct links with the Templars, and within the church there are several effigies marking the point where Templars from the area were buried between the twelfth and fourteenth centuries.[49]

Like the Merry Men, the Templars were the target of the county sheriffs. Although sheriffs were appointed to uphold the law and maintain order within the geographical areas for which they were responsible, the sheriff of the legend has become synonymous with villainy and corruption. It is not merely that he seeks to capture the outlaws and punish them, which would be reason enough for listeners to the ballads to consider him the enemy. He does manage to capture Robin in the *Monk* ballad, although the exact circumstances have unfortunately been lost.[50] In the *Gest* he is mentioned as an enemy from the start. Following Robin's insistence that his followers must not molest a 'good fellow', he refers to the Sheriff of Nottingham as one to beat and bind.

> 'The hye sherif of Notyingham,
> Hym holde ye in your mynde.'[51]

This suggests that the two men have encountered one another before, possibly as described in the other early ballads, but in the *Gest* it is Little John who first comes to the sheriff's attention. In fytte 3 Little John impresses the sheriff when demonstrating his archery skills and is invited to become his servant. Little John agrees, vowing, unknown to the sheriff, to do a poor job.[52] The ballad goes on to describe Little John's journey back to Robin

Hood, after about twelve months, with the sheriff's cook and several of his possessions. The feud escalates further when the sheriff is tricked into captivity in Sherwood Forest.[53]

During the early fyttes of the *Gest* Robin Hood is located in Barnsdale rather than Sherwood, and it is in Barnsdale that he makes reference to the sheriff as an enemy. Barnsdale was probably outside the Sheriff of Nottingham's jurisdiction, although it was classified at various times throughout the Middle Ages as being in the counties of Nottinghamshire, Lincolnshire, Derbyshire and Yorkshire.[54] Many of the key encounters with the sheriff do take place in Nottingham: in the *Monk* ballad Robin is praying in Nottingham and in the *Potter* ballad he sells pots there. We do not know of any other sheriffs pursuing Robin, but they may have done so. In the *Scotichronicon* Robin murders in Barnsdale a prowling viscount who may have been an official from Yorkshire rather than the Sheriff of Nottinghamshire.

The ballad of *Guy of Gisborne* sheds further light on the geographical questions. In the ballad, set in Barnsdale, the sheriff hires a bounty hunter to capture Robin Hood for him. Gisborne, who may have come from Lancashire, seeks to track down Robin Hood but fails and is brutally killed by Robin. The Sheriff of Nottingham also encroaches into Barnsdale to follow up the work of the bounty hunter. The willingness of the Sheriff of Nottingham to employ the services of a bounty hunter to hunt Robin down in Yorkshire demonstrates that he is fully prepared to act outside the formal boundaries of his authority to secure Robin's capture.[55]

Changes in the role of sheriff in the reign of Edward I had led to the appointment of the new 'Conservators of the Peace'. For the first time since the Norman invasion sheriffs were to be elected rather than appointed by the king, but in practice this seems to have happened only very rarely.[56] Edward I's reforms did not develop as far as he had intended during his reign, although changes to the role of sheriff did continue under Edward II. For the first time in England's history, officers were appointed in every county. Building on his father's efforts to promote the role of sheriffs as Conservators of the Peace, Edward II introduced a new requirement that they should constantly reside within their own counties. However, the Conservators were also allowed to raise posse comitatus – groups of able-bodied men over the age of eighteen charged with helping to enforce the law.[57] The system, however, was open to abuse by the sheriffs and at times led to an ineffective regime and corruption of the office. An example of this is given in the *Gest* when the sheriff raises a posse comitatus to attack Sir Richard's castle:

> Lythe and listen, gentylmen,
> And herkyn to your songe,
> Howe the proude shyref of Notyngham,
> And men of armys stronge
>
> Full fast cam to the hye shyref,
> The contré up to route,
> And they besette the knyghtes castell,
> The walles all aboute.[58]

Parallels begin to emerge here with the sheriff who, according to popular culture, abuses his power for personal benefit. The early ballads do not back this up entirely: in the *Gest* and the *Monk* ballads the sheriff seems to be doing little more than expected of a man in his position. That is not to say that sheriffs were never corrupt. Historically, the sheriff Sir Robert Ingram was referred to as being in league with outlaws, and John de Oxenford, a sheriff from 1334 to 1339, was himself later outlawed.[59] The ballads do not mention whether Robin and his men had committed any crimes, but if they were Templars the sheriff would have pursued them in any case.[60] By operating in the border regions of Yorkshire and Nottinghamshire, Robin Hood and his Merry Men would have cleverly exploited the limitations and uncertainties imposed on the Conservators of the Peace by the terms of their appointment that restricted them from operating outside their own area of jurisdiction. In practice, however, the sheriffs probably would not have hesitated to stray slightly outside their geographical boundaries in order to fulfil their responsibility to capture outlaws, particularly in the case of the Merry Men, who were also known to operate within the Sheriff of Nottingham's own jurisdiction.

Whatever the reasons, the sheriff's feud with Robin Hood and his men is clearly personal as much as a matter of duty. Despite this, as we know from the ballads, the sheriff is actually unaware of who Robin Hood is. In the *Potter* ballad he dines with a potter, entirely unaware that the potter is Robin in disguise. In the *Gest* his reaction to falling victim to Little John's trickery suggests that he is also driven by personal pride and a desire for revenge. The legendary rivalry is present throughout the ballads, and if these texts are to be taken as our only sources the Merry Men are concerned only with avoiding arrest and targeting the Sheriff of Nottingham and the clergy. However, popular tradition suggests they had another objective, out of character for outlaws and even for the religious orders of the time: they wanted to promote good fellowship and do good for the poor.

8

TO ROB FROM THE RICH
TO GIVE TO THE POOR

As we have seen, the initial purpose of the Knights Templar was to protect pilgrims *en route* to the Holy Land, and this remained their *raison d'être* until their demise.[1] It was a selfless and charitable aim. The Templars themselves received charity from rich noblemen but never used it for self-benefit. They were both military escorts and warriors, but in order to achieve the purpose of the Order they required funding. In addition to receiving charity they were also bankers. At the time, their techniques often resulted in the religious authorities raising moral questions about how a religious order should use its funds, but what the Templars received was devoted entirely to the support of the cause for which the Order was established. In addition, the Order offered valuable guarantees to the rich who deposited money with them. The Templars could protect their clients as Christians and also, as bankers, protect their financial interests while they were fighting in the Holy Land. Yet they were a religious institution, and, given that usury was banned by the Church, it was inevitable that the moral question of how the money should be managed would arise.[2]

To the Templars the question was irrelevant; the money went to support the army in the Holy Land. Despite this, figures within the Church voiced serious concerns about the means by which the Templars raised their money and the way in which it was spent. The Templars are recorded as having disbursed charity at home, but the majority of the money was used for funding their activities in the Holy Land. However, when the Crusades were lost the situation changed. It may have been acceptable to raise money to fund a holy war, but now the Templars were simply bankers. Without loyalty to a particular nation, they were mercenaries with significant financial backing and resources who were seen by Philip IV and others as a powerful and potentially dangerous threat. To justify their continued existence the Templars would have needed a new cause. They were very rich, but for individual members the vow of poverty remained in force.

'To rob from the rich to give to the poor' is an expression often applied to Robin Hood and his Merry Men. It is one of the key themes associated with the legend. According to this roman-ticized view, they were a band of selfless, high-minded men who sought to redistribute the wealth of the rich into the pockets of the needy rather than simply keeping it for themselves, and par-ticular emphasis is placed on Robin's insistence on targeting corrupt noblemen. But what evidence is there to suggest that such things occurred? Robin's followers are instructed to adhere to a strict code of conduct that requires them not to harm a 'good fellow', which already distinguishes them from common outlaws. Robin's kindness in providing a loan for Sir Richard at the Lee is an early example of his willingness to help the poor, and stealing from the monk constitutes robbing from a rich person. Even at this stage, there is evidence to suggest that Robin Hood has a repu-tation for being a generous outlaw. Yet despite his tendency to do 'poor men much good' the ballads do not ascribe to him the lofty purpose that we sentimentally assume today.[3] Popular tradition refers to the Merry Men's tendency to rob from the greedy rich and give to the poor, but whether this was the purpose of the fellowship is unclear. Was the fellowship formed to help the poor? Did they need to become outlaws in order to achieve this? Why would a criminal place himself in greater danger of capture by sharing with strangers money that he stole and could more safely keep for himself? These questions are made even more perplexing by Robin's refusal to accept repayment of the loan he had made to the knight as the Virgin Mary had already rewarded his piety. Typically an outlaw would take whatever he could get.

When the local Templar preceptories were ransacked after the Papal Bull was issued, the looters mostly found food or furniture but little money.[4] From this we can deduce that either the individual preceptories had little of value or more likely the Templars fleeing the Inquisition took with them most of the money their preceptories had possessed. They would have been rich, yet they remained bound by their oath of poverty. Previous life experience as a Knight Templar would go a long way to explain the disciplined reluctance of the Merry Men to become mere bandits and their rule of doing 'poor men much good', unlike men such as Adam de Gurdon who lived the criminal life of a ruthless highwayman. When considering the Templars' charitable aim, it seems in keeping with their religious character that they should want to give to the needy and be willing to remain poor themselves.

As we have seen, the core values of the Merry Men in the ballads correspond closely with those of the various military-religious orders active during the Middle Ages: they abide by a vow of poverty, remitting the money they acquire to a common fund controlled by the fellowship as a whole; they show obedience to their master; they seem to observe a vow of chastity; they are highly trained and skilled in military combat; and, most interestingly, they are dedicated to Christianity, displaying particular devotion to the Virgin Mary. The work of writers such as Pyle, and the later ballads, portray the Merry Men as a frivolous forest fraternity enjoying feasts and entertaining guests, yet the early ballads say more about the hardships of life in the forest. In the *Gest* the sheriff himself describes their life as being worse than in a monastery or a hermitage:

'This is harder order,' sayde the sherief,
'Than any ankir or frere;
For all the golde in mery Englonde
I wolde nat longe dwell her.'

'All this twelve monthes,' sayde Robyn,
'Thou shalt dwell with me;
I shall the teche, proude sherif,
An outlawe for to be.'[5]

Throughout the ballads Robin's devotion to Christianity is highlighted over and over, although this cannot be said of the religious authorities described in the stories.[6] The behaviour of the abbots, bishops and monks who are the enemies of the out-laws seems the opposite of what one would expect from men of their calling. Historically the religious authorities were indeed often corrupted by power. Authority was shared among landowners, and a third of all land was owned by the Church, which also profited greatly from religiously motivated donations and bequests in wills. The *Gest* and the *Monk* ballads reveal that the monasteries harbour great wealth, and the monks, bishops and abbots are driven by secret motives of greed and lust. In contrast, Robin Hood is devoutly religious.[7]

The Merry Men have been forced to endure the harsh circumstances of life outside the law, although ironically these conditions are in keeping with their values. Their behaviour is reminiscent of what is expected of a monk and, despite being forced to resort to desperate measures in order to survive, they remain respectful of the sacraments. For the Templars there were three important and guiding principles and beliefs, all very much connected, to which members of the Order were bound strictly to adhere, namely: respect for the mysteries of Christianity, belief in the efficacy of the sacraments and trust in Christ's promise of everlasting salvation. These principles are notably lacking from the clerics who appear in the stories, and the ballads are quick to remind us of this. The monk in the *Monk* ballad is guilty of betrayal, the abbot in the *Gest* is concerned with the repayment of the loan by the knight, and the Bishop of Hereford in the ballad of the same name is motivated by politics and power to the extent that he is as much a threat to Robin Hood, despite Robin's piety, as the Sheriff of Nottingham.

The sacraments have always been an important aspect of Christianity. The Templars' faith was highlighted by belief in their efficacy. Robin Hood's devotion to his Christian faith is no less strong. At the beginning of the *Monk* ballad he plans to attend mass in Nottingham, inspired by his faith and not having been able to hear mass for a fortnight. He is undeterred by Much the Miller's son's concern that the sheriff may be on the look-out and that he should not take the risk of being captured.[8] Robin's faith is stronger than his desire not to get caught. Such devotion is also evident in Bower's *Scotichronicon* and the *Gisborne* ballad. In the latter Robin is losing in a fight to Gisborne but calls on Mary for strength and succeeds in killing Gisborne.

> 'Ah, deere Lady!' sayd Robin Hoode,
> 'Thou art both mother and may!
> I thinke it was never mans destinye
> To dye before his day.'

Robin thought on Our Lady deere,
And soone leapt up againe,
And thus he came with an awkwarde stroke;
Good Sir Guy hee has slayne.[9]

The lost rhyme mentioned by Bower also highlights Robin's devotion to the mysteries of Christianity and the sacraments. In *Scotichronicon* Bower refers to Robin's reluctance to finish mass even though he knows that the sheriff is lying in wait for him. When he and his men are subsequently victorious over the sheriff, they credit their success to Robin's decision to finish the mass.[10] As in the *Monk* ballad, we read of a Robin Hood whom many would identify from the early ballads as an outlaw yet still a devoutly religious man. In addition to his faith in the sacraments, we also see evidence of his trust in his salvation by choosing to attend mass – and complete the ceremony – when he could be killed or captured. Bower acknowledges his dedication and comments: 'God harkens to him who hears mass regularly.'[11] Evidence of Robin's reverence of Christianity is particularly illustrated by his devotion to the Virgin Mary, noted in the *Gest* when he takes £800 from the monk. Earlier he refers to how he has not received the money, fearing that the Virgin Mary is angry with him.[12] Little John points out that the monk has it, and he is from St Mary's Abbey in York. Robin later celebrates the recovery of the money, claiming the Virgin Mary is the truest of all women.[13] She is the main object of his prayers.[14] His devotion is taken further in the *Monk* ballad when he is witnessed praying before the rood at the church of the Virgin Mary in Nottingham despite the possibility that he will be spotted, which he is, and subsequently he is captured. Sir Richard at the Lee is equally devoted to the Virgin, suggesting in turn that devotion to her constitutes being a good fellow. It was also customary for fraternities in the Middle Ages to choose a patron saint, and the Virgin Mary was not uncommon, particularly later in the Middle Ages.[15] In the twelfth century she became patron of the Knights Templar.[16]

Although there is a certain irony in the choice of a woman as the patron of an all-male chivalric order, the worship of Mary in the Middle Ages was symbolic. In addition to being the mother of Christ, she was also the Queen of Heaven, and to be in service to her was to be in service to the highest possible authority. The main Templar belief was that the greatest thing a man could do was to serve a higher ideal or truth, and in the Middle Ages this was often represented by Mary.[17]

Throughout the history of the Knights Templar, admiration of the Virgin Mary was displayed on countless occasions. The Abbot Bernard of Clairvaux demonstrated an extraordinary reverence for her in the early days of the Order.[18] One of the Templars who was questioned, William Raven, confirmed that he willingly joined the Order and agreed to the vow that he was to serve God and the Blessed Virgin Mary until the end of his life.[19] Jacques de Molay also showed great reverence to her, even as he was about to be executed: 'I pray you towards the Virgin Mary, to whom Our Lord Christ was born . . .'

The conditions of Templar life were undoubtedly hard. A typical day began at dawn, with matins devoted to Mary. The Templar Rule instructed that prayers should be said first thing in the morning and at specific intervals throughout the day.[20] Robin Hood's routine is no less devout. The *Gest* refers to his pattern of hearing mass:

> Every day or he wold dune
> Thre messis wolde he here
> The one in the worship of the Fader,
> And another of the Holy Gost,

The Thirde of Our dere Lady,
That he loved allther moste.[21]

In modern English this refers to Robin's routine of hearing three masses daily before he dines: one for the Father, one for the Holy Spirit and one for Mary. Robin's routine revolved around these devotions, which were further emphasized by his devotion to other saints. The veneration of saints was, and is still, an important feature of Christianity. Veneration of a saint can take a number of forms such as praying before the shrine of the saint or on the day allocated by the Church to mark the saint's life of devotion.

One of the most common venerations was for Mary Magdalene, celebrated throughout Christianity on 22 July. This saint has always inspired widespread devotion, and in the Middle Ages she was a particularly popular choice for many of the guilds. Exactly who she was remains uncertain. In the gospels of Matthew, Mark and Luke there are similar descriptions of a scene describing Jesus being anointed, mostly in the home of Simon the Leper in Bethany, by an unnamed woman. She is described as a sinner but without further clarification. Although she is not named in any of the gospels, tradition from the third century onwards identified her as Mary of Bethany, the sister of Martha and Lazarus, the man Jesus brought back from the dead.[22] The first attempt to identify Mary Magdalene, Mary of Bethany and the woman who sinned as the same person was made by Pope Gregory in 591. In the West her veneration is a celebration of the woman to whom Christ appeared after his resurrection, rather than as the unnamed sinner. Interestingly the Eastern Orthodox Church refers to them all, probably correctly, as three separate people. In a famous sermon Pope Gregory referred to Mary as a 'peccatrix', meaning a sinner.

How she came to be labelled as a prostitute is not entirely clear. It may be that the word '*peccatrix*' was confused with '*meretix*', meaning prostitute, or perhaps Pope Gregory's assertion that the woman's sin was that she was unchaste, that is, did not abstain from sex, became interpreted as meaning prostitution.[23]

In the Bible there are several different references to Mary Magdalene. In one example she is referred to as a woman from whom Jesus drove out demons: 'And certain women, which had been healed of evil spirits and infirmities, Mary called Magdalene, out of whom went seven devils . . .'[24] Later Mary accompanies Jesus on his last journey to Jerusalem. She witnesses the crucifixion and remains at Jesus' feet until the body is taken down from the cross. She is then one of the women who journeys to the tomb to anoint Jesus' body, only to find a flock of angels in its place. She informs Peter and John of what she has seen. The Gospel of John refers to Mary as being the first person to see the risen Lord.[25]

This is the woman who was canonized by the Church. In keeping with the Templars' practice of venerating saints, Mary Magdalene was viewed as an important figure, and celebration of the feast day of Mary Magdalene was mentioned in the Rule.[26] The Templars were particularly devoted to the martyrs, to whom their own lives were dedicated. Strangely there seems to have been more emphasis on the female martyrs than the male.[27] The Red Cross on the Templar mantle was itself a sign of martyrdom, and when the Order was suppressed the executed Templars themselves became martyrs in the eyes of those who survived them. Similar beliefs are expressed in the ballads. In addition to his own devotion to Mary Magdalene, Robin seems to be concerned with demonstrating acts of bravery in keeping with martyrdom, something also illustrated by his gallantry in defending the castle of Sir Richard and a willingness to risk being killed or captured instead of missing mass. Martyrdom might also explain the presence of scarlet mantles, as the colour was often associated with mar-tyrdom.[28] Dedication to the martyrs provides an explanation of the importance of Mary Magdalene to Robin Hood in the *Gest*, while the Templars' dedication to her explains the importance of the Church of Mary Magdalene in Barnsdale to the historical Knights Templar of Campsall.

One of the most interesting features of Robin Hood's role in the stories is the contradiction between his devotion to his religion and his willingness to steal from religious officials. Throughout the ballads Robin identifies knights and squires as potentially good fellows, but abbots, monks and bishops do not fall into this category. When identifying people to beat and bind, he ear-marks bishops and archbishops as enemies:

> 'These bisshoppes and these archebishoppes,
> Ye shall them bete and bynde.'[29]

In *Scotichronicon* Bower commends Robin Hood for plun-dering wealth to give to servants of the Church, whereas the ballads suggest the opposite. Instead of showing affection towards the religious, which one would expect of a pious man, he demonstrates leniency to most of those he waylays but invariably treats clerics harshly and without consideration. This seems to imply that he has a blatant disregard and disrespect for the Church and casts doubt on his status as a pious man, but in fact he does not steal directly from the Church but, instead, makes an example of particular religious officials. In the *Gest* there are several references to the greed of the abbot and the monk. In the scene with Sir Richard repaying the loan the religious men are more interested in the money than in the evidence that he is a good Christian, even though they knew that he had been fighting overseas for England.[30] Ironically, if the abbot had given Sir Richard more time, the knight would have given him a bonus! Later, the abbot is roundly punished for his wickedness when Robin Hood steals the money that Richard at the Lee repaid to the monastery and accepts it as Richard's repayment to him, refusing more money from the knight on the basis that what he had already received has come as a gift from the Virgin Mary.[31]

Robin's piety and reverence for his religion in fact highlight the role of the 'religious' as the villains of the story. It is unclear whether the religious men portrayed in the ballads were genuine figures, but their behaviour certainly has some basis in fact. The Church was fabulously wealthy, and ordinary people held Benedictine monks, the monks of the Robin Hood story, in low esteem.[32] In the fourteenth century Church officials were popular targets of the gangs of outlaws roaming the forests, and many areas close to Barnsdale were plagued by criminal activity.[33] Members of the religious orders and other Church officials often carried large amounts of money and valuable items, yet they were relatively unprotected so they were easy prey. Clergymen were often murdered by their assailants. In contrast, Robin Hood's reluctance to resort to killing to achieve his aims is frequently mentioned in the ballads. Although Guy of Gisborne, two sheriffs and several of their men are killed, religious figures are released unharmed.[34] Little John murders a monk in the *Monk* ballad as punishment for his betrayal of Robin to the sheriff, and Much kills a page to ensure the secret remains hidden, but no one of higher religious status is murdered. In the *Gest* the monk is forced to dine with Robin Hood, and similar situations arise in ballads such as *Robin Hood and the Bishop* and *Robin Hood and the Bishop of Hereford*. On each occasion Robin steals from them but then makes them dine with him and even promotes his piety by hearing mass before sending them on their way.

The tendency of the Merry Men not to harm fellow Christians despite their contempt for religious officials is very much in keeping with the philosophy of the Templars. The Templar Rule set out the Order's purpose to protect pilgrims and emphasized the sin of harming fellow Christians.[35] The Merry Men show courtesy towards captured clergymen despite taking their money; this is not an act of reverence, as Robin Hood makes an example of them, but it does observe the law of the Order. The Templars were renowned for upholding this law, and it was for this reason that they did not fight on the side of any particular nation as to do so would have involved the killing and even potential massacre of Christians.[36] Robin Hood's dislike of the abbots is particularly apparent, and he targets them as much to make a nuisance of himself as to hurt them. At the start of the *Bishop* ballad Robin sees the cleric coming and hides, knowing that the bishop will have him hanged if he is caught. To disguise his identity, Robin trades clothes with a woman whom he has helped in the past and tricks the bishop into captivity. As usual, the bishop is robbed.[37]

There is more here than mutual dislike. In the eyes of the Church Robin Hood is a criminal. In striking contrast to Sir Richard at the Lee, the monk in the *Gest* refers to Robin as a man of whom he has never heard anything good:

> 'Who is your mayster?' sayd the monke;
> Lytell Johan sayd, 'Robyn Hode.'
> 'He is a stronge thefe,' sayd the monke,
> 'Of hym herd I never good.'[38]

It is clear throughout the ballads that the outlaws have enemies on two fronts: the Church and the sheriff, plus the bounty hunter Guy of Gisborne. The feud with the Church does not seem to be confined to quarrels with individuals but is much more broadly based. In the *Monk* ballad this is demonstrated when the monk catches Robin Hood praying in a church. The text explains that the monk has a personal antipathy towards Robin, who had earlier robbed him of £100,[39] yet by informing the sheriff of the outlaw's whereabouts the monk himself violates the sacred right of sanctuary recognized by all churches throughout the Middle Ages.[40] This extended to convents, monasteries and even the houses of bishops. Sanctuary may have allowed criminals to escape justice, but it also enabled the innocent, wrongfully accused, to find protection in time of need.[41] Sanctuary was granted to all, irrespective of their status in the eyes of the law, particularly when worshipping at mass as Robin was. For this reason, outlaws frequently sought refuge in churches, knowing that they would be safe.[42]

Robin Hood, we are aware, has made many enemies in the Church; there is enmity between the Merry Men and the Church as an institution. Similarly, having been outlawed by Rome, the Templars were at war predominantly with the Church rather than with the Crown of England. The *Monk* ballad develops the matter further when the monk reports Robin Hood to the sheriff. In the dialogue between the sheriff and the monk Robin is described as a 'kynggis felon'.[43] The term, meaning 'king's felon', refers to Robin Hood's status in the eyes of the law. It refers to a person charged with criminal, rather than civil, offences. Authority to deal with civil offences was vested in the sheriffs and local courts; criminal offences, on the other hand, were within the jurisdiction of the Crown. Robbery and murder fell within the latter category, but it is not known whether Robin Hood committed such crimes before he was outlawed. Killing the king's deer constituted a breach of the peace, the penalties for which were severe, ranging from losing an eye to being hanged, and would undoubtedly have motivated someone sought by the authorities to become an outlaw. Sedition against the king, his realm or his army was also a criminal offence.

In the *Gest* Robin Hood speaks of his love of the king and eventually becomes a valet in the royal courts.[44] This is an odd development for someone previously described as a 'king's felon', particularly in the light of his intense dislike of county officials. Throughout the ballads Robin seems to maintain a love for England, and it seems reasonable to suggest that a similar love shown by another might qualify that person as a 'good fellow'.

> 'I love no man in all the worlde
> So well as I do my kynge;
> Welcome is my lordes seale;
> And, monke, for thy tydynge.'[45]

How an outlaw can maintain love for the king is difficult to comprehend. According to popular tradition, Robin was a staunch supporter of King Richard at a time when the king was fighting overseas. As a victim of the regency of Prince John, it was possible to defend true kingship despite his outlawed status. In the case of the 'disinherited', who were outlawed for fighting against the king, it would simply not have been possible. Templar loyalty to the Crown, on the other hand, is less difficult to understand. They had earlier enjoyed good relations with the Plantagenet kings, who often placed them in positions of authority as advisers, negotiators, ambassadors and even royal officials. Based on the evidence that exists, it appears that Edward I treated them with the utmost respect.[46] Edward II did not want to jeopardize relations with the Templars, and his reluctance and hesitation in implementing the commands of the Papal Bull demonstrate his sympathy for the Order. This could not have gone unnoticed by the Templars. In a similar vein, the king shows reluctance to punish the Merry Men in the *Monk* ballad when he realizes that they have tricked him, but he lets the matter pass because of Little John's loyalty to his master.

> 'I gaf theym grith,' then seid oure kyng;
> 'I say, so mot I the,
> For sothe soch a yeman as he is on
> In all Inglond ar not thre.
>
> 'He is trew to his maister,' seid oure kyng;
> 'I sey, be swete Seynt John,
> He lovys better Robyn Hode
> Then he dose us ychon.'[47]

Although the saying 'to rob from the rich to give to the poor' is never specifically mentioned in the early ballads, there is evidence of Robin's tendency to help the poor. As established early on in the *Gest*, he does not steal from 'good fellows', and this may indicate doing 'poor men much good'. The Merry Men do not seem to profit from their gains, and to do so would not be in keeping with their code of conduct. The *Gest* also provides a further indication, perhaps the most important of all. The first fytte in the ballad, as we have seen, refers to Robin Hood's meeting with a poor knight who has fallen on hard times. We learn that the knight owes an abbot the sum of £400 and that he cannot afford to repay it. His lands are forfeit to the monastery as security on the loan, which he acquired in order to save his son from punishment after he killed a knight from Lancaster and a squire. In order to help this good fellow, Robin offers to lend the money to the knight. The loan is made using money taken from a common fund.

'Come nowe furth Litell Johnn.
And go to my tresouré,
And bringe me foure hundered pound,
And loke well tolde it be.'

Furth than went Litell Johnn,
And Scarlok went before;
He tolde oute foure hundred pounde
By eightene and two score.[48]

The common fund is a mark of a fellowship, but it is unclear at this stage whether it is made up of the proceeds of common theft or money acquired from earlier legitimate fund-raising activities. Nevertheless, the outlaws clearly do not own the money individually. They live together as a fellowship in a humble manner without any trappings of wealth, and everything they own is shared. This is perhaps the most interesting characteristic shared by the Merry Men and the Templars. The Merry Men individually are pledged to poverty, supported by a common fund that is used for the good of the fellowship, and, like the Templars, the money can be loaned out for good use. The Templars were encouraged to give alms to the poor, and there is evidence that they did so throughout their existence.[49] If there was no Crusade under way, or any other pressing call upon the money, the Order could use their knowledge of banking to do poor men much good.

The structure of the *Gest* ballad is curious and has been the topic of much discussion over the years. The events described take place over a period of several years and include a number of Robin Hood stories that have otherwise failed to survive in ballad form. To specify the timescale is to confirm when the ballads were set. When Robin meets Sir Richard at the Lee, the latter's comments suggest a military campaign or perhaps a pilgrimage that was either current or had recently occurred. The knight speaks of having been beyond the sea.[50] The livery of white and red worn by his men would be an accurate description of a Crusader uniform, suggesting that he has been on a Crusade.[51] At the peak of the Templars' existence, noblemen travelling to the Holy Land on Crusade, on a pilgrimage or for any other reason would often deposit money with the Order or take out a loan from them. The *Gest* describes a similar situation. The knight is clearly aware of the laws on usury, as were the Templars, and they were usually circumvented by various means and devices. In this case, the knight offers twenty marks and a gift of bows and arrows to Robin Hood at the time of repayment. Perhaps being a patriot and a fighter for the cause – a Crusader – is a further reason why Sir Richard is considered a good fellow, and it is the Templars' vow to protect pilgrims that influences the Merry Men to help him. If the *Gest* was set shortly after the Templars were outlawed, historically the knight may have been referring to the Hospitaller-controlled Crusade of 1308–10.[52] While military action in the Holy Land had subsided after 1291, Pope Clement V did grant Crusade privileges to those who assisted the Hospitallers in the relief of Cyprus and Armenia. Edward II supported the Crusade but gave no official aid. Any knight who decided to join the Crusade had to go at his own expense, and as many as five hundred knights from England were said to have done so. There was a profitable trade in indulgences at this time, supposedly in aid of the Hospitaller Crusade. The Archbishop of York generated nearly £500 in two years, largely from indulgences, and at this time it was no longer necessary to swear a vow before money was handed over.[53] This seems to demonstrate the laxity of the Church at this time and is particularly interesting as Robin Hood's main feud was with the clergy of York.

Another characteristic of the Merry Men shared with the military-religious orders of the time is the absence of female companions. The early ballads refer simply to seven score yeomen. This has also been a major talking point and has even led to suggestions that Robin Hood was homosexual. However, it is made clear in the ballads that Robin's devotion to the Virgin Mary is to protect him altogether from deadly sin:

> Robyn loved Oure dere Lady:
> For dout of dydly synne,
> Wolde he never do compani harme
> That any woman was in.[54]

Reference in the *Gest* to Robin Hood being free from deadly sin suggests that he observed a vow of chastity. The Templars wore items associated with the Virgin Mary as symbols of chastity, and even at the time of the Order's demise the devotion of its members to Mary remained of great importance. During their trials, the Templars who were tortured informed their inquisitors that the chastity cords worn around their waists had once come into contact with an object, usually the pillar, from the church of the Virgin Mary in Nazareth where Christ had received his annunciation.[55] Since the vow of celibacy seems to be central to the values of the Merry Men, many may be disappointed to learn that this casts doubt over the authenticity of Robin's famous female companion.

9

A HIDDEN DIVINITY

In many ways, the events described in the early ballads are quite consistent. Robin Hood and his Merry Men frequently encounter strangers, some of whom Robin helps in times of difficulty, some he robs, and others he fights before inviting them to join the band. There is a pronounced animosity towards religious officials and the sheriff; Robin and his followers kill but only in retribution or self-defence. No matter what happens, the outlaws always seem to benefit financially, but, despite their successes, they do not profit by more than they need or are due. This alone may not fully justify the 'rob from the rich to give to the poor' philosophy that has helped to make Robin Hood so legendary, but in the early ballads he is already noted as an outlaw who helps the poor.

One of the most highly developed skills attributed to the Robin Hood of legend is archery, emphasized throughout the ballads. The *Gest* tells of him shooting before the king and praises the archery skills of Little John and Gilbert of the White-hand. Guy of Gisborne testifies to Robin's proficiency and skill in achieving victory:

'Gods blessing on thy heart!' sayes Guye,
'Goode fellow, thy shooting is goode,
For an thy hart be as good as thy hands,
Thou were better then Robin Hood.'[1]

The *Potter* ballad gives a notable appraisal of Robin Hood's archery in the opening stanzas. After the usual scene setting, the audience is introduced to 'one of the best that ever bore a bow':

Herkens, god yemen,
Comley, courteous, and god,
On of the best that yever bare bowe,
His name was Roben Hode.[2]

Even in the fifteenth century, many of the key aspects of the legend as we know them today are in place. However, there are some clear differences from later tradition. The king is clearly not King Richard the Lionheart at this stage, and the ballads do not support the notion that Robin provides staunch opposition to Prince John's regency. There is no direct evidence of his support for the peasant class or, before 1521, that he is a nobleman. The scene at the knight's castle in the *Gest* is one of several encounters illustrating the military capabilities of the Merry Men, yet Robin's reputation as a formidable fighter and opponent may have been exaggerated by Major's praise of Robin and his reference to one hundred bowmen.[3] While there is evidence of Robin Hood fighting with strangers who later become accepted into the outlaw band, some of the most famous of the Merry Men have yet to appear.

One person not mentioned in the early ballads is the rotund and jolly friar who becomes an indispensable member of the

Merry Men, Friar Tuck. He is portrayed in popular tradition as a fierce warrior and capable swordsman, the equal of any of the others. His involvement as the only holy man among the Merry Men is out of context with Robin's vendetta against the Church but in keeping with the Merry Men's devout piety. The first clear mention of Friar Tuck is found in a fragment of a Robin Hood play entitled *Robin Hood and the Knight*, also known as *Robin Hood and the Sheriff*, thought to date from around 1475.[4] Tuck is introduced as an established member of the band during a sword fight with the Sheriff of Nottingham, but no explanation is given of how or when he joined them.[5] The date of 1475 is early in the development of the legend and, despite claims by some previous commentators that Tuck is a late addition, the presence of the hot-headed holy man at this stage indicates that the character was already familiar to audiences of the fifteenth-century plays.

The first literary account of Friar Tuck's recruitment into the Merry Men comes in a play named *Robin Hood and the Friar*, dated around 1560.[6] It is similar in plot to the *Ballad of Robin Hood and the Curtal Friar*, which is thought by many scholars to have originated in the fifteenth century, despite only appearing in later collections such as the Garland of 1663.[7] In the ballad, Robin Hood talks of his willingness to journey even a hundred miles to meet a man who could match him in combat. Will Scarlock laughs and tells Robin of a friar from Fountains Abbey who would be his match. Robin Hood is delighted at the news and vows not to eat or drink until he meets him.[8]

The ballad continues with Robin's journey to Fountains Abbey where he finds the friar by the riverside. Robin addresses him in a provocative manner, forcing the friar to carry him across the stream to avoid getting wet. On reaching the other side, the friar draws his sword and orders Robin to take him back. Robin does so before drawing his own sword and commanding the friar to take him back over again. The friar obeys but stops abruptly halfway across, throwing Robin into the water, and an epic sword fight follows. With the fight in full flow, Robin requests a favour. The friar naïvely agrees, and Robin blows his horn. The Merry Men appear over the open ground, and the friar is outnumbered. Insisting on a favour in return, he whistles loudly and is soon joined by a number of vicious dogs, at which point Robin ends the fight.[9]

The events in this ballad are in keeping with early tradition. As usual, Robin battles with a stranger who proves himself a worthy opponent. The normal sequence of events continues as the opponent is accepted into the outlaw band, although in this particular ballad the friar chooses friendship rather than joining a fellowship.[10] The plot of the ballad is in keeping with the *Robin Hood and the Friar* play but less specific about the friar's identity. In the play Friar Tuck is named, while the ballad refers only to a 'curtal friar'. The dating of the play to 1560 confirms that the story dates back further than the ballad and perhaps even further in oral form. The play entitled *Robin Hood and the Sheriff* confirms that Tuck as a character was known by 1475, but whether the identification of the friar as Tuck in both the ballad and the play was based on assumptions or definitive knowledge is unclear. In both stories the friar is a formidable fighter, and there can be little doubt that the play was the source from which the account in the ballad was drawn. Equally, evidence that the friar was present in the early tradition is difficult to clarify. The fact that Tuck does not appear in the *Gest, Monk, Gisborne* or *Potter* ballads is in part offset by his appearance in the plays around the same time, yet the early ballads refer to the Merry Men as yeomen only.[11] The Garland copy of the ballad from 1663 was post-Reformation and came at a time when friars no longer existed in England.[12] Equally significant is that there were no friars during the reign of King Richard I.

Despite this, various theories have originated over the years to seek to authenticate the role of the friar. Supporting the King Richard I legend is a tale regarding a monk evicted from Fountains Abbey in 1156 for his unwillingness to abide by the strict code of the monastery. The word 'friar' comes from the French word 'frère', meaning 'brother'. In the *Sheriff* play Tuck is referred to as Frère Tuke, indicating that he could have been a monk, a chaplain or even a Templar.[13] The Sloane Manuscript, which places the date of Robin Hood's birth around 1160, during the reign of Henry II, is open-minded about the appearance of Tuck. The manuscript leans on the statement in the ballad that Tuck was a friar named Michael, but states that others suggest he was another type of religious man, for friars were not in existence at the time.[14] Child develops the argument for Tuck as a monk by explaining that the term 'curtal' was a reference to being short-frocked, suggesting that the 'friar' was a Franciscan monk.[15] However, if Tuck really lived at Fountains he would have been a Cistercian.[16] The name Friar Tuck was in use as an alias by 1417, when an outlawed Sussex chaplain named Robert Stafford travelled under the name of Frere Tuk.[17] Some scholars have pointed to this as a possible origin for Friar Tuck's later involvement with the Merry Men, but it is equally likely that Stafford chose the alias after hearing it in an earlier rhyme involving Friar Tuck.

The widespread popularity of the ballads has created a further problem. Despite the location of the fight between Robin and the friar given in the ballad, popular tradition has relocated the scene to Nottinghamshire.[18] As the *Curtal Friar* ballad refers to Fountains Abbey in Yorkshire, within thirty miles of Barnsdale, the river where they fought must be the Skell, although the ballad ends with a reference to Fountain Dale:

'And every holy day throughout the year,
Changed shall thy garment be,
If thou wilt go to fair Nottingham,
And there remain with me.'

This curtal frier had kept Fountains Dale
Seven long years or more;
There was neither knight, lord, nor earl
Could make him yield before.[19]

The ballad is arguably referring to an area in Nottinghamshire. In close proximity to the well at Fountain Dale, which is itself regarded as a site of holy importance, a hermitage once existed. The ballad builds on the location of the hermitage by suggesting Tuck took refuge there seven years before the fight against Robin. The nearby Newstead Priory had connections with the hermitage, and a chapel within the nearby moat supposedly contained a shrine. Since that time other legends have grown up around this. Tradition suggests that the friar was evicted from the hermitage after seven years and the canons of Newstead cursed the well. Local legend states that the well flows every seventh year and no other, probably a product of the wording at the end of the ballad. Sir Walter Scott wrote part of his well-known novel *Ivanhoe* in the nearby Fountain Dale House, and this may have increased the significance of the location.

The role of Friar Tuck as one of the Merry Men is not out of place. His addition to the legend provides the outlaws with an extra air of respectability, although he, too, is a capable fighter. The possibility of Knights Templar outlaws being in the company of a man like Tuck would certainly not be inconsistent or out of character, particularly as many of the Order were chaplains. Tuck's character is in keeping with that of both a monk and a warrior. In addition, it seems likely that Robin Hood would need someone to say his masses. The rhyme from *Scotichronicon* refers to Robin hearing mass in the forest, and the *Gest* makes reference to hearing three masses before he dines. The ballads do not clarify who says mass for Robin, whether it is one of the Merry Men or someone from outside their ranks. The absence of Tuck from other ballads is puzzling, but the final stanzas of the *Curtal Friar* ballad may explain this. While the *Potter* and *Gest* ballads refer to men being offered a fellowship within the band of Merry Men, Tuck decides to remain a friar but accepts a friendship.[20] The reference to friendship seems to clarify Tuck's position as an honorary Merry Man rather than a permanent addition and 'good fellow'.

More difficult to authenticate are some of the later additions to the Merry Men whose identities can in part be explained by earlier traditions. The tradition of Allan a Dale as the minstrel stems principally from the seventeenth-century ballad *Robin Hood and Allan a Dale*, in which Robin saves Allan's fiancée from the clutches of an evil knight. The Sloane Manuscript, however, had already included a similar storyline involving Will Scarlock.[21] The recurring theme that Robin Hood fought with passers-by and invited them into his band of Merry Men is evident in the *Gest* and *Potter* ballads, but the events that take place in the later ballads may be explained by his addition to the May Day festivities that were popular throughout Europe in the Middle Ages.

May Day became an international working-class holiday in more modern times, but its origins stem back to pagan times.[22] For the ancient Celts and Saxons, it was a festive holy day celebrating the first planting of the seeds. Traditionally the first day of May was significant to rural communities. From 1240 onwards, rural communities participated in springtime celebrations that officially heralded the first month of summer and the end of a long dark winter.[23] The summer solstice – formerly 25 June –

was known as Midsummer. It fell between the first day of May and the start of autumn on a cross-quarter day – one of many days in a year midway between an equinox and a solstice. The 1 May tradition also stemmed from the Celtic festival of Beltane, a celebration of birth and fertility in springtime.[24]

Following the spread of Christianity in Europe during the Middle Ages, traditional May Day celebrations were outlawed. Although some participation continued on a local scale in the rural towns and villages, many God-fearing citizens obeyed the edicts of the Church and shunned these events, particularly as participants would dress up in costumes that were not unlike those for Hallowe'en today. In the early days the May Day proceedings were led by the Goddess of the Hunt, Diana, and Herne the Hunter, a manifestation of the Celtic horned god. This changed during the later Middle Ages as European peasant societies moved away from hunting as their main livelihood to agriculturally based communities. As the pastoral influence on May Day became more pronounced and the character and way of life of the local communities changed, the gods featured in the plays and other events also changed. Initially Diana became a fertility queen of the fields, and Herne became the Green Man, otherwise known as Puck or Robin Goodfellow, the king of the fields. Some historians have indicated a possible connection between Puck and Robin Hood, identifying Puck, a fairy famous for his trickery, as the inspiration for Robin Hood's cunning nature.[25]

During the fifteenth and sixteenth centuries the Church began to incorporate some of the May Day festivities into its calendar. The proceedings were often adapted to present more Christian values and meanings, with a focus on the Virgin Mary. May became a sacred month. The Christian emphasis on devotion to the mother of Jesus, known as Marianism, gave rise to a new

Queen of May, usually known as Maid Marian. However, the new rituals continued to incorporate some pagan elements.[26] Surviving activities such as dancing around the Maypole are connected to the celebration of fertility in springtime.

It is often assumed that Tuck was one of the Morris dancers during the May Day festivities, usually the dancing partner of Maid Marian, although this seems to post-date the *Sheriff* play.[27] Robin's role in the festivities varied. In the early days he was not the King of May but a character who appeared in various plays to entertain the audience.[28] He would take part in mock battles where he would be challenged to combat by sword, quarterstaff or archery and on horseback. From this time on, Robin's reputation as a formidable opponent gathered pace. By the time John Major wrote *Historia Majoris Britanniae* Robin Hood's role in the proceedings was well known.

The addition of Robin Hood to the May Day festivities was significant in the development of the legend, as around this time Robin became the leading figure in a series of plays based on his new role as a feared fighter. The first of note appears to have been performed in Exeter in 1426–7, ten years after the first recorded May Day festivities in that city.[29] Between 1450 and 1550 Robin was known to have appeared in May Day festivities at twenty-four places in the south of England, portrayed as King of May or otherwise as assisting the king.[30] Strangely, this never occurred in Wales or the north of England, although he did sometimes appear in Scotland.[31] When he was part of the May Day festivities, Robin would typically appear alongside his Queen of May, Maid Marian, leading a procession through nearby towns with the aim of raising money for the Church, often known as 'Church Ales'.[32]

Maid Marian's role in the popular tradition of Robin Hood is almost as legendary as that of Robin himself. She is the only female member of the outlaw band, having supposedly fled to the forest to live the life of an outlaw to escape from the clutches of Prince John. The defence of Maid Marian's honour is as integral a part of the story as Robin's supposed allegiance to King Richard. Robin and Maid Marian later marry before living out their days happily, usually in comfortable gentrified style. Yet Marian is a notable absentee from the early ballads, not least the *Gest* which gives an overview of Robin's life. There is no mention of Marian being present when Robin meets the king or any indication of her whereabouts at the time of his death.

The romance between Robin Hood and Maid Marian seems rather out of character for the pious man of the *Gest*. The early portrayal of the Merry Men as a society of hardened soldiers free from deadly sin makes it difficult to explain the presence of a female companion. Yet her inclusion had a notable effect on the legend. The origin of her character has also become a matter of some debate. One of the earliest associations was made in the French pastoral play *Le Jeu de Robin et Marion* by Adam de la Halle.[33] This play, which is said to date back to around 1283, centres on the story of a French knight who falls in love with a shepherdess named Marion. She spurns the knight's advances, remaining faithful to her lover, named Robin. The remainder of the play recounts the activities of Marion and Robin and their friends.[34] Over the next two centuries this was a popular entertainment in the French May Day celebrations, but it was not known in England at the time.

Nearly a century after *Le Jeu de Robin et Marion* was written, characters of the same name appeared in a 30,000-line poem entitled *Mirour de l'omme*.[35] Written around 1376 by the poet and dramatist John Gower, a contemporary of both Langland and Chaucer, the play focuses on moral topics and includes symbolic representations of the seven deadly sins. The play condemns

Top left: 'Merry Robin Stops a Sorrowful Knight'; top right: 'Sir Richard Pleadeth Before the Prior of Emmet'; above left: 'The Mighty Fight Betwixt Little John and the Cook'; all from Howard Pyle's *The Merry Adventures of Robin Hood of Great Renown, in Nottinghamshire*, 1883. Above right: Robin Hood; from Louis Rhead's *Bold Robin Hood and His Outlaw Band: Their Famous Exploits in Sherwood Forest*, 1912

Woodcut of John Major; from the title page of *In Petri Hyspani Summulas Commentaria*, 1505

DAVID EARL OF HUNTINGDON.

David Earl of Huntingdon; from Sir Walter Scott's *The Talisman*, 1863

King John signs the Magna Carta; from *Cassell's Illustrated History of England*, 1902

Above: Henry III; from *Cassell's
Illustrated History of England*, 1902

Right: Edward I; from *Cassell's Illustrated
History of England*, 1902

Kenilworth Castle, 'where almost all the nobles who were rebelling against
the king had taken refuge', according to Bower *Photograph: Mike Davis*

A gathering of Knights Templar; from a nineteenth-century book illustration

Knights Templar on the battlefield; from a nineteenth-century book illustration

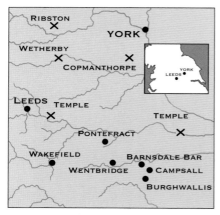

Map of parts of the modern counties of West Yorkshire and North Yorkshire showing Knights Templar preceptories in the old West Riding (marked X) and other places of Templar significance as well as major towns and places mentioned in the ballads

The Church of St Mary Magdalene at Campsall, South Yorkshire *Photograph: Mike Davis*

The Church of St Mary's at Temple Balsall, property of the Knights Templar until 1324

The Church of St Mary's at Edwinstowe, Nottinghamshire; a tradition of the late Middle Ages celebrates the church as being where Robin Hood and Maid Marian were married.

The Church of St Mary's in Nottingham, as mentioned in the *Monk* ballad

'In somer, when the shawes be sheyne': the *Monk* ballad, line 1; Sherwood Forest in summertime

The Major Oak in Sherwood Forest; the tree is thought to be at least seven hundred years old and is often celebrated as the former meeting place of the Merry Men. *Photograph: Mike Davis*

'Itt is merry, walking in the fayre forest': the *Gisborne* ballad, line 3; Barnsdale in summertime

Robin Hood's Well at Skellow, Yorkshire

Wentbridge, near the Sayles Plantation *Photograph: Mike Davis*

'The Merry Friar Carrieth Robin Across the Water'; from Howard Pyle's *The Merry Adventures of Robin Hood of Great Renown, in Nottinghamshire*, 1883

Left: Map of royal hunting forests; from Louis Rhead's *Bold Robin Hood and His Outlaw Band: Their Famous Exploits in Sherwood Forest*, 1912

Below: Fountains Abbey, mentioned in *The Ballad of Robin Hood and the Curtal Friar*
Photograph: *Mike Davis*

Left: 'Robin Hood Meeteth the Tall Stranger on the Bridge'; right: 'Merry Robin Stops a Stranger in Scarlet'; from Howard Pyle's *The Merry Adventures of Robin Hood of Great Renown, in Nottinghamshire*, 1883

Left: 'Ye Sheriff of Nottingham'; right: 'Ye Proud Bishop of Hereford'; from Louis Rhead's *Bold Robin Hood and His Outlaw Band: Their Famous Exploits in Sherwood Forest*, 1912

Kirklees Priory gatehouse, where, according to *The Ballad of Robin Hood's Death*, Robin Hood was murdered; from Joseph Ritson's *Robin Hood*, 1887

'Robin Shoots His Last Shaft'; from Louis Rhead's *Bold Robin Hood and His Outlaw Band: Their Famous Exploits in Sherwood Forest*, 1912

Robin Hood's grave; drawn by Nathaniel Johnston, 1665

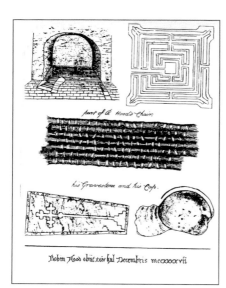

Robin Hood relics at St Anne's Well; originally drawn by John Throsby, 1797, from R. Thoroton's *Antiquities of Nottingham*, 1797

Drawing of a slab that supposedly once covered Little John's grave. It now hangs in the entrance to the Church of St Michael's in Hathersage, Derbyshire. The letters L I reputedly acknowledge Little John. In the *Orygynale Chronykil* Wyntoun refers to him as Litill Iohne.

Little John's cottage at Hathersage; drawing from 1832

Presumed grave of Little John at the Church of St Michael's in Hathersage,
Derbyshire. Inset: Close-up of the headstone *Photograph: Mike Davis*

Supposed grave of Will Scarlock
in the graveyard of St Mary's
Church in Blidworth,
Nottinghamshire

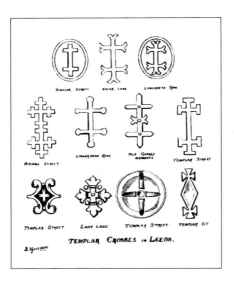

Left: A collection of Templar crosses, based on John Harrison's sketches of crosses that once marked various streets and buildings in Leeds

Left and above: Graves in the graveyard of the Templar Church of St Mary's at Temple Balsall; while the graves are nineteenth century in origin, they contain the original Templar designs and symbols.

Nottingham Castle gatehouse

Wall plaques beneath Nottingham Castle by local
sculptor James Woodford, 1951. From top left:
King Richard the Lionheart joins the hands of
Maid Marian and Robin Hood; Robin Hood and
Little John fighting on a bridge; Robin
Hood, Maid Marian and Friar Tuck with hounds
fighting Guy of Gisborne's men; Robin Hood
shooting his last arrow

Statues by James Woodford, 1951, of Robin
Hood and the Merry Men stand beneath
Nottingham Castle. Clockwise from top left:
Robin Hood; Allan a Dale (front) and
Will Scarlock; Little John (above)
and Much the Miller's son; Friar Tuck
with his back to Little John
Photographs: Mike Davis

the dissolute lives of the Augustine monks and highlights the conduct of Robin and Marion, who enjoy a pastoral existence rather than choosing to obey the teachings of the Church.[36] It seems likely that the Robin and Marion of this play, which in English means the *Mirror of Mankind*, are the same characters as Adam de la Halle's. The personalities of this Robin and Marion cannot be identified with the Robin Hood who condemns the habits of the monks in the ballads. The monks are frivolous and demonstrate characteristics that were unethical at the time, while Robin and Marion, unlike the Robin of the *Gest*, are not free from deadly sin.

By the sixteenth century Robin Hood had become a central character in the May Day festivities in many places, alongside his Queen of May, Maid Marian. But, despite the new connection, they remained separate entities. Maid Marian's role as the new Diana had become widely accepted as Christianization of the pagan festivities continued, while the ballads of Robin Hood were still the most popular stories of the time. Writing in 1508, the poet Alexander Barclay was possibly the first person to connect the two fully with his lines:

> Yet would I gladly hear some merry fytte
> Of Maid Marian, or else of Robin Hood.[37]

Barclay's choice of words coincidentally highlights the possibility of Robin Hood and Marian having a relationship rather than there already being one. In fact, with the exception of the Robin and Marion relationship in *Le Jeu de Robin et Marion*, there is no record of any connection between Robin Hood and Maid Marian until they appear in two plays by Anthony Munday in 1598, 148 years after Robin Hood appears in the ballad of the *Monk*.

In the Munday plays there is a significant change to tradition.

The plays are named *The Downfall of Robert Earl of Huntington* and *The Death of Robert Earl of Huntington*. Unlike in the early ballads, Robin Hood is referred to as a disinherited Earl of Huntingdon who lived during the reign of King Richard I. Major's work had been in print for nearly eighty years by this time, and the period in which *Historia Majoris Britanniae* placed Robin's life was clearly known to Munday. The reference to Robin Hood as a potential earl may also have shaped the content of the play in which Maid Marian's connection to Robin Hood becomes more familiar. In the initial play she is referred to as Lady Matilda Fitzwalter, daughter of Sir Robert Fitzwalter.[38] After Prince John outlaws Robin Hood, the Earl of Huntington, she flees to the greenwood to be with the earl; King Richard later returns to England, and Robert is reinstated. The second play centres on King John coveting Matilda following the murder of Robin. Angered by her rejection of his advances, John has her poisoned, and she dies at Dunmow Priory.[39]

The evidence found in the plays and ballads is seemingly an assemblage of various creations and distortions of actual historical persons introduced to add variety to the stories. Maid Marian, or Marion, or Lady Marion, has varied in the Robin Hood tradition from a Saxon to a Countess of Huntingdon, a lady of noble birth, of Norman birth and even a shepherdess. In some cases she is Robin Hood's childhood sweetheart, in others she is a cousin or niece of King Richard, yet she has also been known to be the daughter of Richard at the Lee. In the plays Marian is an alias of the historical Matilda Fitzwalter. In the later stories Matilda is often used as an alternative form of Marian and vice versa. The historical facts of Matilda Fitzwalter's life are uncertain. The daughter of the nobleman Robert Fitzwalter certainly existed, but the suggestion that she was the unwilling object of King John's attentions was not recorded until the 1300s. Tradition has it that the historical Matilda was poisoned in 1214 in similar circumstances to those described in the play and that her remains were buried at Dunmow Priory, as the play suggests. Historically, in 1212 the king vengefully destroyed every castle in the Fitzwalters' possession. However, history later records the re-emergence of Robert Fitzwalter, who played an important part when King John was forced by the barons to sign the Magna Carta.[40]

Maid Marian's involvement in the Robin Hood ballads is surprisingly limited. As we have seen, she was not included in any of them before the time of the Munday plays, and the first in which she appeared was the ballad of *Robin Hood and Maid Marian*, dating from the seventeenth century. In this ballad, a mere eighty-nine lines celebrating Robin Hood's position as an earl, Marian and Robin share a kiss before they are forced to part. Marian later seeks the outlawed earl and comes to the forest in the disguise of a page. Robin Hood, also disguised, initially mistakes her for a bandit. As usual, he fights the stranger, who causes him much difficulty. Robin admires the stranger's fighting capabilities and is shocked when she reveals her true identity. They return to the greenwood and the feasting begins in earnest.[41]

This storyline is a departure from the early days when Robin Hood, the yeoman, kept the company of men who capably demonstrated military experience. On the other hand, it conforms to the usual pattern of events in which Robin and a stranger fight, the stranger puts up a good show, Robin invites the stranger to join the band, the stranger accepts, and they celebrate. Maid Marian becomes the only member of the band to be clearly referred to as a female, and her nobility is confirmed alongside the identification of this Robin Hood as the Earl of Huntingdon.

Robin's love life was not always straightforward. Sentimentally we may accept Robin Hood and Maid Marian as lovers in the mould of Tristan and Isolde, but Marian was not his only love interest. In another later ballad, dated around 1684, *Robin Hood's Birth, Breeding, Valour and Marriage*, the object of Robin's affections is a woman named Clorinda. In this, another ballad focusing on the gentrified hero, although not the Earl of Huntingdon, Robin Hood is out in the forest when he finds Clorinda, the queen of shepherds. After witnessing her displaying impressive prowess as a hunter by shooting a deer, Robin invites her to dine with him. Later that evening the pair become engaged, and the marriage is celebrated.[42]

Both of these later ballads differ in nature from the early four. The familiar sequence of events occurs – Robin meets a stranger, culminating in a feast and a new addition to the Merry Men – but the gentrified protagonist is no longer a hero among men. Instead, this outlaw is a more romanticized object of interest for the audience and an inspiration for later writers. Throughout the later stories Maid Marian is firmly established as Robin Hood's lover, some writers making Clorinda an alias of Marian, usually Robin Hood's childhood sweetheart.

Even in the later ballads Marian's appearances are limited. In the ballad of *Robin Hood's Golden Prize* she is mentioned without significance.[43] This ballad is similar in structure to many of the early ones, in which Robin targets the clergy and steals from them, in this case £500, yet rewards them for their piety by leaving them £50 each. An unfinished play by Ben Jonson, entitled *The Sad Shepherd*, includes two acts, written shortly before his death, concerned with a pastoral drama featuring the character Maid Marian as a shepherdess and an experienced fighter and hunter. The pastoral play *Le Jeu de Robin et Marion* had described a shepherdess named Marion, and this was probably Jonson's inspiration, but it was the first time Maid Marian had been referred to as a shepherdess. In addition, neither de la

Halle's play nor Gower's *Mirror of Mankind* refers to Marion as a maiden. The influence of the pastoral plays on the character of Maid Marian is clear in the later ballads, but it is unlikely that they were the primary influence on the development of her character.[44]

The presence of Maid Marian alters the legend significantly, particularly as it seems, at least at first sight, to contradict the character of Robin Hood portrayed in the early ballads. The *Monk* and *Gest* ballads give considerable emphasis to Robin's piety and devotion to the Virgin Mary. They also point clearly to his chastity. Popular culture, however, makes little reference to this and apparently displaces his affection for the Virgin Mary on to Marian. However, closer scrutiny suggests a more surprising and complex development. As mentioned, the Christianization of the May Day games saw Maid Marian supplanting Diana, the goddess of the hunt, but the celebrations of fertility in springtime remained and still concentrated on devotion to Mary. Maid Marian represents in human form the divine goddess Virgin Mary, her chastity emphasized by Marian's identification as a maiden. Maid Marian's presence does not detract from Robin Hood's devotion to the Virgin Mary; it merely takes an alternative form. Maid Marian's position among the Merry Men has no effect on her chastity. Her maidenhood remains protected throughout.

The addition of Maid Marian to the Robin Hood stories is part of a progressive evolution of the May Day games into a Christianized and then gentrified legend, perhaps drawing on the French pastoral tradition. But in the following centuries the ballads and stories give birth to a new character: the champion of the downtrodden, instigator of peasant revolt, Saxon, nobleman and benefactor of the poor. Arise Sir Robin of Locksley.

10

SIR ROBIN OF LOCKSLEY'S BIRTH, BREEDING, VALOUR AND MARRIAGE

For Robin Hood the yeoman, his addition to the May Day proceedings proved significant in terms of developing the legend. We have seen how the man from the ballads was integrated into new situations and featured alongside new characters, particularly through the plays, but the May Day festivities were never celebrated on a national scale and neither was Robin Hood.[1] His role was subject to local variations and interpretations. In some places he was king or an assistant to the king, but elsewhere he simply appeared in various plays without assuming any particular importance.[2] At least four of the ballads had appeared in text by the mid-sixteenth century, but by that time his involvement in the May Day festivities had probably done more than the rhymes to spread his popularity.

It is somewhat surprising, considering that Robin came from Barnsdale in Yorkshire, that activities involving him featured more in the south and the Midlands than the north. During the Middle Ages audiences of the rhymes in the south of England viewed the north as a dark place, home to villains and evil spirits who inhabited the forests and preyed on passers-by. Whatever Barnsdale was really like, southerners could enjoy such tales, pieced together from people who had travelled there in the past.[3]

Speculations about the audiences for whom the tales of Robin Hood were composed have been mixed.[4] As a yeoman, his adventures could potentially appeal to peasants, gentlemen, noblemen and, of course, other yeomen. But as time went by his role came to serve a number of symbolic functions and ideals.[5] For the lower classes he was heroic: a man standing up to corrupt officials and clergy; a courteous leader; an outlaw, yet a man who did much good for the poor; a fantastic archer; a formidable fighter; a figure of devout piety; a man free of deadly sin who respected women; who, according to Bower, supported the Church; and who, according to Major, steadfastly defended and upheld superior moral standards. As the old saying goes, he was 'all things to all men'. As printing became more common in England during the sixteenth century, it was only a matter of time before his appeal became more widespread. The early rhymes that had been recited by the minstrels for well over a century were now making their way into the houses of the nobility and the court. As King of the May, Robin was a courteous host and ruler, and it was perhaps for this reason that even the King and Queen of England enjoyed tales of this yeoman outlaw. In 1510 Henry VIII dressed up as Robin Hood to excite the ladies of the court, and in 1515 he watched from the stands as a formal play was put on for him at Shooter's Hill.[6]

> The king and quene, accompanied with many lords
> and ladies, rode to the high ground on Shooter's Hill
> to take the air, and as they passed by the way, they
> espied a company of tall yomen clothed all in green,
> with green whodes and bows and arrows, to the number
> of 90. One of them calling himself Robin Hood, came
> to the king, desiring him to see his men shoot, and the

king was content. Then he wistled, and all the 90 archers shot and losed at once, he then whistled again, and they shot again; their arrows wistled by craft of the head, so that the noise was strange and great, and much pleased the king, the quene, and all the company. All these archers were of the king's guard, and had thus appareled themselves to make solace to the king. Then Robin Hood desired the king and quene to come into the green wood, and see how the outlaws live. The king demanded of the quene and her ladies, if they durst venture to go into the wood with so many out-laws, and the quene was content. Then the horns blew till they came to the wood under Shooter's Hill, and there was an arbour made of boughs, with a hall and a great chamber, and an inner chamber, well made and covered with flowers and sweet herbs, which the king much praised. Then said Robin Hood, 'Sir, outlaws breakfasts is vensyon, and you must be content with such fare as we have.' The king and quene sat down, and were served with venison and wine by Robin Hood and his men. Then the king and his party departed, and Robin and his men conducted them. As they were returning, they were met by two ladies in a rich chairiot, drawn by five horses, every horse had his name on his head, and on every horse sat a lady, with her name written; and in a chair sat the Lady May, accompanied with Lady Flora, richly appareled, and they saluted the king with divers songs, and so brought him to Greenwhich.[7]

By this time the legend was widely known and enjoyed, but Robin was not especially popular among the nobility.

Regardless of what type of yeoman he was, the term denotes a commoner.[8] Yet the ambiguity of the ballads made Robin flexible. It is perhaps for this reason that his popularity, having already endured for over a century, continued to retain its appeal during the early years of the reign of Henry VIII. The absence of a specific historical timescale for the life of the character added to his flexibility for the contemporary ballad writers. Building on the king's enthusiasm for Robin Hood, two new ballads were composed, set during the reign of this monarch.

Popular during the seventeenth century and surviving in the *Percy Folio*, the ballad of *Robin Hood and Queen Catherine* is set in the court of Henry VIII but includes material similar to that of many of the early Robin Hood ballads, including the *Gest*.[9] Although this later work is dated around 1642, King Henry VIII and his queen were probably familiar with the story in the ballad, at least in rhyme form. In the ballad, the queen makes a wager on an archery tournament and summons Robin Hood to compete. Robin obliges and wins the tournament for her.[10] The identity of the queen has never been confirmed: Henry VIII had three wives named Catherine, the most likely being Catherine of Aragon.[11]

Henry VIII also featured in an anonymously written eighteenth-century ballad entitled *Robin Hood's Chase*. In this tale Robin Hood participates in an archery tournament in similar circumstances to the *Catherine* ballad. After the tournament Robin learns that the king is chasing him so he flees with his men to the north. Following their escape Robin suggests that they were pursued because the queen wished to see him. The men head to London to see the queen and learn that this was not the case. At the request of Queen Catherine the king grants Robin a pardon and calls off the chase.[12]

The ballads of *Robin Hood and Queen Catherine* and *Robin Hood's Chase* were not, nor were they intended to be, historically accurate. Their presentation of the outlaws in a more glamorous light was a significant move away from the historically influenced earlier ballads towards the development of the famous Robin Hood that appeared in the eighteenth-century broadsides and garlands. Not only did Robin's popularity sweep through the royal courts but it made the identification of any factual basis for him more difficult. It is no longer possible to determine whether the lower-classes at the time regarded Robin Hood as a historical figure – Bower suggests that the people were aware he was a disinherited rebel – or as an entirely fictitious one. By the mid-sixteenth century the early accounts had been largely replaced in public awareness by a series of stories of more theatrical than historical value.

By 1520 Robin's popularity was beginning to wane.[13] The fact that May Day festivities had never been celebrated on a national level led to their demise, and as public participation fell away so did Robin Hood's legendary status. In 1555 the Scottish Parliament banned celebrations of Robin Hood or people dressing as Robin, Little John, Maid Marian or the 'Abbot of Unreason'.[14] Robin Hood's reputation as a courteous host was still legendary, but the stigma of an unruly reputation from the early ballads, in which death and robbery occurred, remained. There is evidence from the time that the term 'Robin Hood' was used to describe a felon in the same way as it had in the thirteenth century.[15] One particularly intriguing example, given in a petition to Parliament in 1439, cited Piers Venables of Aston in Derbyshire as an itinerant felon after he had appeared with his gang at the May Day festivities in Tutbury in a 'manere of werre, riot, route and insurrection arraid . . . who having no liflode, ne sufficeante of goodes, gadered and assembled unto him many misdoers, beynge of his clothynge, and, in manere of insurrection, wente into the wodes in that countrie, like it

hadde be Robyn Hude and his meyne'.[16] In 1498 the term was
intentionally used as an alias by a man named Roger Marshall
when leading a gang in Willenhall causing an affray.[17] It was
also the stimulus for two men to rise up against the Yorkist
government in 1469 under the names Robin of Holderness and
Robin of Redesdale and for a mob in Norfolk to block a road
and threaten people with their cries: 'We are Robynhodesmen,
war, war, war.'[18] Even in the seventeenth century the term was
associated with villainy. At the time of the Gunpowder Plot, Sir
Robert Cecil branded Guy Fawkes and his band of conspira-
tors as 'Robin Hoods' after their attempt to destroy the Houses
of Parliament.[19] The famous Elizabethan explorer Sir Walter
Raleigh, when charged with treason against Queen Elizabeth I,
is reported to have responded with the words, 'For me to make
of myself Robin Hood, a Watt Tyler, a Kett or a Cade . . . I was
not so mad.'[20]

The stories of Robin Hood had always been officially disapproved, but by the mid-sixteenth century they were
commonly associated with criminal behaviour rather than
moral objections to authority, at least in the eyes of officials.
Historia Majoris Britanniae was an important addition to the
Robin Hood legend. It arrived at a time when printing was
becoming more common in England and the stories were
becoming more widely known. It is noticeable that, either by
coincidence or through deliberate intent, the shift in Robin
Hood's character came not only at a time when the stories were
circulating more widely but when their popularity in the May
Day festivities was waning. Owing in part to his popularity with
the king, for the first time he was beginning to make his mark on
the upper classes. As most of the lower classes were illiterate, it
is reasonable to assume that the ballads would have been read
only by the educated, mainly nobility. Stories of a yeoman were

less likely to appeal to noblemen, but every Robin Hood ballad represents resistance to authority. It was not just the poor who were forced to live under a strict, oppressive yoke of authority. The nobles were highly taxed, most worked very hard, and during the Tudor period they felt the imposition of authority from both Crown and Church. They, too, it could be argued, were victims of a repressed society. There is no reason why nobles could not enjoy the original stories of Robin Hood, but as a gentrified character he was more appealing to a new audience. Robin represented different things to different people, but for most he was a man standing up to unjust authority at a time when it reigned supreme.

It seems reasonable to believe that, before the work of Major, Robin Hood did not have a definitive historical setting, particularly as there is a tendency in the surviving ballads not to name officials clearly or designate the time period. The first attempts to determine Robin Hood's place in history came in the chronicles of Wyntoun and Bower, but even their influence was limited.[21] Wyntoun's *Orygynale Cronykil* was written to satisfy the aims and requirements of his patron and was probably unfamiliar to people south of the border and beyond. Equally, Bower's *Scotichronicon* was intended only for scholars.[22] It is unlikely that these works would have been widely known to the lower classes at the time who, according to Bower, enjoyed the ballads above all others. Major's influence, however, extended more widely. His chronicle, unlike the work of his predecessors, did not centre on Scotland but was intended for a European audience. Although this did not benefit the illiterate, the easier, modern Latin that he used had a wider appeal than the rough language of Bower. This is significant when placing Robin Hood as a historical character. The time periods for his life mentioned in the chronicles, 1283, 1266 and 1193, all appear to be little more than guesswork given that we have no knowledge of the chroniclers' sources, but it was Major's opinion that found acceptance. Major's choice to publish his book in Paris, rather than Scotland, gave it the potential to reach a wide audience.[23] Mass-market readership in turn led to increased familiarity, and Major's views became accepted as history.

King Henry VIII's antiquary, John Leland, who travelled widely throughout England and Wales, provided further evidence for a historical figure and recorded details of Robin Hood's grave at Kirklees. Included in his chronicle, written in 1540, were the words: 'Kirkley monasterum monialum ubi Ro:Hood nobilis ille exlex sepultus',[24] which can be roughly translated as: 'Kirklees Monastery where Robin Hood that nobleman who was outside the law lies buried'. The reference to a nobleman demonstrates that Major's 'Dux' had clearly caught on. The location of Kirklees corresponds with the ending of the *Gest* and with the later ballad of *Robin Hood's Death*, but the hero of the *Gest* was, of course, a yeoman.[25]

Major was the first of the chroniclers to identify a number of prominent characteristics of Robin Hood: not only was he possibly a nobleman but he robbed only from the wealthy, enriched the poor and was courteous to women.[26] A similar picture emerges from the work of John Stow. Once a tailor living in London, Stow became a historian and acquired many historical manuscripts. Yet he achieved little more than regurgitating Major. He wrote: 'Poor men's goods he spared, abundantly relieving them with that which by theft he got from abbeys and houses of rich earls.'[27]

Richard Grafton, the man who penned the *Chronicle at Large* in 1569, had earlier been printer to Edward VI, who reigned from 1547 to 1553. Grafton's work built on Major's but firmly described Robin Hood as an outlawed earl. His chronicle refers to the earl's financial constraints and goes into detail about a 'pamphlet' that confirmed the activities of Robin Hood's life cross-referenced by the confiscation of his lands, proof of which is found in the records of the Exchequer during the reign of King Richard I. As noted in Chapter 2, this potentially ties in with the activities of David, Earl of Huntingdon, but Grafton is clearly talking about the man of the ballads.

Every new reference to Robin Hood at this time reinforced information provided previously before adding something new. The discovery of the Sloane Manuscript continued the trend. Building on the activities of Robin Hood in the *Gest*, this five-and-a-half-page text was the first attempt to profile Robin Hood's life, placing the time at which he lived outside the law firmly in the reign of King Richard I. It also added one now highly contentious aspect to the legend: the site of Robin's birth.

> Robin Hood was borne at Lockesley, in Yorkeshire, or after others, in Notinghamshire, in the days of Henry the second, about the yeare 1160; but lyued tyll the latter end of Richard the Fyrst.[28]

This was the first mention of Locksley as the birthplace of Robin Hood, and, not for the first time, the work of one anonymous contributor succeeded in turning the legend on its head. Bearing in mind that the writer of the manuscript was clearly familiar with the *Gest*, going into detail about the loan scene with Richard at the Lee and mentioning many other events from the ballad, it is puzzling that he refers to Robin living during the reign of Richard the Lionheart when the *Gest* clearly refers to an Edward. The writer must have been aware of the work of Major and probably Grafton, but the text breaks up when referring to Robin's social class.

> He was of wo[?] parentage, but was so riotous, that he
> lost or sould his patrimony, and for debt became an
> outlawe.[29]

This is also similar in content to the work of Grafton, and whichever was the earlier may well have been the other's source. It also firmly demonstrates the cascading effect of the legend. There is still no mention of Robin Hood's role as a leader of peasant revolt, but many of the other popular elements of the modern tradition are starting to appear. The link between Robin Hood and Sir Robin of Locksley is now familiar, but the manner in which this originated is strange. There is a village called Loxley in Yorkshire, close to Sheffield, but its association with the legend has never been authenticated. The influence of the Fitzwalter family on the legend may be at work again, as Robert Fitzwalter's brother-in-law, William de Lovetot, from Huntingdon was later recorded as becoming the Lord of Hallam. In the later ballad, *Robin Hood's Birth, Breeding, Valour and Marriage*, reference is made to Locksley in Nottinghamshire.[30] No such place exists in Nottinghamshire, but it is possible that the reference is to the village in Yorkshire and that confusion resulted from a series of border disputes that occurred periodically throughout the Middle Ages. Despite the lack of evidence for Locksley, the reference in the Sloane Manuscript has since been accepted as incontrovertible fact in much the same way as Major's duke, Munday's Earl of Huntingdon and the May Day's Maid Marian. Within a century of the publication of the *Gest* Robin Hood was already a completely different character. He was now Sir Robert of Locksley, Earl of Huntingdon.[31]

One of the most important ballads that asserted his status as an earl was Martin Parker's *A True Tale of Robin Hood*, penned in 1632. Parker was renowned for being one of the most respected professional ballad writers of the time, and this was one of the few attempts to produce a ballad as a summary of Robin's life as an outlaw. Based on the 'Truest Writers of our English Chronicles', inevitably including Major and Grafton, Parker begins by making reference to both gentry and yeoman status before describing Robin Hood as the Earl of Huntingdon.

> Both Gentlemen, or Yeoman bould,
> Or whatsoever you are,
> To have a stately story tould,
> Attention now prepare.
>
> It is a tale of Robin Hood,
> That I to you will tell,
> Which being rightly understood,
> I know will please you well.
>
> This Robbin, so much talked on,
> Was once a man of fame,
> Instiled Earl of Huntingdon,
> Lord Robert Hood by name.[32]

Despite the absence of persuasive evidence, Parker lays claim to the historicity of the myth with the following strange subtitle of his ballad:

> A brief touch of the life and death of that Renowned
> Outlaw, Robert Earl of Huntingdon vulgarly called
> Robbin Hood, who lived and dyed in AD 1198, being
> the 9 yere of the reigne of King Richard the first,
> commonly called Richard Cure de Lyon.

Carefully collected out of the truest writers of
our English chronicles. And published for the
satisfaction of those who desire too see
Truth purged from falsehood.[33]

Moving on from Grafton, and clearly aware of Munday's
plays, Parker centres on the supposedly historical earl but makes
it obvious that he is referring to the same person as the outlaw of
the *Gest*. As with Grafton, the earl is outlawed for debts during
the reign of King Richard I. After taking to the forests of Yorkshire and Lancashire, he lives with a band of loyal men who earn
a living by robbing from the clergy, and he uses some of his money
to aid the poor.[34] In similar circumstances to the *Gest*, King
Richard agrees to pardon Robin Hood. Some of the outlaws flee
to the Scottish king, whereas Robin soon contracts a fever and is
bled, not by a prioress but by a treacherous friar who bled too
much of his blood.[35]

Despite Parker's claim of 'truth purged from falsehood', the
Gest is clearly his source. We see the clergy being robbed in a
similar manner to the monk of the *Gest*; Robin shares his money
as he did with Richard at the Lee; the king agrees to pardon him
in Nottingham; and the ballad ends when the outlaw dies in
treacherous circumstances. Parker may not have been familiar
with the Sloane Manuscript as there is no mention of Locksley.

The ballad of *Robin Hood's Birth, Breeding, Valour and
Marriage* was particularly influential in outlining the romantic
aspects of Robin's character, but like the *True Tale* ballad it
attempts to illustrate his early years, only this time in a somewhat comical way. Rather than portraying Robin in the same
way as in the chronicles, the early stanzas refer to a selection of
famous ballad heroes. In the opening six stanzas we learn that
Robin Hood is not the Earl of Huntingdon but is of born of

gentry through to his mother being the sister of Squire Gamwell of Gamwell Hall in Nottinghamshire.

> Her brother was Gamwel, of Great Gamwel Hall,
> And a noble house-keeper was he,
> Ay, as ever broke bread in sweet Nottinghamshire,
> And a squire of famous degree.[36]

Born in 'Locksley town' in Nottinghamshire, Robin's father is described in the ballad as a capable archer and even the better of Adam Bell, William of Cloudesley and Clym of Clough.[37] There is also reference to the Jolly Pinder of Wakefield. The pinder, probably George a' Greene, was a popular ballad hero of the time and even starred in a Robin Hood ballad entitled *The Jolly Pinder of Wakefield,* although it was Robin Hood who met the pinder, not his father. A curious family tie is then made to his mother's uncle, a knight called Sir Guy who is famous in the county of Warwickshire. The reference to the knight at first appears meaningless, but the reference to the other ballad heroes may provide a clue to his identity.

> His mother was neece to the Coventry knight,
> Which Warwickshire men call Sir Guy,
> For he slew the blue bore that hangs up at the gate,
> Or mine host of The Bull tells a lye.[38]

Famous for his chivalrous adventures, Sir Guy of Warwick was a popular ballad hero between the thirteenth and seventeenth centuries. After falling in love with Lady Felice, the lowly Guy travels far and wide, smiting various giants, dragons and other deadly opponents before returning home to wed his beloved after proving himself a man. Yet, despite his love for his new wife, his violent past continues to haunt him, and he leaves for a pilgrimage to the Holy Land before living out his life as a hermit.[39] The ballad of *Robin Hood's Birth, Breeding, Valour and Marriage* is not historical but helps embellish the legend of Robin Hood with famous names appealing to the reader.[40]

The reference to Squire Gamwell is an interesting feature that fits neatly with the ballad of *Robin Hood and the Newly Revived*.[41] Until the eighteenth century the Merry Men of the early ballads had not been provided with an origin. This changed as new ballads emerged with various explanations for how the band was formed. In the case of the ballad of the *Newly Revived*, Robin Hood is out in the forest with Little John when he spies a finely dressed stranger shooting deer. Impressed by the man, Robin invites him to join the Merry Men, but he spurns the offer and threatens Robin. They fight with swords, and as the fight progresses Robin asks the stranger his name.

> 'In Maxwell I was bred and born,
> My name is Young Gamwell.
>
> 'For killing my own fathers steward,
> I am forc'd to this English wood,
> And for to seek an uncle of mine;
> Some call him Robin Hood.'[42]

The reference to Gamwell ties in with Gamwell Hall from the *Breeding* ballad. The *Newly Revived* ballad is also similar in plot to the ballad of *Robin Hood and the Bold Pedlar*. It features a pedlar rather than a stranger in scarlet. Robin Hood fights with the pedlar, named Gamble Gold, who this time is identified as Robin's mother's sister's son, and he joins the band. The encounter with the cook and the potter in the early ballads seems to have set the scene for many of the later encounters that are products of modern tradition rather than historical origin. Little John famously meets Robin Hood on a bridge, but that story does not appear until the eighteenth century. In twentieth-century tradition Much the Miller's son fights after Robin demands the miller's flour bag, as he believes him to be concealing goods, and even Maid Marian joins in similar circumstances.

It is fair to say that by the eighteenth century the Robin Hood legend had become almost wholly fictitious. The development of Robert of Locksley's character brought into being a new hero who was very appealing to the nobility. However, the hero of the ballads was still ambiguous. In some cases, the time period was set firmly in the reign of King Richard I, but Robin still lacked a clearly defined status, allowing him to appeal to gentry and lower classes alike.

Following on from the *Gest*, *Monk* and *Potter* ballads, a collection of Robin Hood ballads survives in mid-seventeenth century copies acquired by Bishop Thomas Percy. In this collection there are eight ballads: *Robin Hood's Death*; *Robin Hood and Guy of Gisborne*; *Robin Hood and the Curtal Friar*; *Robin Hood and the Butcher*; *Robin Hood Rescuing Three Squires*; *The Jolly Pinder of Wakefield*; *Little John a Begging*; and *Robin Hood and Queen Catherine*. The *Death* ballad is considered by Child to be in keeping with the early ones; the *Gisborne* ballad is accepted as being fifteenth century; the *Curtal Friar* ballad and the *Butcher* ballad are regarded as being older than the *Percy Folio*.[43] The *Butcher* ballad is identical in plot to the *Potter* ballad, whereas the *Three Squires* ballad concentrates on Robin's desire to help others, combined with his enmity towards the Sheriff of Nottingham as he saves the lives of innocent men who are due to be hanged. In the *Jolly Pinder* ballad the pinder takes on Robin's usual role of charging people a toll by attempting to force Robin to pay to enter Wakefield. Robin refuses and a sword fight ensues. Robin invites the stranger into the band, and he agrees to join the Merry Men at Michaelmas, in order that he may first see out his contract with his current master.[44] The story of *Little John a Begging* is more reminiscent of the conflicts with the monks in the *Gest*, as Little John steals from four men posing as beggars after highlighting their dishonesty when they pretend to have no money, thus emphasizing their status as 'poor fellows'.

In all of these ballads the yeoman outlaw still occupies centre stage. The similarities between those collected by Percy, such as the *Butcher, Death* and *Curtal Friar* ballads, and earlier texts give firm indications that the stories were based on earlier rhymes. The ballads of *Little John a Begging* and the *Three Squires* appear to be more original, but they also concur with the events of the *Gest* and the Merry Men rescuing Robin Hood in the *Monk* ballad. There is still no suggestion that Robin Hood consistently gives money away to the poor, but his rescue of the squires may represent doing 'poor men much good', just as the *Queen Catherine* ballad refers to Robin Hood's loyalty to the king and queen despite his outlaw status.

Most of the later ballads continue this trend, although the antics of the Merry Men become more and more far fetched. The ballad of the *King's Disguise and Friendship with Robin Hood* highlights the change of era to the 1190s and loyalty to King Richard, whereas ballads such as *Robin Hood and the Prince of Aragon* demonstrate romanticized exaggeration, as Robin battles with giants before Will Scarlock marries the captured princess. The somewhat farcical ballads of the eighteenth century onwards continue to portray the outlaws as selfless heroes and fearless fighters. In this sense, the philosophy of the ballads never really changes.

Over the years, many authors highlighted the idealism that the Robin Hood tradition came to represent. Shakespeare refers to Robin Hood in *The Merry Wives of Windsor, Henry IV Part II, Two Gentlemen of Verona* and *As You Like It*. In the last there is a specific mention of Robin Hood when Charles, a wrestler at court, speaks to Oliver de Boys about an exiled duke who has taken a journey into the Forest of Arden to avoid his enemies:

> OLIVER DE BOYS: Where did the old duke go?
> CHARLES: They say he's already in the Forest of Arden, and a
> many merry men with him; and there they live like the old
> Robin Hood of England. They say many young gentlemen
> flock to him everyday, and fleet the time carelessly, as they
> did in the golden world.[45]

There is a suggestion here that, following Major, Shakespeare viewed Robin Hood as a duke. It is not certain that he had read Major's works, but it seems fairly likely.

Shakespeare's reference to the 'golden world' is intriguing. This may be an expression of his own rather than a common phrase, but he clearly expected his audience to understand his meaning. *As You Like It* was written in 1599, shortly after the great Elizabethan explorers set off to South America, following up the early expeditions by the Spanish conquistadors. By that time Sir Walter Raleigh had made one unsuccessful expedition searching for the lost land of El Dorado, and the Spanish had plundered much gold from the cities of the Incas, Chibchas and Aztecs. The lives of the people of the Americas may have been thought to be carefree, but it is unlikely that Shakespeare was talking about them. He probably meant to suggest the carefree life, unburdened by responsibility and duty, that Robin Hood lived in the forest. Of course, the sheriff's depiction of the forest as tougher than any hermitage or monastery was a more accurate assessment of the life of an outlaw, yet in a poetic sense Sherwood or Barnsdale was Robin's Garden of Eden.

However, it is more likely that the term 'golden world' referred not to a place but to an era.[46] The most likely model for this was the golden age of antiquity, as described in Ancient Greek and Roman mythology. According to the poet Hesiod there had been a time when the people lived in absolute peace:

> They lived like gods without sorrow of heart, remote and free from toil and grief: miserable age rested not on them; but with legs and arms never failing they made merry with feasting beyond the reach of all evils. When they died, it was as they were overcome with sleep, and they had all good things; for the fruitful earth unforced bare them fruit abundantly and without stint. They dwelt in ease and peace upon their lands with many good things, rich in flocks and loved by the blessed gods.[47]

It is also possible that Shakespeare was applying the notion of a paradisiacal past to England itself. Although he lived during what is today often regarded as the golden age of English history, it would not then have been so described. He would have been looking further back in time. The term 'Merrie England' today usually refers to the period between 1350 and 1520, when the peasant way of life was developing, and Shakespeare may have had that period of history in mind.[48] In *As You Like It* Adam is particularly representative of that way of life, as demonstrated by his decision to give up all of his worldly possessions to join the old duke in the forest and live off the land:

ADAM: . . . I have five hundred crowns, the thrifty hire I saved under your father, which I did store to be my foster-nurse when service should in my old limbs lie lame and unregarded age in corners thrown: take that, and he that doth the ravens feed, yea, providently caters for the sparrow, be comfort to my age! Here is the gold; all this I give you. Let me be your servant: Though I look old, yet I am strong and lusty; for in my youth I never did apply hot and rebellious liquors in my blood, nor did not with unbashful forehead woo the means of weakness and debility; therefore my age is as a lusty winter, frosty, but kindly: let me go with you; I'll do the service of a younger man in all your business and necessities.

ORLANDO: O good old man, how well in thee appears the constant service of the antique world, when service sweat for duty, not for meed! Thou art not for the fashion of these times, where none will sweat but for promotion, and having that, do choke their service up even with the having: it is not so with thee. But, poor old man, thou prunest a rotten tree, that cannot so much as a blossom yield in lieu of all thy pains and husbandry. But come thy ways; we'll go along together, and ere we have thy youthful wages spent, we'll light upon some settled low content.[49]

Bower's reference in *Scotichronicon* to tragedy and comedy was undoubtedly intended as an insult, yet it is an accurate description of the ballads. And, while the early ballads focused on both, the later ballads and stories centred largely on the comedy. In the later ballads Robin frequently battles with strangers, as illustrated in the *Tanner, Ranger, Tinker* and *Scotchman* ballads, and loses, only for them to join his band of outlaws. This resulted in the addition of many new characters, including the minstrel Allan a Dale, the tanner Arthur a Bland, Will Stutly and David of Doncaster who appears in the *Golden Arrow* ballad. Hood remains shrewd, successfully cheating and hoodwinking people with the aid of disguises such as dressing as a friar or a tinker, but his tendency to commit murder diminishes. He becomes less of a ruthless outlaw and more a man defending the rights and freedom of the oppressed, making him a good role model for children. The tales in the children's novel *The Merry Adventures of Robin Hood*, by Howard Pyle, frequently illustrate this, calling on many of the ballads, and developing Robin's philanthropic ideal. King Richard I is mentioned by Pyle, as are several of the Merry Men including some new ones, but Prince John has no role as an opponent, nor does Robin assist in raising any ransom for the king. The farcical antics of the characters, added by the presence of the minstrel, bear no resemblance to the heavy deeds of the *Monk* ballad, and now the term 'Merry Men' has a new meaning, portraying the characters as bumbling sidekicks rather than hardened soldiers.

It was not until the nineteenth century that Robin was first referred to as a Saxon. *Histoire de la Conquête de l'Angleterre pas les Normands* by Jacques Nicolas Augustin Thierry developed the idea, and his theory has since prompted numerous historical investigations aiming to show that Robin was a Saxon lord disenfranchised following the Norman Conquest.[50] The ethnic element was developed in Sir Walter Scott's *Ivanhoe* where Robin Hood is cast in a familiar role as an ally of King Richard I. The title of Sir Robin of Locksley has since become inseparable from the legend, highlighting his new role as a Saxon nobleman whose lands were unjustly confiscated. His bearing as a figure of peasant revolt now starts to gather pace, and the key elements of the modern legend are in place. The Knights Templar are mentioned in *Ivanhoe* but with no particular reference to Robin Hood.

In 1908, almost seven hundred years after the term 'Robin Hood' appeared on the rolls of English magistrates, the character was brought to the big screen for the first time in the silent movie *Robin Hood and His Merry Men* directed by Percy Stow. In 1938 Hollywood created arguably the greatest Robin Hood movie of all time and the most important. *The Adventures of Robin Hood*, starring Errol Flynn, Olivia de Havilland, Basil Rathbone and Claude Rains, was set in the period after Richard I had been captured in Austria. His younger brother, Prince John, ruled as regent and faced staunch opposition from Sir Robin of Locksley and his Saxon rebels, who were attempting to thwart John's plans to oust his brother and claim the throne. Robin, with the aid of his companions including Much the Miller's son, Will Scarlett, Friar Tuck and Little John, sets out to prevent the prince from usurping the throne and winning the hand of the Lady Marian Fitzwalter. The film drew from a number of the ballads, including parts of the *Gest*, *Robin Hood and the Curtal Friar* and *Robin Hood and Little John*, and focused on Robin's rivalry with the Norman knight Sir Guy of Gisborne rather than the Sheriff of Nottingham, although the sheriff still appeared. For the first time Robin was depicted as a national hero, not as a courteous outlaw who did poor men much good but as 'King of outlaws and Prince of good fellows'.[51]

11

HERE LIES BOLD ROBIN HOOD?

Even the briefest of comparisons between the *Gest* ballad and the Errol Flynn movie illustrates the vast transformation that the legend has undergone. It not only provides an accurate measurement of how far the stories of the yeoman outlaw have been exaggerated but demonstrates that the man celebrated locally in the May Day games in the sixteenth century was perceived as a national hero in the eyes of audiences of the twentieth century. Poetic licence had already seen the depiction of the outlaw become progressively more glamorized, particularly by poets such as Keats and Tennyson in the nineteenth century, yet their work had merely helped create a romanticized ideal rather than developing any particular interest in clarifying the historicity of the character. Such poetic creations brought with them a sense of immortality to the ballad hero.

By the twentieth century the tales of Robin Hood had become almost completely fictional, but that did not prevent them from being manipulated and exploited for commercial and publicity purposes. Scattered throughout the country there are countless so-called proofs of his existence. Houses that no longer exist were said to have been his former homes; stones mark the spots where his arrows supposedly landed; numerous roads, lanes, ways and even wells are named after the outlaws; churches claim to be their places of rest; areas of forest have developed reputations as meeting points; and even inns have been known to boast of their custom and inevitably profit immensely as a result. In 1819 Joseph Hunter recorded evidence of Robin Hood's birthplace near Loxley in Yorkshire, while Roger Dodsworth endorsed the story that Little John lived in a cottage at Hathersage, in close proximity to the graveyard in which he was laid to rest. Nottingham benefited significantly from the tourist trade, having developed a Robin Hood larder, two caves, a grave and a couple of wells by the seventeenth century.[1]

Although such claims of authenticity appeared pleasing to the antiquaries, the practice, beginning in the sixteenth and seventeenth centuries, of preparing and making publicly available evidence, of varying degrees of credibility, to substantiate elements of the legend has had a damaging effect on its development and traditions. In turn, this gave rise to a profitable trade and exploitation of the Robin Hood legend. St Anne's Well in Nottingham, for example, gained a reputation as Robin Hood's Well, and the nearby pub profited from tourists captivated by claims that it displayed items, such as a cap, chair, slipper and bow that the ballad hero had once possessed. In addition, clients were given the opportunity to be initiated into the Robin Hood brotherhood – for a small fee.[2]

While Robin Hood's fame opened up tourist opportunities that have been exploited across the country, areas that can lay better claim to authenticity, such as those mentioned in the early ballads, have gone surprisingly unnoticed. In Yorkshire, Robin Hood's grave has attracted many visitors over the centuries and even gave rise to a bizarre trend for relic hunters and the superstitious to break away parts of the grave slab as a cure for toothache.[3]

The authenticity of the site is open to doubt, but its inclusion in the earliest ballads has given it a degree of credibility.

The earliest accounts of Robin Hood's death began to emerge in the fifteenth century, or earlier. The *Gest* makes reference to Robin returning to the forest after being pardoned by the king before he is murdered while being treated for an ailing stiffness in old age. The traditional depiction of Robin Hood's eventual death was clearly known to the author of the *Gest*, which in turn suggests that the oral tradition of Robin Hood's death may be as old as any of the early traditions. According to the *Gest*, after fifteen months in the king's service Robin had lost most of his wealth through generosity. His life in the service of the king was undoubtedly comfortable compared with the harshness of existence in the forest, yet after witnessing men shooting in the forest Robin yearns to return to the life he left behind:

> Somtyme I was an archere good,
> A styffe and eke a stronge;
> I was comted the best archere
> That was in mery Englonde.[4]

The *Gest* goes into very little detail about Robin's life at court. He enters the king's service after being pardoned but soon realizes that his life in service has cost him his happiness. He asks the king for a seven-day leave in honour of Mary Magdalene. The king grants this, but the ballad suggests Robin never returns, and, in fear of retribution should he later do so,[5] he sees out the remaining twenty-two years of his life as an outlaw until illness persuades him to go to Kirklees Priory to be bled.[6] The *Gest* describes Robin's death while being treated at the hands of a treacherous woman, one of his own relations.

Yet he was begyled, iwys,
Through a wycked woman,
The pryoresse of Kyrkely,
That nye was of hys kynne.[7]

Historically, Kirklees Priory was a Cistercian nunnery located four miles north-east of Huddersfield in the parish of Dewsbury in Yorkshire. Established during the reign of Henry II, the priory was founded by the Lord of Clifton in honour of St James and the Virgin Mary. The nunnery flourished throughout the Middle Ages before becoming a victim of Henry VIII and the dissolution of the monasteries in 1535, although the priory survived until 1539. Henry subsequently gave the building to John Tasburg and Nicholas Savill, before it was bought first by Robert Pilkington and then the Armitage family. The building itself was later destroyed, leaving only a neglected gatehouse. In the late sixteenth century Kirklees Hall was constructed near by using some of the stones salvaged from the original nunnery.[8]

The traditional description of Robin's death at Kirklees is in many ways separate from the rest of the legend. While the other ballads describe the activities of his life, the death scene has brought into being a legend of its own. The first indication of the Kirklees tradition is given in the closing stanzas of the *Gest*, although it does little more than confirm that Robin died at Kirklees. The reference to the prioress is vague, but it states that Robin was the victim of a conspiracy between the prioress and a man named Roger of Doncaster.[9]

The later ballad, entitled the ballad of *Robin Hood's Death*, two versions of which survive, the earliest in the *Percy Folio*, provides a more developed account of the death tradition consistent with the *Gest's* ending. *Robin Hood's Death* is described by Child

as 'in the fine old strain', and its early numbering, Ballad 120 in
Child's Popular Ballads Volume III, dates it around the same time
as the *Potter* ballad.[10] The ballad is largely in keeping with the pattern of the early ones. After Robin decides to seek medical attention
at Kirklees, he dismisses the advice of Will Scarlock that he should
take fifty men with him and is accompanied only by Little John.
On the journey they argue over who should bear his bow.[11] After a
wager, they eventually continue to Kirklees where along the way an
old woman laments Robin and predicts his death. Robin ignores
her and continues to Kirklees.

According to the *Gest*, the prioress is Robin's kin, whereas in
the *Death* ballad she is described more vividly as Robin's 'aunt's
daughter'.[12] The ballad goes into detail of how Robin meets his
death while in the care of his cousin.

> She laid the blood-irons to Robin Hoods vaine,
> Alacke, the more pitye!
> And pearct the vaine, and let out the bloode,
> That full red was to see.
>
> And first it bled, the thicke, thicke bloode,
> And afterwards the thinne,
> And well then wist good Robin Hoode,
> Treason there was within.[13]

The end of Robin Hood's life is as treacherous as it is grue-
some. Weakened by lack of blood, Robin wearily blows on his
horn and is soon joined by Little John who, on arrival at the
priory, finds his master dying.[14] With Little John at his side, Robin
Hood is able to take some solace in his demise as he mortally
wounds his cousin's lover in retribution for his part in the
murder. The man, known as Roger of Doncaster in the *Gest*, is

identified as Red Roger in the *Death* ballad but is probably the same man. The identity of the prioress, however, is not revealed in either ballad.

Following this act of treachery Little John vows to set fire to the priory, but is prevented from doing so by Robin who abides by the code of his Order to the end. With his final breath, a weakened Robin draws the ballad to a close.

> 'I never hurt fair maid in all my time,
> Nor at mine end shall it be,
> But give me my bent bow in my hand,
> And a broad arrow I'll let flee;
> And where this arrow is taken up,
> There shall my grave digged be,
>
> 'Lay me a green sod under my head,
> And another at my feet;
> And lay my bent bow by my side,
> Which makes my music sweet;
> And make my grave gravel and green,
> Which is most right and meet.
>
> 'Let me have length and breadth enough,
> With a green sod under my head;
> That they may say, when I am dead
> Here lies bold Robin Hood.'
>
> These words they readily granted him,
> Which did bold Robin please:
> And there they buried bold Robin Hood,
> Within the fair Kirkleys.[15]

The *Death* ballad is more in keeping with the early tradition than with the later. Its account is reasonably credible, given what we know of the history of the priory. It was in existence during all the possible lifetimes of Robin Hood, and it was not always renowned for its integrity. Between 1306 and 1315 it was embroiled in an intense scandal after revelations came to light about unruly behaviour in the cloisters of three nuns, Alice Raggid, Elizabeth Hopton and Joan Heton.[16] Although the priory was undoubtedly held in high regard as a house of worship, life in a priory or nunnery did not always attract the devout. Unwanted daughters of the nobility, outcasts and even murderesses commonly took refuge in the priories. By the fourteenth century such sites were havens for unwed mothers. The poor conduct and lack of integrity of the three nuns singled out for their misdemeanours is in keeping with that of the prioress and Red Roger, who were known to have been involved in forbidden activities.[17] It is also not unlikely that Robin Hood sought medical attention at Kirklees as, like many other priories, it was regularly visited by the weak and ailing seeking medical attention in return for a donation.

Evidence of Robin Hood's death at Kirklees is not restricted to the ballads. Situated within the grounds of the old priory is the outlaw's supposed grave. Over the years the site has attracted its fair share of interest, particularly from relic hunters and Robin Hood pilgrims. The *Death* ballad refers to Robin's death at Kirklees and locates his grave at the place where his last arrow fell. Today a large monument protected by iron railings survives on the reputed site. The exact location of the grave, however, approximately six hundred yards from the priory gatehouse where Robin supposedly shot his last arrow, is dubious. According to authors such as Richard Rutherford-Moore, six hundred yards was almost twice the distance of which an archer of the time would have been capable.[18] In the *Gisborne* ballad we hear that Robin Hood shot 330 yards at the best:

> And sett them three score rood in twin,
> To shoote the prickes full neare.[19]

The issue of Robin Hood's grave is a historian's nightmare, particularly as there is no consistent record of what actually existed. The story of the grave gained a degree of credence owing to its inclusion in various chronicles by scholars from the Middle Ages, but its plausibility has diminished over the centuries. Leland was the first person to chronicle the Kirklees tradition with the lines roughly translating: 'Kirklees Monastery where Robin Hood that nobleman who was outside the law lies buried'.[20] Whether his statement was intended as a description of the grave or he was merely quoting an inscription that was once on the grave, later to become illegible, cannot be determined. None of these words was recorded as being found on his tomb. It appears that Leland did at least visit the grave. The same might be true of Grafton, who later gave the following account:

> The prioresse of the same place caused him to be buried by the highway-side where he used to rob and spoyle those that passed that way. And upon his grave the sayd prioresse did lay a very fayre stone wherein the names of Robert Hood, William of Goldesborough and others were graven. And the cause why she buryed him there was for the common passengers and tra-vailers knowing and seeying him there buryed might more safely and without fear take their jorneys that way, which they durst not do in the life of the sayd out-lawes. And at eyther end of the sayd tombe was erected

a crosse of stone, which is to be seene there at this present.[21]

Grafton makes no mention of the shooting of the arrow; he claims that the site of Robin's grave was chosen by the prioress.[22] This gives weight to the contention that Robin was murdered by a prioress. The idea that Robin Hood died at the hands of the prioress may be attributable to the *Gest*, but what Grafton says is consistent with the account in the Sloane Manuscript that Robin was buried under a great stone on the wayside.[23] As the *Death* ballad only survives in the *Percy Folio* it is important that an early reference exists, which it does. Grafton's reference to a cross of stone at either end of the grave differs slightly from the testimonies of later commentators. His suggestion that the cross was present at the time of writing indicates that he visited it, although there is some doubt about this, as he confuses Kirklees with Bircklies.[24] Further evidence for the tomb was recorded by the Elizabethan antiquarian William Camden in the fifth edition of his epic *Camden's Britannia*, a county-by-county description of Great Britain providing a geographical and chronological survey of Britain's historical monuments. By 1607 there were seven editions of this work, the first in 1577, which were revised in 1789 and included a reference to the grave of Robin Hood:

At Kirklees nunnery Robin Hood's tomb with a plain cross on a flat stone is shewn in the cemetery. In the ground at a little distance by two grave stones, one which has the inscription for Elizabeth de Staynton, prioress there.[25]

Although he was criticized for plagiarism and inaccuracy by the herald Ralph Brookes, Camden was well respected and acquired a reputation for accuracy. He is known to have drawn on the works of both Leland and William Lambarde, but he has been commended for his ability to question his sources before accepting them as fact. Throughout his lifetime he continued to add to *Britannia* and revise its content.[26] His extensive travels throughout the British Isles to inspect his sources at first hand adds to the likelihood that he saw the grave and was clear about its location. The assertion that Robin's grave lay in close proximity to that of the former prioress – his possible murderess – Elizabeth de Staynton differs from the present location, which in turn gives rise to the possibility that Grafton and Camden were not referring to the same site. De Staynton's grave is located in the priory garden, but the site of Robin Hood's, on a hillside close to where the priory once stood, is consistent with what was earlier recorded by Grafton. Instead, Camden's suggestion may tie in with claims that another grave existed within arrowshot of Kirklees.

Grafton and Camden both supported the claim that a stone grave slab existed, and in 1665 the Tory pamphleteer and antiquary Dr Nathaniel Johnston completed a drawing of it.[27] Johnston, who was physician to Lady Armitage at the time, can surely be given credibility for having personally seen the grave, which he illustrated as having a stone cross with Calvary steps atop the slab. The stone, which was already considerably weathered by Johnston's time, displayed a barely legible engraving reading:

Here lie Roberd Hude, Willm Gold burgh, Thoms . . .

The description of the stone is consistent with the Sloane Manuscript and seems to confirm that Grafton was referring to the same cross. There is thus some consistency between all reports of what the grave looked like all the way through to 1665. No one has identified Willm, probably William, Gold-burgh or Thoms, probably Thomas, but Grafton's explanation that the location of the grave was decided by the prioress suggests that they were also outlaws. Following on from the reference that the grave was a comfort to passers-by who had once feared for their own safety, the *Chronicle at Large* states that they would not have journeyed so freely during the lives of the outlaws.[28]

Thomas Gale, the Dean of York between 1697 and 1702, left behind in his papers the words of a curious epitaph claiming Robin Hood to have been the Earl of Huntingdon.[29] Gale implied that this epitaph was inscribed on Robin Hood's grave at the time, yet this is open to doubt as none of the other visitors to the grave made note of it. The language used has also been questioned, as it appears to be written in some form of archaic English or perhaps even Scottish. The epitaph reads:

> Hear undernead dis laitl stean
> laiz Robert earl of Huntingtun
> near arcir ber az hei sa geud
> an pipl kauld im Robin Heud
> sick utlawz az hi an iz men
> vil england nibr si agen
> obiit 24 kal dekembris 1247.[30]

The translation by Francis Child reads:

> Here underneath this little stone
> Lies Robert Earl of Huntingdon
> No archer as he was so good
> And people called him Robin Hood
> Such outlaws as he and his men
> England will never see again.
> Died 24th calends of December 1247.[31]

By the time Gale became Dean of York, approximately a century had passed since Anthony Munday had written his plays depicting Robin as the Earl of Huntingdon. Gale would undoubtedly have been familiar with the plays. Despite slight differences, parallels can also be drawn between that epitaph and the end of the *True Tale* ballad. On the grave, referred to by Parker as the stone which the prioress laid, were the words:

> Robert Earle of Huntington
> Lies under this little stone
> No archer was like him so good
> His wildnesse named him Robbin Hood
> Full thirteen yeares, and something more
> These northern parts he vexed sore
> Such out-lawes as he and his men
> May England never know agen.[32]

Besides the different wording, the date of death is also different from that suggested by Gale. Parker's reference to 4 December 1198 is more in tune with the Major tradition. Gale's date of 1247 was never recorded before this time and may have been his own creation. The manner of dating is unsatisfactory in every way. The kalend, or calend, mentioned in the epitaph refers to the first day of each month in the Roman calendar. If genuine, this gives the epitaph a much older pedigree, probably relevant to the time of Richard I. In keeping with the Roman calendar, the date is usually determined by counting the number of days past the kalend of a month. Its usage here appears to be incorrect. The reference to 24th kalend December indicates that Robin died on Christmas Day – twenty-four days past the first of the month. The epitaph's wording in modern English is similar to Parker's, making it likely that Parker's note in the *True Tale* ballad was referring to Gale's epitaph.

> The epitaph, as records tell,
> Within this hundred yeares
> By many was discerned well,
> But time all things outweares.[33]

In 1715 the historian of Leeds, Ralph Thoresby, wrote of the grave: 'near unto Kirklees the noted Robin Hood lies buried under a grave-stone that yet remains near the park, but the inscription scarce legible'. Other antiquaries report similar accounts. In the same year a certain Richard Richardson included the following in a letter to Thoresby:

> The inscription upon Robin Hood's grave was never legible in my time; and it is now totally defaced; insomuch that neither the language nor character is to be distinguished; only you may perceive it was written about the verge of the stone. I have heard Dr Armitage say, that he could read upon it *Hic jacet Robertus Hood, filius secundus Comitis de Huntingdon,* but I must own, tho' he was a person of merit, I give little credit to this report. [34]

It is unclear exactly what he meant. The words 'Here lie Roberd Hude, Willm Gold burgh, Thoms' are written on the verge and are legible in Johnston's drawing, but there is no mention of this by later antiquaries. Bearing Richardson's comments in mind, this inscription may have been badly damaged by 1715, generating later confusion. Neither Thoresby nor Richardson made earlier mention of the epitaph, although Thoresby did refer to Gale's papers in his appendix which includes the wording on the epitaph. Richard Gough later explains the absence of the epitaph on the grave in his *Sepulchral Monuments of Great Britain*, *1786*:

> The figure of the stone over the grave of Robin Hood
> (in Kirklees Park, being a plain stone with a sort of cross
> fleurée thereon), now broken and much defaced, the
> inscription illegible. That printed in Thoresby Ducat.
> Leod. 576, from Dr Gale's papers, was never on it.[35]

This is clearly intended to dismiss the new custom of identifying Robin Hood with Robert, Earl of Huntingdon. It is hardly surprising that the inscription was illegible by this time, given its exposure to the elements, and suggestions that the grave was damaged and defaced can probably be explained by its age. Gough, however, goes further by suggesting that the site had been excavated earlier that century.

> The late Sir Samuel Armytage, owner of the premises
> caused the ground under it to be dug a yard deep, and
> found it had never been disturbed; so that it was probably brought from some other place and by vulgar
> tradition ascribed to Robin Hood.[36]

It is normal practice for a grave to be dug to a depth of two yards rather than one. Bearing in mind the apparent casualness of this attempt, it cannot be taken for granted that if the ground had been dug deeper nothing further would have been found. Equally, the lack of physical remains may prove to be of relevance to Camden's claim that Robin Hood's grave was in closer proximity to that of the former prioress. This in turn may support the story that an unmarked grave was excavated during the eighteenth century after it had been damaged when restoration work was carried out on the site.[37] The fact that Samuel Armitage did carry out work on the alleged site of the grave indicates that the slab must have been moved at least temporarily or a new one put in its place. Gough's reference to the excavation suggests that the grave had been tampered with before 1786, which calls into question the state of the grave at the time of *Sepulchral Monuments*. His drawing is similar to Johnston's, and the differences can probably be attributed to their different styles of sketching. The diagram by Gough is identical to that drawn by John Throsby in 1797 and, strangely, may tie in with a somewhat mysterious story by Thomas Gent, a respected artist, topographer and chronologist from York. Writing in 1730, he refers to the tomb of Robin Hood with an effigy on it and tells a peculiar story of how the tomb was moved by a knight. As related by Ritson:

> That his tombstone, having his effigy thereon, was order'd, not many years ago, by a certain knight to be placed as a harth-stone in his great hall. When it was laid over-night, the next morning it was 'surprisingly' removed – on or to – one side; and so three times it was laid, and as successively turned aside. The knight, thinking he had done wrong to have brought it thither, order'd it should be drawn back again.[38]

Although Gent maintains that this was only a story 'to be judged by the reader at his pleasure', this may tie in with the work of Sir Samuel Armitage. It is unfortunate that Gent does not name the knight in question. Given that the slab was taken away during excavations, then later replaced, and also that it had weathered according to Gough, it seems fairly likely that the story is based on truth – even if the ghostly antics of Robin Hood were exaggerated.

Another respected person credited with having drawn the grave was the Reverend Joseph Ismay. He was induced into the parish of Mirfield as vicar in 1739 and for the next thirty-nine years kept records of the everyday life and history of the parish. His diaries of interesting observations proved to be a rich source for historians and caught the eye of Sir Samuel Armitage who later appointed Ismay as tutor for his children.[39] Following his appointment, Ismay investigated the grave of Robin Hood, completing similar drawings between 1752 and 1754, one of which was included in Whitaker's *History of Loidis and Elmete* in 1816. Despite Ismay's claim that his drawings were rough sketches, the cross differs from that drawn by Johnston, Gough and Throsby. Whether the roughness of Ismay's drawings can really account for this is doubtful, although the fact that the excavation had been carried out by that time might explain its altered state. The writing on either side of the cross is difficult to read, but on the left side it appears to read: 'Sir Simon Armitage ordered two stone pillars to be erected by Robin Hood's grave in the park with the inscription found amongst the papers of the learned . . .' Here the text breaks off, but Ismay was clearly referring to Gale. The other side of the sketch includes Gale's epitaph, which would later be added to the grave itself, ending with the words 'assumed to have been bled to death Dec 24th 1247'.[40] Although Ismay does not say whether the cross is the original, since dilapidated, or a replacement, his mention of the epitaph being added on the order of Sir Simon gives an indication that this was the first time the epitaph had been present on the grave. Ismay also confirms that by this stage the grave had been enclosed in order to protect it from intruders seeking bits of the gravestone which by popular superstition were thought to provide a cure for toothache. He explains:

> Ye sepulchral Monument of Robin Hood near Kirklees which has been lately impaled in ye form of a Standing Hearse in order to preserve the stone from the rude hands of the curious traveller who frequently carried off a small Fragment of ye stone, and thereby diminished it's pristine Beauty.[41]

Following a tour of the grounds in 1758, a man named John Watson cited similar references to Ismay and previous commentators in his unpublished notes.

> At some distance from this in an inclos'd Plantation is Robin Hood's tomb, as it is call'd; which is nothing but a very rude stone note quite two yards long, & narrow in proportion; it has the figure of a cross, cut in a manner not common upon it; but no inscription, nor does their appear ever to have been any letters upon it, notwithstanding Mr Thoresby has publish'd a pretended one found amongst the papers of Dr Gale Dean of York.[42]

Watson also makes light of the earldom theory. The lack of inscription suggesting Robin Hood was the Earl of Huntingdon may be explained by the age and dilapidation of the grave, but the epitaph probably never existed. Certainly there was no date recorded by the early antiquaries, and this casts doubt on the authenticity of the epitaph left behind by Gale.

To further complicate matters, two more epitaphs had come into existence by 1746.[43] The mention of the uncommon cross appears to be a reference to the one drawn by Ismay only four years earlier and may also be the one that was drawn by Johnston, since weathered, or perhaps a replacement by the Armitages. Nevertheless, questions regarding the authenticity of the grave have become irrelevant. The slab with the cross and Calvary stepped base that once existed do so only in diagrams. The dilapidated monument and dubious inscription that stands behind enclosed railings on the present site has also become a victim of the earldom theory, illustrating that even the physical remnants associated with the legend have changed with the times.

Unsurprisingly, the remains of the Merry Men have also become the focus of a certain amount of speculation. Little John is reputed to have three graves, one in Ireland, where he was allegedly executed, another in Scotland and, most famously, one in Hathersage in Derbyshire where he is reported as having lived in a cottage until the end of his life.[44] Tradition refers to Little John having buried Robin Hood before heading to Hathersage and digging his own grave in the churchyard of St Michael's Church which now includes a tombstone commemorating the site. The original tombstone is a Calvary-based cross which is consistent with the diagrams of Robin Hood's grave. The respected seventeenth-century antiquarian Roger Dodsworth also acknowledged the reputed site of Little John's grave:

> And he came acquainted with Little John, that kept the kine; which said John is buried at Hathershead in Derbyshire, where he hath a fair tomb-stone with an inscription.[45]

This grave was excavated in 1784; a gigantic thighbone measuring 29½ inches was found, but it later disappeared.[46] Little John's alleged bow was recorded as being on display in 1625, but this has also disappeared without trace, as have his cap, his cottage and any credibility.

Even Will Scarlock could not escape speculation. Within eight miles of Mansfield, in the heart of old Sherwood Forest, a curious unmarked grave stands near the iron gate of the churchyard of St Mary's in Blidworth. Tradition holds that Scarlock was buried in an unmarked grave after being murdered by one of the sheriff's men. In the following years, the site of the grave was marked with the apex of the old church, ironically in the shape of an arrow. The strange headstone, unlike any other in that graveyard, remains undisturbed to this day, with no written indication of whose remains are buried beneath it, and there is little to no chance of confirming or disproving that it is the burial site of Will Scarlock.

12

TRUE TALES OF ROBIN HOOD

The story of Robin Hood is about a legend as much as it is about a man. What began over six centuries ago as a collection of tales telling of a good yeoman who 'walked on ground' has developed so considerably that what existed then is only vaguely recognizable in the hero of 21st-century film and television. Any factual information and evidence about him that may have once existed has become so clouded and distorted by changes, additions and even outright fabrication in subsequent centuries that it is difficult to decide whether his tales are to be believed or just enjoyed. When it comes to history, we understand, rationally, that he didn't exist. That is what most people have come to believe, because that is what we have been told. When we are introduced to the stories of bold Robin Hood in childhood, we are susceptible to the powerful messages they convey. Yet in our naïvety we cannot appreciate that our image and perception of Robin differ enormously from those of our ancestors. No longer are the tales about a good outlaw who 'did poor men much good', as described by the minstrels of the Middle Ages who acted out their rhymes in the medieval surroundings of the courts, towns or forests as a cheap form of entertainment for those of 'freeborn blood'. Now we are given a new hero: a gallant nobleman in Lincoln green who roamed the forests of ancient England, robbing from the rich to give to the poor, 'feared by the bad, loved by the good'. The modern tales are not about history; they are allegories illustrating a struggle against tyranny and oppression by a man championing the rights and welfare of the poor and downtrodden yet, at the same time, heroically defending true kingship.

This is what the Robin Hood legend has become. For most people, whether or not a real person existed has become unimportant. We are presented with an ideal: a man of high moral principles that he steadfastly upholds, despite his outlaw status. He is a victim, yet he still stands up for the innocent. He is a nobleman, but he still fights on behalf of the common man. This theme remains as attractive and enduring in its appeal to the audiences of today as it was in the past.

The durability of Robin's legend through the ages is largely unrivalled, but in the process, rather like the Neverland of Peter Pan, his Sherwood Forest has become a realm of the imagination where he lives for all time in the good company of his Merry Men. Ever vigilant, never ageing or dying, a constant thorn in the side of the Sheriff of Nottingham and Prince John, he sets about freeing the oppressed alongside his beloved Maid Marian, whose love never diminishes, like the perpetual springtime in which Sherwood Forest remains as it was in Shakespeare's 'golden world'. It is surprising that such adulation should be lavished on an outlaw, yet the Robin Hood of the early ballads was just that. And how did an apparently real person who first appeared in the chronicles and ballads as a humble woodsman subsequently come to be portrayed as a heroic nobleman? These changes were quite gradual, as we have seen. Over the years, distortion of the oral tradition and the creativity of new ballad writers have presented historians with a challenge. In literature

Robin has often been described as a figure concerned with defending the rights of the peasants, but the early tales do not support this. He is depicted as an outlaw who has no love for authority, but he is not identified as being committed to a particular cause. In the early tales the peasantry are barely mentioned, and until the work of John Major there are only limited indications of Robin's tendency to help the poor. Robin's reputation in the early ballads as a rebel against authority would have been appealing to the lower classes at a time when authority was oppressive and taxes were heavy, but his cause and aims were not clearly linked with a desire to improve the lot of the common people. He stole from his enemies, but what he did with the proceeds is not altogether explained. Judging by the *Gest*, he used some to help the poor but not on the scale that we sentimentally celebrate. That he was a violent man is hardly surprising, since almost all the outlaws of the time were. Indeed, that was most often the reason why they were outlawed. But even in the early ballads Robin can be seen as a man of noble intentions. He is pious, courteous and loyal, and his bravery is beyond doubt. His capability as a formidable fighter is clear, as is his reputation as an archer. While he may not have distributed his money as far and wide as modern tradition suggests, he was still a generous outlaw who demonstrated altruistic behaviour and morals unusual for most outlaws.

History is unclear whether he actually existed, but this is not surprising given six centuries of dissimilar and conflicting sources of evidence. The search for a historical Robin Hood is often portrayed as an attempt to authenticate a medieval superman. Yet if Robin Hood did exist the first thing to clarify is exactly what we are looking for. Is the search for Robin Hood the search for a good yeoman, as he was regarded in the fifteenth century? The King of May, popular in the sixteenth century? An

Earl of Huntingdon, as described in the seventeenth century? A romantic icon, as he appeared to the poets of the eighteenth and nineteenth centuries? The Saxon nobleman and leader of peasant revolt familiar in the nineteenth and twentieth centuries? Or, as depicted in modern cinema, the prince of thieves?

If Robin Hood did exist as he appeared in the medieval ballads, then he was a yeoman, an ordinary man who roamed the greenwoods of Barnsdale and Sherwood. The early ballad writers may have glamorized him, but that is perhaps an inevitable effect of poetry. The stories of Fulk FitzWarin, Eustache the Monk, Hereward the Wake and William Wallace have all been embellished and glamorized to some degree, yet they were all real people. Some distortion and change of the early legend over the course of time is also, perhaps, inevitable. The story fascinated people in the Middle Ages, it made its way into the court of the king, Shakespeare acknowledged it, as did many other famous writers, and the tales have graced the big screen for a century. The way Robin Hood has been portrayed by movie stars such as Errol Flynn and Kevin Costner is the outcome of a 600-year journey, and their portrayals of his adventures have brought enjoyment to millions of viewers. Yet even in film his character has changed with the times.

In order to separate fiction from history it is necessary to return to the start of that journey. The early ballads may have glamorized Robin's character but they are the best evidence available. In contrast, the later ballads are poor, largely repeating the early traditions but without vitality. They are clear works of fiction. The early ballads illustrate poverty, fellowship and the harshness of life in the greenwood. If a man like Robin Hood did exist in the circumstances described in the early ballads, he was a humble but extraordinary man who, despite being an outlaw, helped the poorest members of society.

Wyntoun, Bower, Major and Grafton, the four earliest chroniclers, all make reference to the popularity of the ballads. By including Robin Hood in their chronicles they clearly intend to provide him with a historical pedigree, but their reports are far from uniform. This incompatibility suggests an absence of authenticity and makes acceptance of any of them difficult. They cannot be accurately referring to the same person since they do not even agree on a time period, yet they all claim they are referring to the man of the ballads. Of the chronicles, *Historia Majoris Britanniae* has become the most widely accepted; it locates Robin Hood's life as a historical person in the period 1189–99. Widespread distribution of Major's history gradually bred familiarity, and since the sixteenth century his view has been accepted as the most likely, although no historian has ever been able to confirm its accuracy. The work of Grafton contributed equally to an extensive belief in the Lionheart connection, and he was the first chronicler to refer to Robin Hood as an earl. But his source is unverifiable. If the 'auld and auncient pamphlet' he mentioned did exist, its whereabouts are unclear.[1] Grafton states that records of the exchequer provide proof, but these have either been lost or they never existed.

If we none the less accept Major and Grafton as reliable sources, Robin Hood was a historical nobleman, possibly an earl. Neither suggests that he was a yeoman, or that he was the Earl of Huntingdon. When considering Robin Hood's change of status from yeoman to earl, the importance of Anthony Munday's plays should not be underestimated, but they cannot be considered as historical sources. The Robin Hood depicted by Munday did not exist. The suggestion that Robin was Robert, Earl of Huntingdon, comes primarily from the unauthenticated writings of Dr William Stukeley in the eighteenth century.[2] Robert, son of David, would have inherited the title if he had outlived his father, but that did not happen. However, the real-life tales of the young Robert's father, David, Earl of Huntingdon, may have been integrated into the later legend. This man was truly loyal to King Richard I and a staunch opponent of Prince John. David's disappearance from history between 1190 and 1194 is unexplained, but its timing closely matches Major's dates for the life of Robin Hood. We know that the historical earl reappeared to support Richard in the siege of Nottingham Castle, a deed performed by Robin Hood in many of the later Robin Hood tales, and indeed it is included at the end of the Errol Flynn film.

What became of the earl during those four missing years is a matter for speculation. John Fordun claimed that David fought in the Crusades alongside Richard during this period. This is not impossible, but it went unnoted by any of the contemporary chroniclers. Another story suggests that, while travelling back from the Holy Land, David was shipwrecked off the coast of Egypt; he was later taken to Constantinople before being recognized by some English merchants and returned home.[3] His involvement in the Nottingham rebellion further demonstrates his loyalty to the king and his opposition to Prince John. The fact that his activities were unrecorded in the four years Richard was on Crusade also suggests that he may have been away from his home and duties during Richard's absence. It cannot be ruled out that David took to the forests around 1193 and subsequently became Robin Hood, but this is impossible to prove. In around 1211 David was in severe debt, which concurs with Grafton's assertion that Robin Hood was an earl outlawed for debt. David's links to two of the Ranulfs, Earls of Chester, also supports the possibility that he was the Robin Hood described by Langland. It should also be noted that, according to the shipwreck story, David attributed his deliverance to the Virgin Mary and founded a monastery at Lindoris.[4]

Parker's *True Tale* ballad was possibly influenced by Munday's plays and more directly by the work of Grafton and Major, but it could be referring loosely to Earl David. It refers to 'Lord Robin Hood' being outlawed by Prince John during the reign of King Richard I. Parker then clearly uses details from the *Gest*, describing the earl's feud with the abbot of St Mary's, and develops the outlaw's tendency to help the poor. Robin dies before King Richard pardons him, which was not true of David, Earl of Huntingdon, who assisted Richard in 1194 and died during the reign of Henry III. Reference in the ballad to the King of Scotland is interesting, however, as the Earls of Huntingdon traditionally had links with the Scottish monarchy. The Scottish King at the time, William the Lion, was David's brother.

None the less, an earl is not a yeoman and therefore could not be the Robin Hood of the ballads. Many of the antiquaries are unconvinced by suggestions that Robin Hood was an earl. Bishop Percy is one of many recorded as having serious doubts about the historicity of the earldom theory and emphasizes the point in his *Reliques of Ancient English Poetry*:

> The most ancient poems on Robin Hood make no mention of this earldom. He is expressly asserted to have been a yeoman in a very old legend in verse preserved in the archives of the public library at Cambridge in eight fyttes.[5]

Also unconvincing are suggestions that Robin Hood was a Saxon. His identification as a Saxon, previously mooted by the French historian Jacques Nicolas Augustin Thierry in his *Histoire de la Conquête de l'Angleterre pas les Normands*, is an important feature in Walter's Scott's novel *Ivanhoe* and several retellings of the story since that time, but there is no reference to it in the chronicles or early ballads. The Norman–Saxon divide high-lights the theme of tyranny and oppression portrayed in the later versions of the legend that draw particularly on Walter Scott's description of the imposition of the Norman Yoke.[6] The idea that the Norman Conquest put an end to a Saxon golden age has undoubtedly been exaggerated, yet history does recall times when the Saxon–Norman conflict took centre stage. The concessions set out in the Magna Carta were restrictions on the rule of the Norman king, and they reclaimed some 'pre-Norman' rights, albeit only for the gentry. Whether they benefited the Saxons directly, however, is less clear, particularly as the barons were mostly Norman. The concept of the Yoke was central to the Peas-ants' Revolt of 1381 when men such as Tyler and Straw took the argument on directly, seeing liberation from Norman rule as a step towards the achievement of a utopian society free from autocracy, sometimes referred to as Merrie England. Tyler and Straw believed the Bible taught that there was no place for the aristocracy and that the unforgiving, indiscriminate nature of the Black Death had demonstrated that all were equal in the eyes of God.[7]

The philosophies of Merry England and the Norman Yoke may be argued as being significant in our appreciation of the events that led to the signing of the Magna Carta, the Peasants' Revolt and even the English Civil War, but their relevance during the reign of Richard I cannot be clearly determined. Walter Scott's decision to highlight cultural differences and ethnicity disputes undoubtedly developed Robin Hood's portrayal as an outlawed Saxon nobleman, although the Saxon association was first mentioned in Ritson's collection when referring to the Lincoln green livery as grass green or Saxon green: 'His coat is of Saxon green, his waistcoat's of a plait.'[8]

Scott also depicted Robin as an ally of King Richard I. Modern-day presentations of the legend continue to portray the

Saxon Robin Hood as a supporter of Richard, but in reality this would be surprising since Richard the Lionheart was himself a Norman. Nevertheless, this did not deter Scott from highlighting the importance of ethnicity when he penned *Ivanhoe*:

> Norman saw on English oak.
> On English neck a Norman yoke;
> Norman spoon to English dish,
> And England ruled as Normans wish;
> Blithe world in England never will be more,
> Till England's rid of all the four.[9]

The idea of Merry England was undoubtedly an unrealistic portrayal of life for the majority of the peasant class. However, once the Black Death was over some of the survivors were able to enjoy the life of 'Merrie England'. The country was experiencing a labour shortage, so labourers had their pick of work and landowners could no longer bully their workers. For the first time the peasantry had a bargaining tool. The concept of the yeoman farmer emerged from this: men free to choose where they worked and for how long. Renting land from a lord, who was now incapable of running his estates profitably, the farmer was bound to hand over a certain amount of the produce to the manor but was free to choose what he did with the rest. Over the years this became common practice.[10]

The improved living conditions after the Black Death did not last. In an attempt to block increases in the prices that peasants were demanding for their produce, the Statute of Labourers imposed a wage freeze in 1351. However, prices continued to rise, and the peasants once more suffered as conditions began to return to the way they had been before the Black Death. Richard II betrayed his humble subjects still further as he attempted to fund his continuing war against the French with a poll tax.[11] The subsequent revolt could be argued as significant for the later Robin Hood legends, with the Saxons rebelling against the Norman autocracy, but no such revolt took place during the regency of Prince John. The ideal of Merry England later became inseparable from Robin Hood after it appeared in William Hazlitt's essay *Merry England*, later also included in his *Lectures on the English Comic Writers* under the heading 'St George for Merry England':

> The beams of the morning sun shining on the lonely glades, or through the idle branches of the tangled forest, the leisure, the freedom, 'the pleasure of going and coming without knowing where', the troops of wild deer, the sports of the chase, and other rustic gambols, were sufficient to justify the appellation of 'Merry Sherwood', and in like manner, we may apply the phrase to Merry England.[12]

Although the ballad hero can never be accepted as a historical figure from the twelfth century, parallels between Robin Hood, the nobleman of later tradition, and Fulk FitzWarin should not be completely overlooked. FitzWarin, an authentic historical landowner and nobleman, was stripped of all his possessions and titles following a quarrel with King John and took to the woods as an outlaw. From there he took his revenge and humiliated the king.[13] His career was similar to that of the Robin Hood of recent centuries, and it could certainly be argued that parts of Fulk's legend may have overlapped with Robin Hood's to create a wronged nobleman. Indeed, Fulk, too, had connections with Ranulf, Earl of Chester. Less convincing, however, are arguments that the early Robin Hood ballads were works of fiction inspired by the lives of Fulk and others such as Gamelyn, Eustache the Monk and Hereward the Wake. Similarities have been adduced: Hereward dressing as a potter; Eustache operating from a forest hide-out; Fulk waylaying a caravan of merchants in similar circumstances to Little John and Much waylaying monks and yeomen in the *Gest*; dining with the enemy; and Fulk using trickery and disguise to capture King John.[14] This line of argument has its strengths, but there are also a number of weaknesses. Operating from a forest hide-out, using disguise and robbing monks is typical enough behaviour for an outlaw. There are also several instances where an obvious source for plot details in the *Gest* is not known. The loan in the *Gest* seems to be quite original, as is much of the storyline involving the knight. Support for the true-life outlaws theory, however, seemed to increase after one of Thomas Wright's printed essays on Robin Hood, in a collection from 1846, coincidentally appeared alongside pieces on Hereward, Eustache and Fulk. This is somewhat ironic as Wright's essay was actually an attempt to identify Robin Hood as 'the green man of mythology'.[15]

Evidence that the term 'Robin Hood' was used generically to describe criminals as early as the thirteenth century probably had no bearing on the man from the ballads but is of great importance when it comes to understanding the history of the time.[16] The term 'Robin' or 'rabun' seems to have been used to describe someone who robs or steals. Similarly, 'hood' implied a hoodlum, or someone wearing a hood.[17] Bearing in mind that outlaws were on the run from the law, often wearing hoods to disguise themselves, the description probably needs no further explanation. Nevertheless, it is noticeable that no records of 'Robin Hoods' have been found in the rolls before the reign of Richard I. This could indicate that a historical Robin Hood from the twelfth century inspired the use of the term, but it is not proof. It is possible that the first Robert Hod, who was recorded on the rolls thirty-one years after the recapture of Nottingham Castle and some twenty-two years before Gale's estimated date of death for Robin Hood in 1247 (as proposed by L. V.D. Owen), could have influenced the legend, but it may simply be a coincidence.[18] If we accept that Robin was active during the reign of an Edward rather than Richard I, as suggested in the *Gest*, the term 'Robin Hood' would have already been in use to describe a lawbreaker. In addition, there is evidence in the ballads to support the view that Robin Hood was labelled in this way. In the *Potter* ballad the proficiency and elegance of Robin's trickery make it impossible for the sheriff to recognize him.[19] In the *Gest* ballad, when the poor knight and later the monk enter Robin's hut, Robin removes his hood before addressing his guest.[20] Given that, according to the ballads he robbed from the rich and frequently used disguise, there is a strong likelihood that 'Robin Hood' may be an alias rather than a proper name. Yet, according to the chroniclers, this is not so. In the chronicles of Wyntoun, Bower and Major the outlaw is always named Robert. It would be helpful to understand why this is, as Robin is never referred to as Robert in the surviving ballads.

According to Bower, Robin Hood was a historical outlaw who became active following Simon de Montfort's defeat at the Battle of Evesham. This view appears quite convincing considering Bower's theory that Robin took to the forests with his accomplices from among the 'disinherited' to avoid the royalists, but it is by no means conclusive. Bower's depiction of Robert Hood bears a remarkable resemblance to Roger Godberd. Godberd was a well-known murderer, and his involvement in fighting against the king's army at Sir Richard Foliot's Fenwick Castle largely corresponds with the encounter between the sheriff and Robin at the castle of Sir Richard at the Lee. Godberd was said to have had control of a hundred men, which is similar to Robin Hood's seven score yeomen, and his encounters in Nottinghamshire parallel the activities of Godberd and his men. In addition, it was the former Sheriff of Nottingham, Reginald de Grey, who eventually captured Godberd.[21] Despite this, there is no obvious evidence that Godberd plied his trade in Barnsdale. Indeed, references to Sherwood are also susceptible to criticism after previous mention of Charnwood in Leicestershire was misinterpreted as Sherwood.[22] Robin Hood is famous as an outlaw of Sherwood, but the early references to Barnsdale make this his home. In *Scotichronicon* Bower never refers to Sherwood, and this may indicate that Godberd was not the man in question.

What became of Godberd after his trial remains unclear. Most likely he died, although it is possible that he was pardoned and returned to his farm.[23] This is rather different from the ending of the *Gest* and Robin Hood's death at Kirklees. Also missing here is any mission. In the ballads Robin Hood and his men have no purpose other than to steal from archbishops or bishops and not to molest one who would be a 'good fellow'. After becoming outlawed after the Battle of Evesham, however, Godberd's life became one of constant criminal activity.[24] His tendency to prey on travellers and carry out indiscriminate killings is at variance with Robin Hood's principle of not molesting one who would be a good fellow but very much in keeping with Bower's reference to Robin Hood as having inflicted 'a vast amount of slaughter on the common and ordinary folk, cities and merchants'. Although the early Robin Hood ballads are violent they do nothing to support Bower's suggestion that Robin was responsible for such widespread violence. The long-awaited capture of Godberd in 1272 was a political move on behalf of the Crown, and his subsequent imprisonment was punishment for his role in the rebellion. In the *Gest* the unidentified King

Edward was to Robin 'a comely king', whereas it is difficult to imagine that Edward I was Godberd's comely king. In addition to the fact that Edward was on Crusade at the time Godberd was captured, his father, Henry III, was still alive. Although Edward had a tendency to support the barons before the outbreak of the war, it would not have been possible for Godberd to be an outlaw in rebellion against the king and, at the same time, support true kingship. Equally, it would have been extremely unlikely for Henry III to let Godberd go unpunished in the way that the king did Robin Hood in the *Monk* ballad.[25]

Child is particularly critical of Bower. He says of Fordun that he is a man of judgement and research and that his statements and opinions are entitled to respect, but he accuses Bower of interpolating the work of Fordun with the 'most absurdest fictions'.[26] Bower's reference to Roger Mortimer and John D'Eyville being active around 1266 offers some credibility to his argument, yet Fordun's failure to include the passage in the original document, combined with claims of inaccuracy in Bower's work, leaves *Scotichronicon* difficult to accept without an earlier source. The idea that the 'disinherited' continued to cause trouble throughout the reign of Edward I may offer some support for Bower and Wyntoun, yet it is difficult to accept that scattered groups of rebels who fled after the defeat at Evesham were still active as late as 1283. Also problematical here is the absence of any mention of Inglewood in the Robin Hood ballads. It is possible that none has survived; it is also possible, as suggested by William Motherwell, that the rhymes varied by geography and that people in Scotland knew some that the English did not.[27] Nevertheless, it may also be that the similarities with Adam Bell offer insight into the thoughts of the seventy-year-old Wyntoun.[28] The only possible reference to Inglewood comes in the *Gest* and is concerned with excessive deer hunting in Plompton Park, which is otherwise irrelevant to the ballad. The pro-Scottish nature of the chronicle calls its objectivity into question. The *Orygynale Cronykil* is greatly influenced by Wyntoun's own pro-Scottish and anti-English beliefs, and his records of Robin Hood in 1283 are otherwise unsupported and without clear sources.

It seems probable that more than one historical person influenced the later legend. Earl David is a plausible candidate for the post-Major Robin Hood, whereas Godberd may well have been the man Bower wrote about. Yet neither accurately matches the yeoman ballad hero who lived during the reign of an Edward. Historical evidence of a yeoman is never easy to find. Of the outlaws that history does recall, their background is usually of knightly descent. Godberd had connections with the nobility, as did Eustace de Folville.[29] If a historical Robin Hood lived during the reign of an Edward, then history places him between the reigns of Edward I (1272–1307) and Edward III (1327–77). Given that by 1377 some elements of the legend were already in place, this can be narrowed down further.[30] A man from Rockingham Forest arrested in 1354 for poaching and trespassing gave his name as Robin Hood. Rather than providing an original historical candidate for Robin, this incident probably confirms that there was already a widespread awareness of the legend at the time.[31]

In order to identify the time period in which the ballads were set, it is necessary to understand which king was on the throne at the time. According to the *Gest*, the king ventured to Nottingham to infiltrate the Merry Men. In 1300 Edward I passed by Nottingham on the way to Caerlaverock;[32] Edward II was there in 1323 and 1324 on his way back from the north, and Edward III was also in Nottingham in 1330 following the arrest of Roger Mortimer and his mother, Queen Isabella.[33] Joseph Hunter's theory regarding Robert Hood of Wakefield draws particular attention to the events of 1322 surrounding the rebellion of Thomas of Lancaster against Edward II and the king's circuit through the royal hunting forests of Yorkshire and Lancashire the following year.[34] Edward II is recorded as being present in Nottingham between 9 and 23 November 1323. The *Gest* also states that Robin was once in the employment of the king, and Joseph Hunter later identified a Robyn Hode working as a valet in the king's household around this time.[35] In the *Chamber Journal* Hunter found that a yeoman was in service at this time: 'A. Henri Lowe, Colle de Ashruge, Will de Shene, Joh. Petimari, Grete Hobbe, Litell Colle, Joh. Edrich, Robyn Hode . . .'[36] In a genuine attempt at making sense of Robin's return to the green-wood at the end of the *Gest*, Hunter tells us that the valet left the king's service around 21 October 1324. This, however, does not conclusively confirm that this Robyn Hode was ever an outlaw, or eliminate the possibility that he was in service before Edward came to Nottingham. Hunter's attempt to identify this man as the law-abiding Robert Hood of Wakefield is based almost entirely on coincidence; Hunter was cautious about his own theory.[37]

Despite this, many factors seem to support the notion that Edward II was the king in question. Hunter's time period is convincing, with his reference to Plompton Park in the *Gest* potentially tying in with Edward II's trip.[38] The *Gest* refers to a deer shortage, which was recorded in the forests of northern England as an after-effect of the Earl of Lancaster's faltering rebellion.[39] The ballads may provide other clues. The description given in the *Monk* ballad of the grim gaol conditions that Robin Hood endured fits the period.[40] In addition, the story of the sheriff organizing a posse to take Robin Hood at the castle of Richard at the Lee is consistent with the laws on Conservators of the Peace in place at the time, although the sheriff should not have encroached into Yorkshire.[41] Perhaps the most important clue is the personality of the king. Although Longshanks was undoubtedly capable of the cunning associated with the monarch in the *Gest*, it seems out of character for the 'Hammer of the Scots' to dress as an abbot simply to locate an outlaw. His harshness and even war crimes committed against the Scots, notably Wallace, cannot be identified with the character of the monarch of the *Gest* or the forgiving monarch of the *Monk* ballad. The reference to Edward as a comely king is equally unlikely, although he did father fifteen children with his wife, Queen Eleanor, and a further three in his second marriage to the much younger Marguerite of France.[42] Edward III was described as comely in a poem written around 1339, which predates the *Gest*.[43] Edward III was undoubtedly a popular king, compared by some with King Arthur. This monarch could certainly have appeared comely to Robin Hood, but it is difficult to imagine that Edward III would dress up as an abbot to infiltrate a group of outlaws. His reputation for pragmatism helped maintain order, which in turn brought him praise, yet the merciless and impulsive streak that he possessed and which later brought about the murder of Mortimer and England's involvement in the Hundred Years' War seems alien to the monarch of the *Monk* and *Gest* ballads.[44]

Edward II was the least king-like of the three. Longshanks and Edward III were astute leaders, but Edward II did not share their ambitions. He became heir to the throne at only a few months of age following the death of his older brother Prince Alphonso, and Longshanks trained him in warfare and statecraft throughout his childhood but without success. Irritatingly for the king, the young prince was more interested in activities such as boating, craftwork, digging trenches and other pastimes considered inappropriate for kingship. This was also reflected in his tendency to favour the lower classes over the nobles throughout his reign.[45] Edward II's affinity with the lower classes is reminiscent of the courtesy shown by the king in the *Gest* towards the yeoman outlaws, a characteristic largely out of keeping with his father and son. Edward II is recorded as enjoying hunting as one of his favourite pastimes, and the pleasure derived by the king portrayed in the *Gest* ballad from indulging in frivolous interests rather than those associated with true kingship also seems in keeping with Edward II's character.

The events described in the ballads also provide an in-depth insight into the personalities of the Merry Men. Piety is evident; experience in military matters and martial skills, particularly archery and sword fighting, are demonstrated throughout the ballads; obedience to their master is shown by all the men, although they did not behave in the same way towards county officials and members of the clergy; harming women is forbidden by their code of conduct; the outlaws have a desire to do poor men good, and they also show kindness to one who would be a good fellow. Strangely, these outlaws do not profit individually from their thievery, and the *Gest* ballad mentions that they have a common fund benefiting the fellowship as a whole. The absence of deadly sin is in keeping with their piety and in turn demonstrates a code of conduct like that of a monastic order. These characteristics point to two likely options, as earlier chapters have argued: they were outlawed monks, or they were part of a Christian military religious order.

The fact that the Merry Men display impressive military capabilities, steal from monks and abbots who are not 'good fellows' and wear a common livery suggests the latter. Their behaviour is in keeping with what was expected of the Christian military religious orders of the time, notably the Knights Templar, who were later outlawed. The absence of a reason why the Merry Men are outlaws and the notable fact that the *Gest* refers to the men as being at Robin's disposal indicates that they were outlawed together. Judging by the ballads, the fellowship is well established, with the Merry Men following a code of conduct that has been in place for many years. The fact that none of them is married and they abide by vows of chastity indicates that they belong to a religious order.[46] Vows of chastity were compulsory for members of Christian military orders, and they were required to keep them throughout their lives. Following the dissolution of the Templars, some former members did marry, but, despite the demise of the Order, their vows of chastity were still upheld by the pope and their marriages were annulled. The importance of the chastity cords, as once touched by the Virgin Mary, was fundamental to the Templars' way of life as they emphasized the Order's dedication to their patron saint.[47]

Although many Templars in England carried out the work of managing the estates, from the end of the twelfth century onwards, appeals for Englishmen to go to the Holy Land were widely broadcast from pulpits and market crosses in many towns and villages.[48] Following the defeat at Hattin in 1187, Gerald of Wales accompanied the Archbishop Baldwin across Wales seeking new members. The 3,000 who agreed to join were said to have been 'highly skilled in the use of spear and arrow, most experienced in military affairs and only too keen to attack the enemies of our faith. They were all sincerely and warmly committed to Christ's service.'[49]

The Merry Men undoubtedly meet these criteria, and it also seems likely that Templar outlaws were active in the region of Barnsdale following their excommunication. Records show that as few as eighteen Templars, including four preceptors, were arrested from the ten Yorkshire preceptories, an average of 1.8

persons per preceptory, which indicates that most Templars departed before the Inquisition arrived.[50] Evidence collected from the time confirms that numerous Templars remained at large in the area and that the Sheriff of York and the king were aware of this. From records connected to the preceptories, we learn that many of the Templars who were arrested were local figures, as illustrated by their use of locative names, and were often recruited into the areas where they had lived most of their lives.[51]

Also located in Yorkshire is Kirklees Priory where Robin Hood was supposedly murdered and later buried. In the heavy woodland in the grounds of the priory, a ruined monument, hidden behind iron railings on private property, commemorates the site where it is said that Robin Hood was laid to rest. There is good evidence that a stone slab with a cross and Calvary steps at the base once existed, as demonstrated in Chapter 11. Based on the diagrams, this grave is remarkably in keeping with the way in which deceased Knights Templar were buried throughout Europe.[52] The cross is consistent with those used by the Order and the base incorporating the Calvary steps was used to illustrate Christ's death on Calvary and also the steps to the Temple of Solomon. The absence of dates and a name on the grave is problematic in terms of clarifying an exact date of death for Robin Hood, but the omission adds weight to the view that this was a Templar grave, as it was common practice for the Order not to include dates and names so that the importance of the individual would never take precedence over the Order in which they served.[53]

Templar influence on the ballads is nowhere more clearly demonstrated than in the early scenes with the knight in the *Gest*. In addition to providing the knight with a loan, something for which the Templars were legendary, a Templar was always required to maintain a poor man at their own expense, which

Robin Hood and his men do in a manner fitting of a Templar.[54] The suggestion that Richard at the Lee was heading off on Crusade, or returning from Crusade, is equally important as this demonstrates that the Templar role of guarding pilgrims on their travels to holy places is being carried out by the Merry Men.

The charges brought against the Knights Templar during their trials cast a blemish on their image that the passing centuries have not entirely eradicated. In recent years it has also been alleged that the Order brought about its own downfall through involvement in dark arts such as sorcery, witchcraft and Devil worship. Whether or not there is any basis to such allegations, the absence of definite information about the Templars after the Papal Bull was enacted allowed such theories to flourish. Records of the Order have largely vanished, and the events of the time are badly chronicled: neither *Scotichronicon* nor the *Orygynale Cronykil* refers to the Templars at all.

Owing to the incomplete nature of the ballads, the illiteracy of yeomen, poor record-keeping at the time, the many contradicting views of the chroniclers and the question marks that remain over the authenticity of Robin Hood's grave, a neat and tidy explanation for the ballad hero will probably never be obtainable. If the events of the ballads and the drawings of the grave are accepted as being historically accurate, they offer support to the theory that Robin Hood was a Knight Templar. If, on the other hand, the ballads were fictitious, their authors were certainly influenced by the Christian military-religious orders of the time, in particular the banking activities of the Templars, and they modelled the Merry Men on them, setting the activities in places closely associated with the Templars.

Whether the ballads provide an accurate historical commentary on the lives of fugitive Templars who evaded arrest in Yorkshire or merely glamorize the Order through fictional depictions is difficult to determine. Based on the historical evidence available from the preceptories before they were abandoned, it can be said that the Templars were living their lives in accordance with their vows.[55] The Templars who were recorded as being at large in Yorkshire and Kent were never accused of causing any harm or trouble. They were outlawed at a time when ruthless men preyed on the vulnerable, but, as was said of Robin Hood, 'so courteous outlaws as they were otherwise never was found'.

POSTSCRIPT

On the wall of the Robin Hood exhibition at the Sherwood Forest country park there is a quotation: 'The spirit of Robin Hood lives for ever in Sherwood Forest and in the hearts of those who seek him.' Similar sentiments are expressed in all the various accounts of the life and deeds of Robin Hood. This is the essence of the Robin Hood story. It is an inspirational legend, rather than a true account of a particular man, demonstrating loyalty to true kingship, noble intentions and resistance to unjust authority.

Centuries of repetition and distortion have had a noticeable effect both on the stories and the character of Robin Hood, and sometimes these changes can be accounted for. Whether the scale and scope of the legend had changed before the ballads were written is now impossible to say. As far as we are aware there is no definitive biography of Robin Hood's life, either in the ballads or written by the chroniclers of the time, that will confirm his historicity or that he was a fictional creation. Perhaps we are missing something. Perhaps a vital piece of information eludes us. It is quite possible that something once existed, perhaps only in oral form, but has not survived. It is known that the Bishop of St Andrews commissioned a biography of William Wallace, but that has long since vanished. Maybe one of Robin Hood's followers wrote about his life. Possibly the legend began with the reminiscences of someone that he assisted: Sir Richard at the Lee, who features in the *Gest*, was almost certainly literate; Little John also plays a prominent role.

When it comes to history, our views are influenced by the records left to us. Guy Fawkes, for instance, will be remembered for his attempt to destroy the Houses of Parliament, but his gallantry at the siege of Calais fighting for the English is rarely acknowledged. Richard I is likely always to be the hero of the Robin Hood stories, and a popular English monarch, despite the fact that he spent so little time in England and used the country primarily as an extra source of income to fund his wars. Likewise, King John may always be viewed as the villain of the Robin Hood saga and the reluctant signatory of the Magna Carta, but he is given at best scant praise for the efficiency of his administration and the more than 1,300 trips he made to the farthest corners of his kingdom. Kings and noblemen are judged by their legacy. When it comes to Robin Hood, we have very little evidence to go on, yet the hero of the ballads transcends the paucity of the historical record. Perhaps this is because we like to remember people who demonstrated noble intentions and ideals. The Bible refers to Moses standing up to the unjust authority of the Egyptian rulers and leading the Israelites to the Promised Land, and Nelson Mandela and Martin Luther King will be remembered for similar reasons. They all encountered difficulties, but they are honoured today for what they achieved. The film *Prince of Thieves* includes an appropriate line, said by the Saracen: 'There are no perfect men, only perfect intentions.' Perhaps this is why Robin Hood remains so firmly fixed in our national psyche. His tales may have been exaggerated, yet for over 600 years his legend has been celebrated. People throughout the ages have enjoyed it, and it seems certain that they will continue to do so for a long time to come. Parts of his legend may remain incomplete, but we can still appreciate what we do know and continue to add to our knowledge. And with this,

> I shall think my labour well
> bestowed to purpose good,
> that it should be said that I did tell
> true tales of Robin Hood.

Notes and References

Details of books, chronicles and so on cited in abbreviated form are found in full in the bibliography.

Chapter 1. A Proud Outlaw

1   *Gest*, stanzas 1–2. The author has updated the lines into modern English.
2   It is impossible to tell the exact number. Some oral traditions may not have survived, whereas others exist only as fragments.
3   Francis Child, *English and Scottish Popular Ballads*, Vol. III, pp. 39–115; Francis Child, *English and Scottish Ballads*, selected and edited by Francis Child, Vol. V, pp. 1, 17, 42–4, 159; Joseph Ritson, Joseph Frank and Thomas Bewick, *Robin Hood: A Collection of the Ancient Poems, Songs, and Ballads, Now Extant, Relative to That Celebrated English Outlaw*, Vol. II, pp. 1–2, 81, 114; Joseph Ritson, *Robin Hood: A Collection of All the Ancient Poems, Songs, and Ballads, Now Extant, Relative to That Celebrated English Outlaw*, pp. 1, 60, 83; J.C. Holt, *Robin Hood*, pp. 15–16; A.J. Pollard, *Imagining Robin Hood*, pp. 6–7; Knight and

Ohlgren, *Robin Hood and Other Outlaw Tales*, pp. 80–86;
Thomas Ohlgren, *Ten Tales in Modern English*, pp. 216–21.

4 Holt, p. 15; Pollard, p. 7; Knight and Ohlgren, pp. 31–4;
Dobson and Taylor, *Rymes of Robin Hood*, pp. 113–22. In
addition, Child claims it may be as old as the reign of
Edward II: Child III, p. 1.

5 Any reference throughout this book to Child refers to the
famous ballad collector who indexed the ballads in 1882–98.

6 *Monk*, stanzas 1–9; Holt, p. 28.

7 There is a break in the text after line 120. According to Knight
and Ohlgren, in the missing period the Merry Men would
learn, perhaps by word of a page, how Robin was captured.

8 The king in this ballad is not named.

9 A Yeoman of the Crown was a position in the royal
household. This sometimes involved being a bodyguard.

10 *Monk*; Child III, pp. 94–102; Holt, pp. 28–30; Maurice
Hugh Keen, *Outlaws of Medieval Legend*, pp. 121–3.

11 Holt, p. 16; Pollard, p. 7; Knight and Ohlgren, p. 167;
Dobson and Taylor, pp. 140–45.

12 *Gisborne* ballad; Child III, pp. 89–94; Holt, pp. 30–33;
Keen, pp. 118–21.

13 Child V, p. 17; Holt, p. 15; Pollard, p. 7; Knight and Ohlgren,
pp. 57–9; Dobson and Taylor, pp. 123–32. Thomas Wright
suggests that the ballad may be as old as the reign of Henry
VI (1421–71). This is also mentioned by Child: Child III,
p. 17.

14 *Potter* ballad, fytte 2.

15 *Potter*, fytte 3; Child III, pp. 108–15; Holt, pp. 33–5; Keen,
pp. 116–18.

16 Ritson, p. 1; Child III, p. 39; Knight and Ohlgren,
pp. 80–86; Holt, pp. 15–17; Keen, pp. 100–103. Some have
suggested the *Gest* may be as old as 1400. Holt refers to

1450 as a safe bet.

17 A fytte usually refers to a song. *Gest*, therefore, comprises eight individual songs.

18 The knight is not named until fytte 6.

19 *Gest*, fytte 1.

20 *Gest*, fytte 2.

21 *Gest*, fytte 3.

22 *Gest*, fytte 4. This is an early reference to Robin's generosity in helping the poor.

23 *Gest*, fyttes 5–6.

24 *Gest*, fyttes 7–8; Child III, pp. 39–89; Holt, pp. 17–23; Keen, pp. 100–115; Ohlgren, pp. 221–38.

25 *Gest*, stanza 456.

26 William Langland, *The Vision of William Concerning Piers Plowman*.

27 Langland, Tiller and Martin, *Piers Plowman*, p. 51.

28 Dobson and Taylor.

29 Wyntoun was probably referring to the forest that once existed in Cumbria.

30 See Chapter 4.

31 Knight and Ohlgren, p. 25.

32 Dobson and Taylor, p. 5; Knight and Ohlgren, p. 26. See also Chapter 3.

33 Knight and Ohlgren, p. 25.

34 Dobson and Taylor, p. 5; Knight and Ohlgren, p. 25.

35 See Chapter 3.

36 Reference to the king is first made in fytte 7 of the *Gest* when Robin refers to Edward as 'our handsome king' (trans. Ohlgren). In the *Monk* ballad the king is not named.

37 He is also known as John Mair.

38 See Chapter 2.

39 Dobson and Taylor, p. 5; Knight and Ohlgren, pp. 26–7.

Chapter 2. A Major History of Britain

1   The *Potter* ballad stanzas 12–25 describe Robin battling with the potter before accepting him as a member of the outlaw band. The *Gest*, *Potter*, *Gisborne* and *Monk* ballads all refer to Robin's superior ability in archery.

2   John Major, *Historia Majoris Britanniae*, edited by Archibald Constable 1892, pp. 156–67.

3   It should be noted that Robin Hood is never once referred to as Robert in the early ballads. In the Munday plays he is referred to in this way, and he is also named Lord Robert Hood in Martin Parker's *True Tale*. While it is conceivable that early rhymes where Robin was named Robert do not survive, the reference to Robert as a forename stems directly from the chronicles.

4   Robin first refers to his men as his 'Mery men' in line 35 of the *Monk* ballad.

5   For discussions on Maid Marian, see Chapter 9.

6   For discussions on the later tradition, see Chapter 10.

7   For Robin Hood's involvement in the May Day proceedings, see Chapters 9 and 10.

8   Alison Weir, *Eleanor of Aquitaine*; John Harvey, *The Plantagenets*, p. 51.

9   John Burke, *History of England*, p. 51.

10 Turner and Heiser, *Reign of Richard the Lionheart*, p. 71.

11 Burke, p. 51.

12 Turner and Heiser, pp. 72–86; John Gillingham, *Richard the Lionheart*, pp. 125–42.

13 Burke, pp. 52–3; Thomas Madden, *A New Concise History of the Crusades*, p. 96.

14 Jean Flori, *Richard the Lionheart, King and Knight*, pp. 155–75.

15 Turner and Heiser, p. 74.

16 Burke, pp. 53–4.

17 Turner and Heiser, p. 225; Gillingham, pp. 241–77; Jeremy Black, *A New History of England Britain*, p. 68.

18 Harvey, *The Plantagenets*; Jacob Abbott, *Richard I*, p. 175.

19 Knight and Ohlgren, pp. 27–8.

20 Richard Grafton's *Chronicle at Large*, 1569, pp. 84–5.

21 See Chapter 10.

22 Holt, pp. 42–3.

23 K.J. Stringer, *David, Earl of Huntingdon 1152–1219: A Study in Anglo-Scottish History*, p. 40.

24 J.C. Holt, *Magna Carta*, pp. 137–8.

25 Stringer, p. 114; Holt, p. 138.

26 Stringer, pp. 40–49.

27 Henry of Huntingdon, *The History of the English People, 1000–1154*, p. 143.

28 Christopher Tyerman, *Who's Who in Early Medieval England, 1066–1272*.

29 Stephen Thomas Knight, *A Complete Study of the English Outlaw*, pp. 29–32. The *Gest* is clearly referring to Barnsdale in Yorkshire.

30 Grafton refers to it as Birklees, but this is probably a misinterpretation of Kirklees rather than an alternative location, as Grafton is clearly familiar with the popular death story.

31 J.C. Holt, *The Northerners*, p. 63. For discussions on Robin Hood's death, see Chapter 11.

32 Chrisopher Hill, *Puritanism and Revolution*; Christopher Hill, *Intellectual Origins of the English Revolution Revisited*, Chapter 17; Marjorie Chibnall, *The Debate on the Norman Conquest*, p. 38; Robert Gibson, *Best of*

Enemies, pp. 4–5; Dennis Dworkin, *Cultural Marxism in Postwar Britain*, pp. 40–41; Rosalind O'Hanlon, *Caste, Conflict and Ideology*, p. 150; Krishan Kumar, *The Making of English National Identity*, pp. 48–9.

33 Kumar, p. 49. In Anglo-Saxon culture a thegn was an official, usually with military significance.

34 Further reading: Hill, *Intellectual Origins of the English Revolution Revisited*. See also Chapter 12.

35 Graham P. Kirkby, Database of Sheriffs of Nottingham. Ecomplanet.com.

36 Knight and Ohlgren, p. 693.

37 *Gest*, fytte 5.

38 Glyn Burgess, *Two Medieval Outlaws: Eustache the Monk and Fouke Fitz Waryn*; Knight and Ohlgren, pp. 693–723; 'Fulk Fitz Waryn', translated by Thomas E. Kelly, found in Ohlgren's *Ten Tales*, pp. 106–67.

39 Knight and Ohlgren, p. 27.

40 In popular culture the meeting in the *Gest* often involves Richard I rather than Sir Richard.

41 Alexander Broadie, *The Tradition of Scottish Philosophy*, pp. 21–7; see also Alexander Broadie, *The Circle of John Mair*.

42 Knight and Ohlgren also make note of this.

43 Broadie, *The Tradition of Scottish Philosophy*, pp. 21–7, 86–90.

44 Further reading: Hugh Thomas, *Rivers of Gold: The Rise of the Spanish Empire*.

45 Significant Scots. ElectricScotland.com.

46 Broadie, p. 22.

47 Keen, p. 177.

Chapter 3. Disinherited

1   Burke, p. 54.

2   Black, p. 70.

3   This conflict followed the nineteen-year winter (1135–54) and the revolt of Henry the Young King against Henry II (1173–4).

4   Burke, pp. 54–5.

5   Ibid, p. 55–6.

6   Ibid.

7   D.A. Carpenter, *The Minority of Henry III*, p. 13.

8   Holt, *Robin Hood*, pp. 52–3, 59, 187–90. References were originally found in the Pipe Rolls.

9   Dobson and Taylor, pp. xxi–xxii; Holt, pp. 52–3.

10 Dobson and Taylor, pp. 10–13.

11 Holt, pp. 188, 190.

12 John Chancellor, *The Life and Times of Edward I*, p. 47.

13 Burke, pp. 56–7.

14 Black, p. 73; Maurice Powicke, *The Oxford History of England, 1216–1302*, pp. 75–8.

15 Carpenter, p. 14.

16 Burke, p. 57. Many historians refer to the war against King John that eventually resulted in the signing of the Magna Carta as being the first Barons' War. Most historians class this as a civil war, making the 1264–5 war possibly England's fourth to that date.

17 Powicke, pp. 187–90.

18 Burke, p. 57; Michael Prestwich, *Plantagenet England, 1225–1360*, p. 116.

19 Chancellor, p. 62.

20 Burke, p. 58.

21 Charles Beard, *The Office of the Justice of the Peace in England and Its Origin and Development*, pp. 17–18.

22 J.R. Maddicott, *Simon de Montfort*, p. 283.

23 Burke, p. 58; Prestwich, p. 116.

24 Ibid.

25 Prestwich, p. 117.

26 Originally from Bower, *Scotichronicon*. See also Child III, p. 41, or Knight and Ohlgren, p. 26.

27 *Scotichronicon*, edited by D.E.R. Watt, p. 357. A similar translation appears in Child V, p. xii.

28 This is particularly reminiscent of the *Monk* ballad where Robin Hood refuses the advice of Much the Miller's son to attend mass.

29 This rhyme was not indexed by Child and is also absent from collections by Ritson and Bishop Percy.

30 In the *Monk* ballad Little John beats Robin Hood in an archery competition. In the *Gest* it is the archery of Little John that impresses the sheriff.

31 *Gest*, fytte 1.

32 Throughout the ballads his name varies between Scarlock, Scathelocke, Sadlock and Scarlet. It is likely that eventually this led to the formation of two separate characters and also suggests that the early ballads were not necessarily written by the same writer.

33 This is seemingly a product of later tradition alongside his tendency to be portrayed as a youngster or dandy.

34 *Gest*, fytte 6.

35 Holt, pp. 98–9; Keen, pp. 196–7.

36 Ibid. See also *Gest*, fytte 6.

37 Holt, p. 98. See also Chapter 12.

38 For an extended discussion on yeomanry, see Pollard, Chapter 2.

39 Pollard, p. 32.

40 In the *Monk* ballad, Little John and Much are named Yeomen of the Crown, which is in keeping with this view.

41 Pollard, p. 32.

42 The role of the yeoman archers in the subsequent centuries became legendary in battles such as Crécy in 1346.

43 Powicke, p. 208; Prestwich, p. 117.

44 See p. 53.

45 Powicke, pp. 209–13.

Chapter 4. Waichmen Were Commendit Gude

1 Burke, p. 58.

2 Maddicott, p. 279.

3 Burke, p. 58.

4 Burke, p. 59; Michael Prestwich, *Edward I*, p. 170.

5 Black, p. 76.

6 Prestwich, pp. 170–201; Chancellor, pp. 92–152.

7 Prestwich, p. 358.

8 Burke, p. 60.

9 Burke, p. 60; Black, p. 76; Prestwich, p. 469.

10 Prestwich, p. 473.

11 Burke, p. 60.

12 Prestwich, p. 427.

13 Black, pp. 76–7.

14 Ibid.

15 Knight and Ohlgren, p. 24; Stephen Thomas Knight, *A Mythic Biography*, pp. 4–5.

16 *The Original Chronicle of Andrew of Wyntoun*, edited by F.J. Armours, 1907, pp. 136–7.

17 Knight and Ohlgren, pp. 24–7.

18 John Major dismisses the idea that Longshanks was guilty of the war crimes suggested by Wyntoun.

19 Prestwich, p. 176.

20 Helen Phillips, *Robin Hood: Medieval and Post Medieval*, p. 8; Child III, pp. 54–5.

21 This is a similarity between Cloudesley and the legend of William Tell.

22 *Adam Bell*, stanzas 7–10. It is worth pointing out for people unfamiliar with the ballad that it centres more on William Cloudesley than Adam Bell.

23 *Adam Bell*, fytte 2.

24 *Adam Bell*, stanza 4.

25 Knight and Ohlgren, p. 25.

26 Powicke, p. 213.

27 Pollard, p. 195; Rupert Willoughby, *Sir Adam de Gurdon and the Pass of Alton, Willougby*; Child V, p. xix; P.V. Harris, *The Truth about Robin Hood*, p. 72.

28 Knight and Ohlgren, p. 24; Knight, p. 4; *Encyclopaedia Britannica*, 11th edn, 1910–11.

29 *Encyclopaedia Britannica*.

30 Knight and Ohlgren, p. 25; Knight, pp. 5–6.

31 *Encyclopaedia Britannica*; Balfour-Melville, *James I King of Scots*.

32 *Encyclopaedia Britannica*; Barbieri, *A Descriptive and Historical Gazetteer of the Counties of Fife, Kinross and Clackmannan with Anecdotes, Narratives and Graphic Sketches, Moral, Political, Commercial and Agricultural*, p. 195.

33 Child V, p. 187.

Chapter 5. A Fellowship of Outlaws or an Outlawed Fellowship?

1   Hereward the Wake was outlawed as a result of his
    pro-Saxon stance and contempt for Edward the Confessor
    prior to the Norman invasion; see *De Gestis Herwardi
    Saxonis*. Eustache the Monk was a mercenary outlawed by
    the Count of Bologne in the thirteenth century; Burgess.
    Fulk was outlawed by King John as a result of a past
    quarrel; see Burgess or Knight and Ohlgren. Adam Bell
    was outlawed for poaching venison; *Adam Bell*, stanza 4.
    The early Robin Hood ballads, however, never offer an
    explanation as to why the hero was outlawed.
2   See Chapter 10.
3   Dodsworth Manuscript, 160, fol. 64b.
4   Child III, p. 175. Child was probably comparing the
    Progress to Nottingham ballad to the early ballads when
    referring to it as comparatively late.
5   Child III, pp. 175–7; Holt, p. 164; Knight and Ohlgren,
    p. 507.
6   Examples of this include *Robin Hood and the Tanner*,
    Robin Hood and the Ranger, *Robin Hood and the Newly
    Revived*, *Robin Hood and the Bold Pedlar* and *Robin Hood
    and the Curtal Friar*. This is a recurring theme in the later
    ballads, but such activity is limited in the early ballads.
7   See also Chapter 10.
8   Pollard, pp. 143–5.
9   Holt, pp. 170–71. The later tendency for duels to take place
    with quarterstaffs was probably influenced by the activities
    of the Merry Men in the May Day celebrations.
10 *Monk*, stanza 4.
11 *Monk*, stanza 9.
12 Definition taken from etymology dictionary.

13 *Potter*, stanza 4; Pollard, pp. 142–3.

14 *Gest*, stanzas 145 and 148.

15 Pollard, p. 33. This is more important in the *Gamelyn* ballad.

16 Ibid, p. 35.

17 *Gest*, stanza 1.

18 Further reading: Pollard, Chapter 2; Holt, Chapter VI; Keen, Chapter 11.

19 Pollard, p. 42.

20 Ibid; Peter Coss, *Aspects of Cultural Diffusion*.

21 *Gest*, lines 323–4.

22 Dobson and Taylor, p. 34.

23 Pollard, pp. 149–50.

24 *Gest*, stanza 14.

25 Pollard, p. 148.

26 *Potter*, line 94; Pollard, p. 138.

27 Pollard, pp. 150–55.

28 *Gest*, stanza 7.

29 *Gest*, stanza 14.

30 *Gest*, fytte 6.

31 *Monk*, stanzas 78–9.

32 *Gest*, stanzas 449 and 391.

33 *Monk*, stanza 15.

34 This is illustrated in fytte 1 of the *Gest* when Robin insists the knight pay for his own meal. Robin later lets him off after accepting that the knight is trustworthy.

35 John Major was clearly aware of this.

36 Knight and Ohlgren, p. 25.

37 De Montfort himself was renowned for his piety.

38 See also Dobson and Taylor.

39 *Gest*, stanza 15.

40 *Gest*, stanzas 13–14; Keen, p. 196.

Chapter 6. The Templars Versus the Bull

1 Burke, p. 61.
2 Prestwich, p. 517.
3 Burke, p. 61.
4 Mary Saaler, *Edward II*, pp. 31–6; Harold Hutchison, *Edward II the Pliant King*, pp. 60–73.
5 May McKisack, *Oxford History of England, 1307–1399*, p. 7; Saaler, p. 47.
6 McKisack, p. 9.
7 Black, p. 73.
8 Burke, p. 61.
9 Saaler, pp. 51–7; Michael Prestwich, *The Three Edwards: War and State in England, 1272–1377*.
10 See pp. 112–14.
11 Keen, pp. 197–201; Holt, pp. 152–7.
12 Knight and Ohlgren, p. 149. The *Oxford English Dictionary* specifically refers to an outlaw as '1. (formerly) a person excluded from the law and deprived of its protection. 2. any fugitive from the law. 3. to put (a person) outside the law and deprive of its protection'.
13 Paul Piers Read, *The Templars*, p. 91; Karen Ralls, *Knights Templar Encyclopaedia*, pp. 134–6, 138; Evelyn Lord, *The Knights Templar in Britain*, Chapter 1.
14 Peter Partner, *The Murdered Magicians: The Templars and Their Myth*, pp. 3–6.
15 Malcolm Barber, *The New Knighthood*, p. 7. While conspiracy stories have since taken on a life of their own regarding the treasures the new Order may have found, history recalls that the Templars were in fact housed on the south side of the Temple.

16 Partner, p. 10; Edward Burman, *The Templars, Knights of God*, pp. 26–7.

17 The Rule is the most valuable document to survive in translation describing the day-to-day life of the Templars. It mainly clarifies a detailed set of regulations regarding the running of the organization. See Ralls, pp. 163–5.

18 Burman, pp. 33–6.

19 Ralls, p. 115; Helen Nicholson, *The Knights Templar: A New History*, p. 141.

20 Burman, p. 45; Sharan Newman, *The Real History Behind the Templars*, pp. 303–13.

21 Burman, pp. 80–81; Lord, pp. 220–35.

22 Burman, pp. 82–7. This was the first example of the transfer of money across borders. Some scholars regard this as the birth of international banking. Some also believe that the concept of the cheque came from here.

23 Burman, pp. 91–7.

24 Lord, p. 236; Nicholson, p. 201.

25 Lord, p. 237; Partner, pp. 69–70.

26 Barber, p. 32.

27 He did not absolve de Nogaret.

28 Burman, *Supremely Abominable Crimes: The Trial of the Knights Templar*, pp. 3–15; Lord, pp. 241–5.

29 Nicholson, p. 237; Sean Martin, *The Knights Templar: The History and Myths of the Legendary Order*.

30 See Malcolm Barber, *The Trial of the Templars*, and 'The Verdict of History' in Lord's *Templars in Britain*, pp. 265–6.

31 Burman, *Supremely Abominable Crimes*, pp. 85–94; Martin, p. 118.

32 Ralls, p. 217; Jack. M. Driver, *The Templars: Holy Warrior Monks of the Ancient Lands*, p. 114.

33 Lord, p. 240.

34 Ibid, pp. 201–19.

35 Ibid, pp. 247–8.

36 Ibid, pp. 248–9.

37 Partner, p. 80.

38 Ibid, p. 13.

39 Lord, p. 250.

40 Ibid, p. 259.

41 Ibid, p. 253.

42 Ibid, p. 251; *Calendar of Close Rolls, 1307–1313*, pp. 179, 189, 106.

43 Lord, p. 254.

44 Driver, p. 118.

45 Martin, pp. 123–4, 140.

46 Lord, p. 266; Driver, p. 118.

47 Burman, *Knights of God*, p. 45. Although no official record ever existed confirming exactly how many members the Order had in total, Malcolm Barber suggests that throughout Europe it was unlikely to have been less than 7,000.

48 Partner, p. 59.

49 Martin, pp. 140–42.

50 Ralls, p. 220.

51 Lord, p. 259; Ralls, pp. 220–21.

52 Lord, p. 260; Ralls, p. 221.

Chapter 7. Into the Greenwood

1 Ralls, p. 62.

2 Burman, *Knights of God*, pp. 91–7.

3 See also Chapter 10.

4 Burman, *Knights of God*, p. 43. In the *Monk* and *Death* ballads Robin Hood insists that Little John accompany him and carry his bow.

5   Burman, *Knights of God*, p. 45. The author estimates that only 10 per cent of the Order were actual knights.

6   Ralls, p. 175; Martin, p. 54.

7   *Gest*, stanzas 70–74.

8   Ralls, pp. 115–16. It is not clear whether the reference to the scarlet mantle is a reference to the colour, first recognized in the English language around 1250, or a type of cloth that was common in the Middle Ages.

9   Ibid, p. 61.

10 It was not until 1324 that the Templar lands were finally given to the Hospitallers.

11 *Gest*, fyttes 6–7.

12 Holt, pp. 45–7; originally established in Joseph Hunter's *Robin Hood*; Child, p. xvi.

13 Each king has a possible connection with Nottingham. For the visits of Edward I and Edward III see pp. 207–9.

14 Lord, pp. 104–5.

15 Lord, p. 105; Holloway and Colton, *The Knights Templar in Yorkshire*.

16 A Corrodian is defined as a pensioner of a religious house, Lord, p. xiv.

17 Lord, pp. 105–7.

18 *Calendar of Close Rolls*, 1307–1313, pp. 179, 189, 106; Lord, p. 252; Ralls, p. 219.

19 See also Ralls, p. 219.

20 *Gest*, lines 9–10.

21 Dobson and Taylor, p. 17.

22 This confirms the location as Barnsdale in Yorkshire rather than Barnsdale in Rutland, which had links to the Earls of Huntingdon.

23 Mr Hunter's critical and historical traits: Hunter, p. 12. I am aware that Hunter's use of inclosure is inaccurate.

24 Leland's *Collectanea*, 1540.
25 Hunter speculates that it was Rolle who composed the *Gest* ballad. His view seems unsupported.
26 NationMaster.com encyclopedia.
27 Parry, *Vagabonds All*, p. 90.
28 Dixon, *Hunting in the Olden Days*, pp. 4–5; Johnson, *The Hunting Directory*, p. 235; Gilpin and Dick, *Remarks on Forest Scenery, and Other Woodland Views*, p. 284.
29 *Gest*, stanza 18.
30 Dobson and Taylor, pp. 22–3.
31 Holt, pp. 83–4.
32 Ibid, p. 107. Wentbridge is mentioned for the first time in fytte 4 of the ballad when Sir Richard claims he helped a wrestler on his way to repay the loan to Robin Hood. The suggestion that the Sayles was Sayles Wood and Quarry seems to have first been put forward by Tim Midgley.
33 Ralls, pp. 124–5.
34 Ibid, pp. 66–7.
35 *Gest*, stanza 13.
36 *Gest*, stanzas 37–40, 243–8.
37 I am conscious that the point about being willing to serve under Robin Hood constituting being a good fellow was also put forward by A.J. Pollard. Although his argument is not related to this book, I acknowledge the importance of his comments.
38 See Chapter 10.
39 For discussion on Robin Hood and the loan, see pp. 131–3.
40 *Gest*, lines 299–302.
41 The Turcoman was an elite riding horse used in the Holy Land.
42 Ralls, pp. 95, 163–5, 224; Read, p. 133; Martin, p. 54; Burman, p. 43

43 Ibid, pp. 26, 157.

44 *Gest*, stanza 77.

45 Ewart Oakeshott, *A Knight and His Horse*.

46 Dixon, *Hunting in the Olden Days*, p. 5.

47 Ralls, p. 62.

48 *Gest*, stanzas 439–41.

49 The author cites his own research and visits to the church here.

50 Knight and Ohlgren, p. 53: the editors believe that a substantial amount of text is missing.

51 *Gest*, lines 59–60.

52 *Gest*, lines 615–16.

53 See also Chapter 1.

54 NationMaster.com.

55 Gisborne wounds Robin, who later calls on the Virgin Mary to invigorate him: *Gisborne* ballad, stanza 39.

56 Beard, p. 28; *Statutes of the Realm*, i, 140.

57 Beard, p. 29.

58 *Gest*, stanzas 317–18.

59 Pollard, p. 185; J.R. Maddicott, *The Birth and Setting of the Robin Hood Ballads*, pp. 276–99.

60 Lord, pp. 247–55.

Chapter 8. To Rob from the Rich to Give to the Poor

1 Burman, *Knights of God*, pp. 26–38; Partner, pp. 3–26; Lord, pp. 5–8.

2 Lord, p. 221.

3 Aside from Major's chronicle and the loan scene in the *Gest*, one of the earliest examples of Robin Hood's reputation is given in Martin Parker's *True Tale of Robin Hood*. The ballad, the first known to concern the Earl

of Huntingdon, plays on Robin having been outlawed for debt and develops the fellowship code of the *Gest* by illustrating his love for the poor. Stanzas 19–21 of the ballad read:

> But Robbin Hood so gentle was,
> And bore so brave a minde,
> If any in distresse did passe,
> To them he was so kinde
>
> That he would give and lend to them,
> To helpe them at their neede:
> This made all poore men pray for him,
> And wish he well might speede.
>
> The widdow and the fatherlesse
> He would send meanes unto,
> And those whom famine did oppresse
> Found him a friendly foe.

4   Lord, p. 240.

5   *Gest*, stanzas 198–9; Pollard, p. 113.

6   Further reading: Pollard, Chapter 5.

7   Pollard, p. 149.

8   *Monk*, lines 21–34.

9   *Gisborne*, stanzas 40–41.

10 See p. 52.

11 *Scotichronicon*.

12 *Gest*, stanzas 206–7.

13 *Gest*, stanzas 268–73.

14 *Gest*, stanza 9.

15 Pollard, p. 149.

16 Ralls, pp. 36–41, 41–3.

17 Ibid, pp. 41–3.

18 Ibid, p. 38.

19 Lord, p. 252.

20 Ibid, pp. 148–9.

21 *Gest*, lines 31–6.

22 Jansen, *The Making of Magdalene*.

23 Kripal, *The Serpent's Gift*, pp. 50–56.

24 Luke 8:2.

25 John 20:11–18.

26 Ralls, pp. 118–24.

27 Ibid.

28 See Chapter 7, note 8.

29 *Gest*, lines 57–8.

30 *Gest*, stanza 89.

31 *Gest*, fyttes 2 and 4.

32 Pollard, pp. 122–5.

33 Holt, pp. 84–5; Pollard, p. 92; Hahn, p. 68; Child V, p. 44.

34 Pollard, p. 114.

35 Lord, pp. 107–8, 252.

36 The exceptions were the strange circumstances at the battles of Dunbar and Falkirk in 1296 and 1298 when the Templar master in Scotland, Brian de Jay, took up arms against the Scots.

37 Child III, p. 191.

38 *Gest*, stanza 221.

39 *Monk*, stanzas 21–3.

40 Knight and Ohlgren, p. 51.

41 *Penny Cyclopaedia of the Society for the Diffusion of Useful Knowledge*, p. 540.

42 In 1473–4 Edward IV is identified as having respected the privilege of sanctuary in the case of a Roger Marshall at

Durham after his escape from gaol: A.R. Myers, *English Historical Documents 1327–1485*.

43 *Monk*, line 85; see also Knight and Ohlgren's endnote, p. 51.
44 *Gest*, fytte 8.
45 *Gest*, stanza 386.
46 Lord, pp. 204–19.
47 *Monk*, stanzas 86–8.
48 *Gest*, stanzas 67–8.
49 Ralls, pp. 132–4.
50 *Gest*, line 388. See also Knight and Ohlgren, p. 155.
51 *Gest*, fytte 2.
52 Christopher Tyerman, *England and the Crusades, 1095–1588*, p. 230.
53 Ibid, p. 241.
54 *Gest*, stanza 10.
55 Ralls, p. 42; Lord, pp. 161–3.

Chapter 9. A Hidden Divinity

1 *Gisborne*, stanza 33.
2 *Potter*, stanza 2.
3 See pp. 31–2.
4 Knight and Ohlgren, pp. 269–80; Holt, p. 16.
5 Child III, p. 90.
6 Knight and Ohlgren, pp. 281–90.
7 Ibid, p. 458.
8 *Friar* ballad, stanzas 1–9. In this ballad, Scarlock's name is spelt Scadlock, although it is undoubtedly the same man as in previous ballads.
9 *Friar*, stanzas 10–33. The ballad refers to the number of dogs as being 'for every man a dog'.

10 *Friar*, stanzas 35–8.

11 The Garland version also refers to the friar as a yeoman. See Child or Knight and Ohlgren's endnote, p. 466. In the interests of consistency, my numbering of the stanzas coincides with their version.

12 Knight and Ohlgren, pp. 458–9.

13 In the play *Robin Hood and the Sheriff*, lines 32 and 36 refer to him as 'Frere Tuke'.

14 The Sloane Manuscript.

15 Child III, p. 121. In another version of the ballad he is described as 'cutted'.

16 Child was also aware of this: ibid. In addition, the Knights Templar developed good relations with the Cistercians: Ralls, p. 54.

17 Child III, p. 41; Holt, pp. 58–9.

18 The American author Washington Irving confused the matter by claiming that Fountain Dale was the location of the fight. Irving, *Abbotsford and Newstead Priory*, p. 237.

19 *Friar*, stanzas 37–8.

20 *Friar*, stanza 34.

21 Sloane Manuscript.

22 Ronald Hutton, *Stations of the Sun*, pp. 224–5. The author even goes as far as to suggest that there is evidence to believe that they antedate history.

23 Thomas Hahn, *Robin Hood in Popular Culture: Violence, Transgression and Justice*, p. 244.

24 Anthony Aveni, *The Book of the Year*, pp. 77–82.

25 Hahn, pp. 239–49; Frank McLynn, *The Lionheart and Lackland*, pp. 243–5; Aveni, pp. 85–6; Andrew Sinclair, *The Sword and the Grail*, pp. 89–107; Knight, *A Mythic Biography*, pp. 202–4. Puck's alias as Robin Goodfellow has successfully convinced some people that Robin

Hood's art of trickery originates from the mischievous fairy. If anything, the name Robin Goodfellow seems to have originated after the Robin Hood ballads appeared in print. It should also be remembered that forest spirits were associated with magic, whereas Robin Hood is a symbol of piety.

26 Hahn, p. 242; Costa, *Mary's Day and Mary's Month*.

27 Knight, *A Complete Study*, p. 104.

28 David Wiles, *The Early Plays of Robin Hood*, pp. 31–42.

29 Pollard, p. 11; Knight and Ohlgren, p. 269; Lancashire, p. 134; Hutton, *Stations of the Sun*, pp. 226–43; Hahn, p. 239.

30 Ronald Hutton, *The Rise and Fall of Merry England*, p. 31.

31 Wiles, p. 3.

32 Hutton, *The Rise and Fall of Merry England*, p. 31.

33 Holt, p. 160.

34 Hutton, *Stations of the Sun*, pp. 270–73.

35 Holt, p. 160.

36 Holt, p. 160; William Burton Wilson, *Mirour de l'Omme (The Mirror of Mankind)*, pp. 119, 279.

37 Jeffrey Richards, *Swordsmen of the Screen*, p. 190.

38 Holt, p. 162; Pollard, p. 15.

39 Holt, p. 162. See also Wiles, *The Early Plays*.

40 Richardson and Everington, *Magna Carta Ancestry*, p. 344; Painter and Qubain, *The Reign of King John*, particularly the seeds of revolt chapter.

41 *Marian* ballad, lines 1–85; Child III, p. 218.

42 Child III, pp. 214–15; *Breeding* ballad.

43 Stanza 1 of the *Golden Prize* ballad:

> I have heard talk of bold Robin Hood,
> Derry derry down
> And of brave Little John,

Of Fryer Tuck, and Will Scarlet,
Loxley, and Maid Marion.
Hey down derry derry down.

44 See also Hutton, *Stations of the Sun*, pp. 270–71.

*Chapter 10. Sir Robin of Locksley's Birth, Breeding, Valour
and Marriage*

1 As seen on p. 143, identified in Hutton's *Rise and Fall of
Merry England*, participation in the May Day games
varied, with twenty-four locations incorporating Robin
Hood into the proceedings as king or assisting the king.
The fact that such events did not occur in the north of
England or Wales indicates that perceptions of Robin
Hood varied. Participation in Scotland occurred: Wiles p. 3;
but Child indicates that the tradition of Robin Hood in
Scotland included many rhymes and ballads still to find
their way into a common collection: Child, p. 187.

2 Holt, p. 159; see also Hutton, *Stations of the Sun*, and
Child III, p. 44.

3 See also Pollard, Chapter 3, in particular pp. 58, 64–5.

4 Further reading: Holt, Chapter VI.

5 Hutton, *Rise and Fall of Merry England*, p. 33; Wiles,
pp. 16–17, 45–53.

6 Holt, p. 161; Hutton, *Stations of the Sun*, pp. 270–71;
Hutton, *Rise and Fall of Merry England*, p. 32.

7 Hall's *Chronicle*, p. 582. Patrick Valentine Harris draws
attention in his book to the point that Maid Marian and
Friar Tuck were not present. The absence of Maid Marian is
no surprise considering Barclay spoke of Robin and Marian
as separate entities in 1508, yet the absence of Tuck is also
quite significant. The fragment of the play from 1475, *Robin*

Hood and the Sheriff, confirms that Tuck was a known
character by the time of the Shooter's Hill performance, but
his absence, in addition to his non-appearance in the ballads,
does suggest he was not regarded as an important character
prior to the play of 1560. See Harris, p. 40.

8 Dobson and Taylor, p. 34.

9 Knight and Ohlgren, pp. 563–4; Child III, p. 197.

10 *Catherine* ballad.

11 Henry's first wife, Catherine of Aragon, formerly the wife
of Henry's brother, married on 11 June 1509, marriage
annulled on 23 May 1533; his fifth wife, Catherine Howard,
married on 28 July 1540, stripped of her role as queen on
22 November 1541 and executed on 13 February 1542; his
sixth wife, Catherine Parr, married on 12 July 1543, died on
5 September 1548, outliving Henry.

12 Ritson, p. 170; Child III, pp. 205–6; ballad of *Robin Hood's
Chase*.

13 Hutton, *The Rise and Fall of Merry England*, p. 67.

14 Holt, p. 161, Pollard, p. 173.

15 See p. 48–9.

16 *Rotuli Parliamentorum*, v. 16.

17 Holt, p. 160; Pollard, p. 174.

18 Holt, p. 58; Pollard, p. 110.

19 Strayer, *Dictionary of the Middle Ages*, p. 435.

20 Sélincourt, *Great Raleigh*, p. 212.

21 At least no other chronicles have survived.

22 Knight and Ohlgren, p. 25. The editors here outline the
point that *Scotichronicon* was not meant for public
consumption.

23 Broadie, p. 23.

24 From Leland's *Collectanea*, 1540.

25 See Chapter 11.

26 In some cases Major has clearly leaned on the ballads.

27 John Stow, *The Annales of England*, p. 227.

28 From the Sloane Manuscript.

29 Ibid.

30 *Birth, Breeding, Valour and Marriage* ballad, stanza 2.

31 The argument that Robin Hood and Sir Robert of Locksley are effectively two separate entities goes to ridiculous lengths. In the first stanza of *Robin Hood's Golden Prize*, Loxley even appears as a character in his own right. Knight and Ohlgren also make note of this: see Chapter 9, note 43.

32 *True Tale* ballad, stanzas 1–3.

33 *True Tale*; Child V, pp. 353–4; Ritson, p. 91; Knight and Ohlgren, p. 602.

34 *True Tale*, stanzas 1–20.

35 The ending is consistent with the *Gest* and the later *Death* ballad. The reference to Robin Hood's men fleeing to the Scottish king is in keeping with traditional family connections between the Earls of Huntingdon and the Scottish Crown.

36 *Breeding* ballad, stanza 6.

37 *Breeding*, stanza 4.

38 *Breeding*, stanza 5.

39 Most of the information on Guy of Warwick is from Richmond, *The Legend of Guy of Warwick*.

40 This was also the view of Knight and Ohlgren.

41 It is sometimes known as *Robin Hood and Will Scarlet*.

42 *Newly Revived* ballad, lines 68–73.

43 *Death* ballad, Child III, p. 103. For the *Gisborne* ballad, Child III, pp. 89–93, see also Chapter 1; *Curtal Friar*, Child III, pp. 120–28; *Butcher*, Child III, pp. 115–19.

44 The feast of Michaelmas falls on 29 September.

45 *As You Like It*, Act I, Scene I.

46 Cairncross, *Shakespeare and the Golden Age*, p. 1; Roe, *John Keats and the Culture of Dissent*, p. 142.

47 From the poem *Work and Days* by Hesiod.

48 Cairncross, p. 1; further reading: Hutton, *The Rise and Fall of Merry England*. See also Chapter 12.

49 *As You Like It*, Act II, Scene III.

50 Keen, p. 183; Harris, p. 45.

51 *Ivanhoe*.

Chapter 11. Here Lies Bold Robin Hood?

1 Holt, pp. 174–9; Keen, pp. 143, 187; Child III, p. 47.

2 Ritson, Frank and Bewick, pp. cxxv–cxxvii; Holt, pp. 178–179; Brome, *An Historical Account of Mr Rogers's Travels*, pp. 90–91; Harris, p. 42.

3 Holt, p. 42.

4 *Gest*, stanza 437.

5 In *Scotichronicon* Bower refers to Robin Hood avoiding the anger of the king and threats of the prince. It is quite conceivable that Bower was referring to stanza 450 of the *Gest* where Robin has fled the king's service and remains an outlaw for the rest of his life.

6 *Gest*, stanzas 450–56.

7 *Gest*, stanza 451.

8 Greenwood and Whitaker, *The Early Ecclesiastical History of Dewsbury in the West Riding of the County of York*, pp. 112–14.

9 *Gest*, stanza 452.

10 Child III, p. 103; Knight and Ohlgren, pp. 592–3. Ritson also supports the ballad's age: Ritson, p. 231.

11 *Death* ballad, stanzas 1–9, as they appear in Knight and Ohlgren. The wager is identical to the circumstances of the

Monk ballad where Robin refuses to pay Little John. They also argue in the *Gisborne* ballad.

12 *Gest*, line 1804, and *Death*, stanza 12.

13 *Death*, version A, stanzas 16–17.

14 *Death*, version A, stanzas 18–19.

15 *Death*, version B, stanzas 16–19.

16 Page, *A History of the County of York*, Vol. 3, p. 170.

17 J.W. Walker located the name of a Roger of Doncaster as a chaplain in the 1300s, although it is impossible to prove this man was involved in any ungodly activities.

18 Further reading: Richard Rutherford-Moore, *On the Outlaw Trail*.

19 *Gisborne*, lines 113–14; in *Robin Hood's Progress to Nottingham* Robin is said to have shot a hart from a distance of 550 yards.

20 See Chapter 10, note 24.

21 *Chronicle at Large*. See Chapter 2, note 20.

22 In the *Gest* the arrow is not mentioned.

23 Keen, p. 178.

24 *Chronicle at Large*.

25 *Camden's Britannia*, 1789 edition.

26 Herendeen, *William Camden*.

27 Harris, p. 36; Holt, p. 41; Keen, p. 180.

28 See Grafton.

29 Keen, p. 179; Holt, pp. 41–2; Harris, p. 38.

30 Ritson, p. xxxviii; Holt, p. 42.

31 Child III, p. 233.

32 *True Tale* ballad; Child III, pp. 107, 233.

33 *True Tale* ballad, stanza 103.

34 Thoresby, *Ducatus Leodiensis*.

35 Gough, *Sepulchral Monuments*, p. cviii.

36 Ibid.

37 Rutherford-Moore.

38 Ritson, Frank and Bewick, p. iv.

39 Phillips, p. 100.

40 The dating of 24 December seems to be incorrect.

41 See David Hepworth, 'A Grave Tale', in Helen Phillips,
    Robin Hood: Medieval and Post Medieval, pp. 91–112.

42 Ibid.

43 Quoted in *Sepulchrorum Inscriptions* from 1727:

> Here underneath this little stone
> Thro' Death's assaults, now lieth one
> Known by the name of Robin Hood
> Who was a thief, and archer good
> Full thirteen years, and something more
> He robb'd the rich to feed the poor
> Therefore, his grave bedew with tears
> And offer for his soul your prayers.

A further inscription is found in *The Travels of Tom Thumb over England and Wales* by Roger Dodsley, dated 1746:

> Here under this memorial stone
> Lies Robert earl of Huntingdon
> As he, no archer e'er was good
> And people called him Robin Hood
> Such outlaws as his men and he
> Again may England never see.

44 Keen, p. 182; Harris, p. 43; Jeffrey Singman, *Robin Hood: The Shaping of a Legend*, p. 108.

45 Dodsworth Manuscript 160, fol. 64b.

46 Keen, p. 182.

Chapter 12. True Tales of Robin Hood

1   See Grafton.
2   Holt, pp. 42–3.
3   Robert Sibbald, *The History, Ancient and Modern, of the Sheriffdoms of Fife and Kinross*, pp. 403–4.
4   Ibid.
5   Thomas Percy, *Reliques of Ancient English Poetry*, p. 104.
6   See the introduction to *Ivanhoe* by Ian Duncan.
7   Further reading: Hutton, *The Rise and Fall of Merry England*, and Hill, *Intellectual Origins of the English Revolution Revisited*, Chapter 17.
8   Ritson, p. xxxiv.
9   *Ivanhoe*, Chapter 27.
10 Burke, p. 65.
11 Ibid, pp. 67–8.
12 William Hazlitt, *Merry England*.
13 See pp. 42–4.
14 Child III, pp. 43, 49, 51, 53, 95, 109, 179, 191, 211.
15 See also Holt, pp. 54–5.
16 See also Dobson and Taylor, pp. 11–12.
17 *Encyclopaedia Britannica* also makes a number of references to the possibility that Hood was a dialectal alternative to 'Wood'.
18 Holt, p. 189; L.V.D. Owen in the *Times Literary Supplement* of February 1936.
19 *Potter*, fytte 2.
20 *Gest*, lines 115–16; 901–2.
21 Keen, p. 196; Holt, p. 98; Brian Benison, *Robin Hood: The Real Story*.
22 Holt, p. 98.
23 Benison.

24 Keen, p. 196.

25 It should also be remembered that de Montfort was an Earl of Chester, although his name, of course, was never Ranulf.

26 Child V, p. x.

27 See Chapter 4.

28 This was also the view of Maurice Keen: Keen, p. 176.

29 Keen, p. xviii.

30 It was in 1377 that Robin Hood was mentioned in *Piers Plowman*.

31 See also Holt, p. 54; Knight and Ohlgren, p. 22.

32 Bradbury, *The Medieval Siege*, p. 142. The reference is not to Nottingham but merely the siege itself in July 1300.

33 Prestwich, *Plantagenet England*, pp. 223–4.

34 Holt, pp. 45–6.

35 Harris, p. 67; originally from Hunter.

36 Harris, p. 67; originally from the *Journal de la Chambre*.

37 Hunter, p. 63.

38 It was Camden who first proposed that Plompton Park was in Cumbria and was hence Hunter's source. Yet there is also a Plompton in Yorkshire and another in Lancashire.

39 Holt, pp. 101–4.

40 Rothwell, *English Historical Documents 1189–1327*, pp. 566–7. Knight and Ohlgren also made note of this: p. 54, endnote 246.

41 See pp. 112–14.

42 It may have been sixteen with Eleanor.

43 Poem IV of Lawrence Minot in 1339 begins:

> Edward oure cumly king
> in Braband has his woning
> with mani cumly knight.

And in that land, trewly to tell,

ordanis he still for to dwell,

to time he think to fight. [II. 1–6]

44 Further reading for Edward III: McKisack, *Oxford History of England, Fourteenth Century: 1307–1399*; Ormrod, *The Reign of Edward III*; Prestwich, *Plantagenet England*.

45 Black, p. 78.

46 *Gest*, stanza 10.

47 See Chapter 8.

48 Lord, pp. 16–19.

49 Gerald of Wales, trans. Thorpe, *The Journey through Wales*, p. 204.

50 Lord, p. 114; Wilkins, *Conciliae Magnae Britannae et Hiberniae*, Vol. 2, pp. 371–2.

51 Further reading: Lord, p. 114, name evidence for Yorkshire.

52 Sinclair, *The Sword and the Grail*, pp. 104–7.

53 Ralls, pp. 183–4.

54 Ibid, p. 133. This was also noted by Andrew Sinclair: Sinclair, p. 106.

55 See Chapter 6.

BIBLIOGRAPHY

Primary sources are acknowledged in the Notes and References.

Alexander, Michael, *Medievalism: The Middle Ages in Modern England*, New Haven and London: Yale University Press, 2007

Aveni, Anthony F., *The Book of the Year: A Brief History of Our Seasonal Holidays*, New York: Oxford University Press, 2004

Barber, Malcolm, *The New Knighthood: A History of the Order of the Temple*, New York: Cambridge University Press, 1994

———, *The Trial of the Templars* (1st edn), Cambridge and New York: Cambridge University Press, 1976

———, *The Trial of the Templars* (2nd edn), Cambridge and New York: Cambridge University Press, 2006

Beard, Charles Austin, *Office of the Justice of the Peace in England in Its Origin and Development,* New York: Burt Franklin, 1961

Benison, Brian, *Robin Hood: The Real Story*, Mansfield: Leslie Brian Benison, 2004

Black, Jeremy, *A New History of England: United Kingdom*, Basingstoke: Palgrave MacMillan, 2002

Bower, Walter and Watt, D.E.R., *Scotichronicon: In Latin and English*, Aberdeen: Aberdeen University Press, 1987

Bradbury, Jim, *The Medieval Archer*, Woodbridge: Boydell and Brewer, 1985

Broadie, Alexander, *The Circle of John Mair: Logic and Logicians in Pre-Reformation Scotland*, Oxford: Clarendon Press, 1985

——, *The Tradition of Scottish Philosophy*, Edinburgh: Polygon, 1990

Burgess, Glyn, *Two Medieval Outlaws: The Romance of Eustache the Monk and Fulk Fitz Waryn*, Rochester, New York: D.S. Brewer, 1997

Burke, John, *An Illustrated History of England*, London: Book Club Associates, 1974

Burman, Edward, *The Templars: Knights of God*, Rochester, Vermont: Destiny Books, 1986

——, *Supremely Abominable Crimes: The Trial of the Knights Templar*, London: Allison and Busby, 1994

Carpenter, D.A., *The Minority of Henry III*, London: Hambleton, 1996

Chancellor, John, *The Life and Times of Edward I*, London: Weidenfeld and Nicolson, 1981

Chibnall, Marjorie, *The Debate on the Norman Conquest*, New York and Manchester: Manchester University Press, 1999

Child, Francis James, *The English and Scottish Popular Ballads*, Vol. III, New York: Dover Publications, 2003, originally between 1882 and 1898

List of ballads as they appear in Child:

115. *Robyn and Gandeleyn*

116. *Adam Bell, Clim of the Clough and William of Cloudesly*

117. *Gest of Robyn Hode*
118. *Robin Hood and Guy of Gisborne*
119. *Robin Hood and the Monk*
120. *Robin Hood's Death*
121. *Robin Hood and the Potter*
122. *Robin Hood and the Butcher*
123. *Robin Hood and the Curtal Friar*
124. *The Jolly Pindar of Wakefield*
125. *Robin Hood and Little John*
126. *Robin Hood and the Tanner*
127. *Robin Hood and the Tinker*
128. *Robin Hood and the Newly Revived*
129. *Robin Hood and the Prince of Aragon*
130. *Robin Hood and the Scotchman*
131. *Robin Hood and the Ranger*
132. *The Bold Pedlar and Robin Hood*
133. *Robin Hood and the Beggar*, I
134. *Robin Hood and the Beggar*, II
135. *Robin Hood and the Shepherd*
136. *Robin Hood's Delight*
137. *Robin Hood and the Pedlars*
138. *Robin Hood and Allen a Dale*
139. *Robin Hood's Progress to Nottingham*
140. *Robin Hood Rescuing Three Squires*
141. *Robin Hood Rescuing Will Stutly*
142. *Little John a Begging*
143. *Robin Hood and the Bishop*
144. *Robin Hood and the Bishop of Hereford*
145. *Robin Hood and Queen Katherine*
146. *Robin Hood's Chase*
147. *Robin Hood's Golden Prize*
148. *The Noble Fisherman or Robin Hood's Preferment*

149. *Robin Hood's Birth, Breeding, Valour and Marriage*
150. *Robin Hood and Maid Marian*
151. *The King's Disguise, and Friendship with Robin Hood*
152. *Robin Hood and the Golden Arrow*
153. *Robin Hood and the Valiant Knight*
154. *A True Tale of Robin Hood*
——, *English and Scottish Ballads*, Vol. V, Boston: Little Brown and Company, 1858
Colton, Trish and Holloway, Diane, *The Knights Templar in Yorkshire*, Stroud: Sutton, 2008
Coss, Peter R. and Lloyd, S.D., *Thirteenth Century England*, Vol. II, Woodbridge: Boydell and Brewer, 1988
Dixon, William Scarth, *Hunting in the Olden Days*, Whitefish, Montana: Kessinger Publishing, 2004
Dixon-Kennedy, Mike, *The Robin Hood Handbook*, Stroud: Sutton, 2006
Dobson, Richard Barrie and Taylor, John, *The Rymes of Robin Hood: An Introduction to the English Outlaw*, London: Heinemann, 1976
Dobson, Richard Barrie, Vauchez, Andre, Walford, Adrian and Lapidge, Michael, *Encyclopaedia of the Middle Ages*, New York: Routledge, 2000
Doel, Fran and Doel, Geoff, *Robin Hood: Outlaw and Greenwood Myth*, Stroud: Tempus, 2000
Driver, Jack M., *The Templars: Holy Warrior Monks of the Ancient Lands*, London: Kandour, 2007
Dworkin, Dennis, *Cultural Marxism in Postwar Britain: History, the New Left, and the Origins of Cultural Studies*, Durham, North Carolina: Duke University Press, 1997
Encyclopaedia Britannica, 11th edn, Cambridge: Cambridge University Press, 1911

Flori, Jean and Birrell, Jean, *Richard the Lionheart: King and Knight*, Edinburgh: Edinburgh University Press, 2007

Gibson, Robert, *Best of Enemies: Anglo-French Relations Since the Norman Conquest*, Exeter: Impress Books, 2005

Gilbert, Henry, *Robin Hood*, Ware: Wordsworth, 1994

Gillingham, John, *Richard the Lionheart* (2nd edn), New York: Times Books, 1978

——, *Richard Coeur de Lion: Kingship, Chivalry and War in the Twelfth Century*, London and Rio Grande, Ohio: Hambleton Continuum, 1994

Gillingham, John and Fraser, Antonia, *The Life and Times of Richard I*, London: Book Club Associates, 1973

Gilpin, William and Lauder, Sir Thomas Dick, *Remarks on Forest Scenery, and Other Woodland Views*, Edinburgh: Fraser, 1834

Green, Barbara, *Secrets of the Grave*, Brighouse, Vermont: Palmyra Press, 2001

Hahn, Thomas, *Robin Hood in Popular Culture: Violence, Transgression and Justice*, Cambridge: D.S. Brewer, 2000

Hallam, Elizabeth, *The Four Gothic Kings: The Turbulent History of Medieval England and the Plantagenet Kings (1216–1377) Henry III, Edward I, Edward II, Edward III – Seen Through the Eyes of Their Contemporaries*, New York: Weidenfeld and Nicolson, 1987

Harris, Patrick Valentine, *The Truth about Robin Hood*, Mansfield: Linney, 1978

Harvey, John, *The Plantagenets, 1154–1485*, London: Batsford, 1948

Herendeen, Wyman H., *William Camden: A Life in Context*, Rochester, New York: Boydell Press, 2007

Hill, Christopher, *Intellectual Origins of the English Revolution Revisited*, Oxford: Oxford University Press, 2001

Hilton, R.H., *Bond Men Made Free: Medieval Peasant Movements and the English Rising of 1381*, London: Routledge, 1973

——, *Past and Present*, 1958, pp. 30–44

——, *Peasants, Knights, and Heretics: Studies in Medieval English Social History*, New York and Cambridge: Cambridge University Press, 1976

Holt, Sir James Clark, *Colonial England, 1066–1215*, London: Continuum, 1997

——, *Magna Carta*, Cambridge: Cambridge University Press, 1992

——, *The Northerners: A Study in the Reign of King John*, Oxford: Oxford University Press, 1961

——, *Robin Hood*, London: Thames and Hudson (1st edn), 1982

——, *Robin Hood*, London: Thames and Hudson (2nd edn), 1989

Howarth, Stephen, *The Knights Templar*, London: Collins, 1982

Hutchison, Harold, *Edward II: The Pliant King*, London: Eyre and Spottiswoode, 1971

Hutton, Ronald, *The Rise and Fall of Merry England: The Ritual Year 1400–1700*, New York: Oxford University Press, 1996

——, *Stations of the Sun: A History of the Ritual Year in Britain*, Oxford and New York: Oxford University Press, 1997

Irving, Washington, *Abbotsford and Newstead Abbey*, London: John Murray, 1835

Johnson, Thomas Burgeland, *The Hunting Directory*, London: Printed for Sherwood, Gilbert and Piper, 1826

Keen, Maurice Hugh, *Outlaws of Medieval Legend*, Toronto: University of Toronto Press, 1978

——, *The Penguin History of Medieval Europe*, London: Penguin, 1991

Knight, Stephen Thomas, *A Complete Study of the English Outlaw*, Oxford: Blackwell, 1994

——, *Robin Hood: A Mythic Biography*, Ithaca, New York: Cornell University Press, 2003

Knight, Stephen Thomas and Ohlgren, Thomas, *Robin Hood and Other Outlaw Tales*, Kalamazoo, Michigan: Medieval Institute Publications, 1997

Kumar Krishan, *The Making of English National Identity*, Cambridge: Cambridge University Press, 2003

Labarge, Margaret Wade, *Simon de Montfort*, Bath: Chivers Press, 1972

Leigh, Richard and Baigent, Michael, *The Temple and the Lodge*, New York: Arcade Publishing, 1991

Lord, Evelyn, *The Knights Templar in Britain*, Harlow: Longman Pearson, 2004

Madden, Thomas, *A New Concise History of the Crusades*, Lanham, Maryland: Rowman and Littlefield, 2005

Maddicott, J.R., *Simon de Montfort*, New York: Cambridge University Press, 1994

Martin, Sean, *The Knights Templar: The History and Myths of the Legendary Military Order*, New York: Thunder's Mouth Press, 2005

McKisack, May, *Oxford History of England, Fourteenth Century: 1307–1399*, Oxford: Oxford University Press, 1963

McLynn, Frank, *Lionheart and Lackland*, London: Vintage, 2007

Musson, Anthony, *Boundaries of the Law: Geography, Gender and Jurisdiction in Medieval and Early Modern Europe*, Aldershot: Ashgate, 2005

——, *Public Order and Law Enforcement: The Local Administration of Criminal Justice 1294–1350*, Woodbridge: Boydell Press, 2001

Newman, Sharan, *The Real History Behind the Templars*, New York: Berkeley, 2007

Nicholson, Helen, *The Knights Templar: A New History*, Stroud: Sutton, 2001

O'Hanlon, Rosalind, *Caste, Conflict and Ideology*, Cambridge: Cambridge University Press, 2002

Ohlgren, Thomas, *Medieval Outlaws: Ten Tales in Modern English*, Stroud: Sutton, 1998

——, and Matheson, Lister M., *Robin Hood: The Early Poems, 1465–1560: Texts, Contexts, and Ideology*, Newark, DE: University of Delaware Press, 2007

Parker, Thomas, *The Knights Templar in England*, Tucson, Arizona: University of Arizona Press, 1963

Partner, Peter, *The Murdered Magicians: The Templars and Their Myth*, New York: Oxford University Press, 1982

Parry, Edward Abbott, *Vagabonds All*, London: Cassell, 1926

Phillips, Helen, *Robin Hood: Medieval and Post Medieval*, New York and London: Cornell University Press, 2003

Pollard, Andrew James, *Imagining Robin Hood: The Late Medieval Stories in Historical Context*, London and New York: Routledge, 2004

Potter, Lewis, *Playing Robin Hood: The Legend as Performance in Five Centuries*, Newark, Delaware: University of Delaware, 1998

Powicke, Maurice, *Oxford History of England, 1216–1302*, Oxford: Oxford University Press, 1963

Prestwich, Michael, *Edward I*, London: Methuen, 1988

——, *Plantagenet England, Oxford History of England: 1225–1360*, Oxford: Oxford University Press, 2007

——, *The Three Edwards: War and State in England 1272–1377*, London and New York: Routledge, 2003

Pringle, Patrick, *Stand and Deliver: Highwaymen from Robin Hood to Dick Turpin*, New York: Dorset Press, 1991

Pyle, Howard, *The Merry Adventures of Robin Hood*, New York: Dover, 1969

Ralls, Karen, *Knights Templar Encyclopaedia: The Essential Guide to the People, Places, Events, and Symbols of the Order of the Temple*, Franklin Lakes, New Jersey: New Page, 2007

——, *The Templars and the Grail*, Chicago, Illinois: Quest, 2003

Read, Paul Piers, *The Templars*, Cambridge, Massachusetts: Da Capo Press, 1999

Rhead, Louis, *Bold Robin Hood and His Outlaw Band – Their Famous Exploits in Sherwood Forest*, New York: Blue Ribbon, 1912

Richards, Jeffrey, *Swordsmen of the Screen: From Douglas Fairbanks to Michael York*, London: Routledge and Kegan Paul, 1977

Ritson, Joseph, *Robin Hood: A Collection of All the Ancient Poems, Songs, and Ballads, Now Extant, Relative to That Celebrated English Outlaw*, London: Printed for Longman, Hurst, Rees, Orme, and Brown, Paternoster Row; and T. Boys, Ludgate Hill, 1820

——, and Bewick, Thomas, *Robin Hood: A Collection of All the Ancient Poems, Songs, and Ballads, Now Extant, Relative to That Celebrated English Outlaw*, Vol. II, London: William Pickering, 1832

Roe, Nicholas, *John Keats and the Culture of Dissent*, Oxford: Oxford University Press, 1998

Rutherford-Moore, Richard, *The Legend of Robin Hood*, Chieveley: Capall Bann, 1999

——, *Robin Hood: On the Outlaw Trail*, Chieveley: Capall Bann, 2002

Saaler, Mary, *Edward II*, London: Rubicon Press, 1997

Scott, Walter, *Ivanhoe*, Oxford: Oxford University Press, 1998

Seward, Desmond, *The Monks of War: The Military Religious Orders*, Harmondsworth: Penguin, 1995

Sibbald, Robert, *The History, Ancient and Modern, of the Sheriffdoms of Fife and Kinross*, London: R. Tullis, 1803

Sinclair, Andrew, *The Sword and the Grail*, London: Arrow, 1994

Singman, Jeffrey, *Robin Hood: The Shaping of the Legend*, London: Greenwood Press, 1998

Stringer, K.J., *Earl David of Huntingdon 1152–1219: A Study in Anglo-Scottish History*, Edinburgh: Edinburgh University Press, 1986

Thirsk, Joan, *Rural England: A History of the Landscape*, Oxford: Oxford University Press, 2002

Thomas, Hugh, *Rivers of Gold: The Rise of the Spanish Empire*, London: Phoenix, 2004

Thoresby, Ralph and Hunter, Joseph, *The Diary of Ralph Thoresby . . . (1677–1724): Now First Published from the Original Manuscript*, London: H. Colburn and R. Bentley, 1830

Turner, Ralph and Heiser, Richard, *The Reign of Richard the Lionheart*, Harlow: Pearson Education, 2000

Tyerman, Christopher, *England and the Crusades, 1095–1588*, Chicago, Illinois: University of Chicago Press, 1996

Waithe, Marcus, *William Morris's Utopia of Strangers: Victorian Medievalism and the Ideal of Hospitality*, Cambridge: D.S. Brewer, 2006

Whitaker, Thomas Dunham and Greenwood, John Beswicke, *The Early Ecclesiastical History of Dewsbury in the West Riding of the County of York*, London: John Russell-Smith, 1859

Wiles, David, *The Early Plays of Robin Hood*, Cambridge: D.S. Brewer, 1981

Wright, Thomas, *Songs and Carols*, London: Percy Society, 1846

INDEX

Abbot of 'Unreason', 155
Abbot of Westminster, 19
abbots, 22, 23, 29, 31, 32, 68, 83, 104, 120, 121, 123, 126–7, 128, 131, 199, 209, 210
Acre, fall of, 90–91
Ad Providam, see Papal Bull
Adam Bell, 65–6, 71, 163, 206, 228, 229
Adam Bell, Clym of the Cloughe and Wyllyam of Cloudeslee, 65
Alexander III, King of Scotland, 62
Alfred 'the Great', King of Wessex, 41
Allan a Dale, 141, 170
Alphonso, Earl of Chester, son of Edward I ('Longshanks'), King of England, 209
Alton, pass of, 67
anticlericalism, *see* Robin Hood, relationship with religious officials
Aragon, Catherine of, Queen Consort of Henry VIII, 154, 243
Aragon, King of, 98
archery, *see* Robin Hood, skills attributed to
Arden, Forest of, 167
Armenia, 133
Armitage family, 176, 182, 185–8, 190
Arthur a Bland, 170
As You Like It, see Shakespeare's plays

Assizes of Arms, 57
Aston, Derbyshire, 155
Austria, 35, 171
d'Avranches, Hugh, 1st Earl of Chester, 39
d'Avranches, Richard, 2nd Earl of Chester, 39

Baldwin, Archbishop, 211
Baldwin II, King of Jerusalem, 89–90
Ballads about Robin Hood
  audience, 15, 17, 76, 148, 151–2, 155, 157
  development of, 160–66, 169–70
  popularity, 25, 27–8, 33, 54, 69, 71, 139, 145, 151, 153–6, 195–7
  Individual titles
  Gest of Robyn Hode, 14, 17–18, 21–3, 24, 25, 29, 33, 40, 43–4, 55–6, 66, 72–82, 84–5, 103–15, 120–23, 126–8, 130–36, 138, 141, 144–5, 149, 154, 158–60, 162, 165–6, 171, 173, 175–7, 181, 195, 199, 203–12, 216, 220–21, 223–4, 226, 230, 235–7, 244–6
  Robin Hood and Guy of Gisborne, 18, 20, 25, 33, 74, 105, 113, 121, 136, 138, 165, 180, 222, 236, 246
  Robin Hood and the Monk, 18–19, 24–5, 27, 33, 55, 65–6, 74–5, 80–81, 112–14, 120–22,

127, 129, 131, 138, 145, 149,
  165–6, 170, 206, 208–9, 221,
  222, 226–7, 233, 246
Robin Hood's Death, 18, 23,
  25, 40, 158, 165–6, 176–9,
  181, 233, 244
Robin Hood and the Potter, 18,
  21, 25, 27, 31, 33, 65, 73–4,
  78, 81–2, 113, 115, 136, 138,
  141, 165, 177, 204
Robin Hood and the Butcher,
  165–6
*Robin Hood and the Curtal
  Friar*, 137–41, 165–6, 171,
  229, 240
The Jolly Pinder of Wakefield,
  163, 165
Robin Hood and Little John,
  73, 171
Robin Hood and the Tanner,
  169, 229
Robin Hood and the Tinker, 169
*Robin Hood and the Newly
  Revived*, 73, 164, 229
*Robin Hood and the Prince of
  Aragon*, 166
Robin Hood and the Scotchman,
  169
Robin Hood and the Ranger,
  169, 229
*Robin Hood and the Bold
  Pedlar*, 73, 164, 229
Robin Hood and Allan a Dale,
  141
*Robin Hood's Progress to
  Nottingham*, 72, 229, 246
*Robin Hood Rescuing Three
  Squires*, 165–6
Little John a Begging, 165–6
Robin Hood and the Bishop,
  127–8
*Robin Hood and the Bishop of
  Hereford*, 121, 127
*Robin Hood and Queen
  Catherine*, 154, 165–6

Robin Hood's Chase, 154
Robin Hood's Golden Prize,
  108, 148, 244
*Robin Hood's Birth, Breeding,
  Valour and Marriage*, 148,
  160, 162–4
Robin Hood and Maid Marian,
  147
*The King's Disguise and
  Friendship with Robin Hood*,
  166
*Robin Hood and the Golden
  Arrow*, 170
A True Tale of Robin Hood, 71,
  160–62, 184–5, 199, 222, 236–7
Balliol, John, 62
Bannockburn, Battle of, 88
Barclay, Alexander, 145, 242
Barnsdale Bar, 106–7
Barnsdale Forest, 20–21, 24, 26, 28,
  32, 40, 44, 52, 54, 59, 64–5, 67,
  72, 105–7, 110–13, 126–7, 139,
  151, 168, 196, 205, 211, 223, 234
barons, 27, 39, 47–51, 53, 57–8, 61,
  79, 88, 109, 147, 200, 206, 225
Barons' War, the first (1215–16),
  39, 47–48, 147, 225
Barons' War, the second (1264–65),
  27, 50–51, 53, 57–8, 206
Beltane, *see* May Day Games,
  origins of
Benedict XI, Pope, 92
Benedictine, Order of, 127
Bengeworth Bridge, 51
bishops and archbishops, *see*
  Robin Hood, relationship with
  religious officials; *see also* Bishop
  of Hereford
Bishop of Hereford, 121, 127
Black Death, the, 200–201
Blidworth, St Mary's Church, *see*
  Will Scarlock, grave
Blondeville, Ranulf de, 6th Earl of
  Chester, 40, 42
Boniface VIII, Pope, 92

Bower ('Bowmaker'), Walter, 26–9,
31, 33, 46, 49, 51, 53, 54, 56, 58–9,
64, 66–9, 71, 74, 82, 84, 121–2,
126, 152, 155, 157, 169, 197,
204–7, 245
Britannia, see Camden, William
broadsides, 155
brotherhood, *see* fraternity
Burghwallis, 107

Caerlaverock, 207
Cambridge, 18, 199
Camden, William, 181–2, 186, 249
Campsall, 111–12, 126,
Canterbury, Archbishop of, 105
Carlisle, 65–6
castles of Edward I ('the iron
ring'), 62
Cecil, Sir Robert, 156
Charnwood Forest, 56, 205
Child, Francis, 15, 18, 21, 69, 72,
139, 165, 176–7, 183, 206, 220,
226, 229, 240, 242
Chronica Gentis Scotorum, 68
Chronicle at Large, 36, 158, 183
church ales, 143
Church, the, 41, 45, 47, 52, 84–5,
90–91, 93, 98–9, 117, 120, 124–9,
133, 137, 142–3, 145, 152, 157
Churchlees, *see* Kirklees
Cistercians, Order of, 139, 176, 240
civil wars of England, 47, 200, 225
Clairvaux, Bernard of, 123
Clement V, Pope, 89, 92–3, 94–5,
97, 98, 101, 105, 133, 211
Clermont, Council of, 89
Clorinda, Queen of the Shepherds,
148
Clym of Clough, *see* Adam Bell
Coke, Sir Edward, 41
Conservators of the Peace,
113–15, 208–9; *see also* Sheriff,
office of the
Coterel gang, 88, 102; *see also*
criminal gangs

courser, *see* horses
criminal gangs, 83, 88–9, 102, 127,
155–6, 205, 207
Crusades, the, 12, 34, 38, 41, 47,
58, 78, 89–92, 94, 97, 107–8, 118,
132–3, 198, 206, 213
Curtal Friar, Robin Hood and the,
see ballads about Robin Hood;
see also Friar Tuck
Cyprus, 91, 133

David I, King of Scotland, 27, 68
David of Doncaster, 170
David of Scotland, Earl of
Huntingdon, 38–40, 42, 44, 48,
159, 197–9, 207
De Gestis Scotorum, 46
Death, Robin Hood's, see ballads
about Robin Hood
*Death of Robert Earl of
Huntington, The, see* Munday,
Anthony
deer hunting, 11, 23, 43, 129, 148,
164, 202, 207–8
Derbyshire, 56, 113, 155, 190
destrier, *see* horses
Diana, Goddess of the Hunt, 142,
145, 149
'Disinherited', the, 51–4, 58, 66,
74, 76, 79, 130, 155, 204, 206
dissolution of the monasteries,
176
Dobson and Taylor, 15, 106–7
Dodsworth, Roger, 72, 174, 190
Doncaster, 21, 106–7
*Downfall of Robert Earl of
Huntington, The, see* Munday,
Anthony
Dunbar, Battle of, 62, 94, 238
Dunmow Priory, 146–7

Edward I ('Longshanks'), King of
England, 14, 26, 50–51, 53–4,
58–9, 61–4, 66–7, 87–8, 92, 94,
113, 130, 206–7, 209, 228, 234

Edward II 'of Carnarvon', King of England, 14, 62, 83, 87–9, 94–8, 101–2, 104–5, 114, 130, 133, 207–10, 220

Edward III 'of Windsor', King of England, 68, 207, 209, 234, 249

Edward 'our comely king', 23, 25, 29, 44, 46, 71–2, 84, 104, 159, 204, 206–7, 209, 221, 249

Edward 'the Confessor', King of England, 41, 229

Eleanor of Aquitaine, Queen Consort of Henry II, 34

Eleanor of Castile, Queen Consort of Edward I, 209, 249

Eleanor Plantagenet, wife of Simon de Montfort, 6th Earl of Leicester, 49

English common law, 41

Eustache the Monk, 13, 42, 71, 196, 203, 229

Evesham, Battle of, 27, 51, 56, 67, 204–6

Exchequer, the 37, 39, 159, 197

Exeter, 143

D'Eyville, John, 53, 58, 206

Falkirk, Battle of, 63, 94, 238

farms and farming, 57, 91, 94, 102, 107–8, 201, 205

Fawkes, Guy, 156, 216

fellow, 78, 80–81, 85, 108, 112, 118, 122, 126, 130–31, 133, 136, 141, 166, 171, 205, 210, 235

fellowship, 78–83, 85, 103, 115, 119, 132, 138, 141, 196, 210–11, 237

Fenwick Castle, 59, 204

Ferrers, William de, Sheriff of Nottingham, 42

Fevere, William Son of Robert le, see Robin Hood, as a surname and criminal label

Fitz Ooth, Robert, fictitious Earl of Huntingdon, 13; see also Stukeley, William

Fitzwalter, Lady Marian, 171; see also Maid Marian

Fitzwalter, Lady Matilda, 146–7

Fitzwalter, Sir Robert, 146–7, 160

Flynn, Errol, 171, 173, 196, 198

Foliot, Sir Richard, 56, 59, 204

Folville gang, 88, 102, 207; see also criminal gangs

Fordun, John, 26–7, 38, 46, 51, 68–9, 198, 206

foresters, 72, 77; see also Yeomen of the Forest

Fountain Dale, 139–40, 240

Fountains Abbey, 137, 139

Franciscan, Order of, 139

fraternity, 73–4, 76–83, 101, 103, 120, 144

Friar Tuck, 137–41, 143, 171, 242–3 as an alias, 139

Fulk FitzWarin, 13, 42–5, 71, 196, 202–3, 229

Gale, Thomas, 183–6, 188–9, 204

Gamble Gold, 164

Gamelyn, 203, 230

Gamwell, 163–4

garlands, 137–8, 155, 240

Garter, Order of the, 79

Gathelus of Greece, 46

Gaveston, Piers, 1st Earl of Cornwall, 87–8

Gelasius II, Pope, 90

Gent, Thomas, 187

Geoffrey, Duke of Brittany, son of Henry II, 34

George a' Greene, see Wakefield, Jolly Pinder of

Gerald of Wales, 211

Gernon, Ranulf de, 4th Earl of Chester, 39–40

Gest of Robyn Hode, see ballads about Robin Hood

Gilbert of the Whitehand, 54, 56, 81–2, 135
Gisborne, Guy of, 20, 28, 53, 113, 121, 127–8, 135, 236
Gisborne, Robin Hood and Guy of, see ballads about Robin Hood
Gisborne, Sir Guy of, 12, 171
Godberd, Roger, 56, 59, 67, 78, 84–5, 204–7
Goídel Glas, see Gathelus of Greece
Goldsborough, William of, 37, 180, 182, 185
Goodfellow, Robin, see Puck; *see also* Green Man
gospels, 124–5
Gough, Richard, 186–8
Gower, John, 144, 149
Grafton, Richard, 36–40, 44, 54, 71–2, 158–62, 180–83, 197–9, 223
Green Man, 142, 203
Gregory I, Pope, 124–5
Grey, Reginald de, Sheriff of Nottingham, 56, 205
Griffith, Llewelyn ap, 62
Gruffydd, Llywelyn ap, *see* Griffith, Llewelyn ap
guerrilla warfare, 56, 63, 84
guilds, 77–8, 124
Gurdon, Adam de, 67, 78, 84–5, 119
Gwynedd, Princes of, 62

Halle, Adam de la, 144–5, 148–9
Hampshire, 48
Hathersage, Derbyshire, *see* Little John, grave
Havilland, Olivia de, 171
Hazlitt, William, 202
Henry II ('Curtmantle'), King of England, 33–4, 38, 42, 139, 159, 176, 225
Henry III 'of Winchester', King of England, 14, 27–8, 48–51, 53–4,
56, 58–9, 61, 66, 72, 84, 94, 199, 206
Henry VIII, King of England, 106, 152, 154, 176, 243
Henry 'the Young', King of England, 33–4, 38, 225
Hereward the Wake, 13, 42, 71, 196, 203, 229
Herne the Hunter, 142
Hesiod, 168
Histoire de la Conquête de l'Angleterre pas les Normands, see Thierry, Jacques Nicholas Augustin
Historia Majoris Britanniae, 29, 31, 36, 45–6, 143, 146, 156, 197
hobbehod, *see* Robin Hood, as a surname and criminal label
Holderness, Robin of, *see* Robin Hood, as an alias
Holy Land, 34–6, 58, 61, 89, 91, 92, 101, 104, 107, 117, 118, 133, 164, 198, 211
Horns of Hattin, Battle of, 91, 211
horses, 22, 55, 103, 109–10, 143, 153, 235
human rights law, 45–6
Hunter, Joseph, 106, 174, 207–8, 235, 246, 249
Huntingdon, Earl of, *see* David of Scotland, Earl of Huntingdon; *see also* Robin Hood, as Earl of Huntingdon
Huntington, Earl of, *see* Munday, Anthony

Inchcolm Abbey, 68
Inglewood Forest, 26, 64–5, 67, 206
Ingram, Sir Robert, Sheriff of Nottingham, 114
Innocent III, Pope, 47
international law, 45
Ireland, 35, 47, 61, 99, 190

Isabella, 'she-wolf' of France,
Queen Consort of Edward II,
87, 207
Ismay, Joseph, 188–90
Ivanhoe, see Robin Hood, in
fiction; *see also* Scott, Sir Walter

James I, King of Scotland, 68
Jamieson, Robert, 18
Jerusalem, 89, 125
John I ('Lackland'), King of
England, 11–12, 33–5, 39, 41–3,
45, 47–8, 72, 94, 130, 136, 144,
146–7, 170–71, 194, 198–9, 202,
216, 225, 229
John of Scotland, Earl of
Huntingdon and 7th Earl of
Chester, 48
Johnston, Nathaniel, 182, 185,
187–8, 190
Jonson, Ben, 148–9
journeyman, 77

Keats, John, 173
Kenilworth, 88
Castle, 53, 58
Dictum of, 58, 66
Kevelioc, Hugh de, 5th Earl of
Chester, 40
King of May, *see* May Day Games
king's felon, 129–30
Kirklees Priory, 23, 40, 158,
175–82, 185–6, 189, 205, 212, 223
history of, 176
prioress of, 37, 162, 176–84, 186
Knights of Christ, Order of the, 98
Knights Hospitaller, Order of the,
92–3, 98, 133, 234
grant of Templar property, 98,
234
Knights Templar, Order of the,
14, 89–99, 101–5, 107–12, 115,
117–18, 120–21, 123, 125–6,
128–34, 139, 140, 170, 210–11,
231, 232, 234, 238, 240

history of, 89–99, 133
origins of, 89–90
decline, 91–7
arrests, 93–9
charges against, 93, 96–7, 213
imprisonment and torture, 93,
95–7
trial of, 97–8
dissolution of, 97–8, 211
assets of, 90–94, 96, 98, 104–5,
107–8, 119, 132–3
as bankers, 91, 92, 93, 94,
117–18, 132–3, 212–13
drapers, *see* hierarchy *below*
espionage and counter
espionage, 101–2
evasion of county sheriffs, 98,
101–2, 105, 112, 115, 130,
211–12
as farmers, 91, 102, 108
graves, 212
hierarchy, 102–4
horses, 103, 109–10
knights, *see* hierarchy *above*
Latin Rule, 90, 104, 109, 123,
125, 128, 232
mantle, 90, 103–4, 125
Mary Magdalene, *see* veneration
of saints
prayers, 123–4
relationship with the
Plantagenet kings, 94, 130
relationship with women, 134,
211
rules of conduct, 90, 101–3, 108,
117–24, 128, 132–4, 211, 212–13
sergeants, *see* hierarchy *above*
Templars in England, 94–7,
98–9, 101– 2, 104–5, 107–8,
111–12, 115, 211–14
in Kent, 97, 105, 214
in Yorkshire, 104–5, 107–8,
111–12, 126, 211–14
Templars in Ireland, 99
Templars in Scotland, 99

veneration of saints, 111–12, 124, 125–6
veneration of the Virgin Mary, 123–4, 211

Labourers, Statute of, 201
Lancashire, 23, 113, 162, 208, 249
Lancaster, Thomas Earl of, 208
Langland, William, 25, 28, 33, 39–40, 144, 198
Leicestershire, 56, 205
Leland, John, 106, 158, 180, 182
Leopold V, Duke of Austria, 35
Lewes, Battle of, 50–51
Leyburn, Roger, 53
Lincoln Cathedral, 25
Lincoln green, 103, 194, 200
Lincolnshire, 104, 113
Lindoris, 198
Little John, 12, 18–20, 22, 26–7, 31, 33, 43, 49, 52, 54–5, 64, 66–7, 69, 73–5, 77, 80–82, 84, 102–3, 106, 108, 112, 115, 122, 127, 131–2, 135, 155, 164–6, 171, 1 74, 177–8, 190, 203, 216, 226–7, 233, 246
  as an alias, 49
  grave, 174, 190
Loch Leven, 68
Locksley, see Robin Hood, legend of, as Sir Robin of Locksley
Longchamp, William, Bishop of Ely, 35
Lovetot, William de, Lord of Hallam, 160
Loxley, as a separate person, 242, 244
Loxley, Yorkshire, 160, 174

Magna Carta, 39, 47, 49, 51, 61, 147, 200, 216, 225
Maid Marian, 13, 32, 112, 143–9, 155, 160, 165, 171, 194, 242
Mair, John, see Major, John
Major, John, 29, 31–3, 36–8,

44–6, 49, 54, 64, 67, 72, 136, 143, 146, 152, 156–61, 167, 184, 195, 197–9, 204, 207, 221, 228, 230, 236, 244
Margaret, 'the maid' of Norway, 62
Marguerite, Queen Consort of Edward I, 209
Marianism, 142
Marshall, Roger, of Wednesday, see Robin Hood, as an alias
Mary Magdalene,
  chapel of, 111
  church of, 111, 126
  veneration of, 110–11, 124–6, 175
Maud of Chester, 38
May Day Games, 141–5, 149, 151–3, 155–6, 160, 173, 229, 242
  origins of, 141–2
  christianization of, 142–3, 149
  King of May, 143, 151–3, 195
  Queen of May, 143, 145, 153, 160
  Robin Hood in, 143–5, 149, 151–3, 155–6, 173, 229, 242
  decline and prohibition, 155–6
Merrie England, see Merry England
Merry Adventures of Robin Hood, see Robin Hood, in fiction; see also Pyle, Howard
Merry England, 168, 200–202
Merry Men, 11–13, 19, 20, 21, 22–3, 24, 32, 40, 54–7, 68, 72–84, 102–5, 107–10, 112, 115, 118–20, 128–9, 131–41, 144, 146, 148–9, 164, 166, 167, 170–171, 190, 194, 207, 210–11, 213, 220, 229
  assets of, 103–4, 109–10, 131–3
  livery and maintenance, 103–4
  military capabilities, 20, 23, 54, 56–7, 75, 77, 136, 210
  new recruits, 22, 73, 78, 81–2, 135, 137–8, 141, 146, 148, 164, 166, 170

origin of, 54, 56–8, 72–84,
102–5, 133, 137, 164, 211
rules of conduct, 79–81, 83–4,
102–4, 108, 118–20, 128,
131–5, 144, 210, 213
social status, see yeomen
structure, 54–7, 74–83, 102–4,
138, 140–41, 170, 211
Meschin, Ranulf le, 3rd Earl of
Chester, 39
meyne, 75, 156; see also Venables,
Piers
mills, 107
minstrels, 27–8, 52, 69, 141, 152,
170, 193
Mirour de l'omme, 144; see also
Mirror of Mankind
Mirror of Justices, 41
Mirror of Mankind, 145, 149
Molay, Jacques de, 92–3, 97, 123
Monk, Robin Hood and the, see
ballads about Robin Hood
monks, 19, 22, 43, 55, 81, 84, 89,
108, 118, 120, 121, 122, 126,
127–8, 129, 139–40, 145, 162,
166, 203, 204, 210
Montesa, Order of, 98
Montfort, Simon de, 6th Earl of
Leicester, 27–8, 49–53, 56, 58,
61–2, 67, 84–5, 204, 230, 249
Montfort, Simon de ('the
younger'), 7th Earl of Leicester,
53
More, William de la, 96
Mortimer, Roger de, 1st baron of
the Marches and Wigmore, 51,
53, 206
Mortimer, Roger de, 1st earl of
March, 207, 209
Motherwell, William, 69, 206
Mowbray, Roger, 104
Much the Miller's son, 19, 43,
54–5, 65, 74, 81–2, 102–3, 107,
110, 121, 127, 165, 171, 203,
226–7

Munday, Anthony, 37–8, 145–7,
149, 160, 162, 184, 197, 199, 222

Newgate, 56
Newstead Priory, 140
Nogaret, Guillaume de, 92, 232
Norman autonomy, 12, 34, 40–42,
62, 171, 200–202
Norman Conquest, 34, 111, 113,
170, 200
Norman–Saxon rivalry, 12, 40–41,
170–71, 200–202, 229
Norman Yoke, 40–41, 200–201; see
also Norman–Saxon rivalry
Normandy, Duchy of, 35
Normans, 12–13, 28, 41–2, 43,
146, 170–71, 200–201
Nottingham, 19, 21, 22–3, 39, 72,
104, 110, 113, 121–2, 140, 162,
174, 198, 207–8, 234, 249
Castle, 39, 198, 204
St Mary's Church, 19, 122
Sheriff of, see Sheriff of
Nottingham
Nottinghamshire, 56, 113, 115,
139–40, 160, 163, 205

Orygynale Cronykil of Scotland,
26, 28, 46, 63–4, 66–8, 157, 207,
213
outlawed gangs, see criminal gangs
Owen, L.V.D, 204
Oxenford, John de, Sheriff of
Nottingham, 114
Oxford, Provisions of, 50

packhorse, 109–10; see also horses
Palestine, 92
palfrey, see horses
Papal Bull (Ad Providam), see
Knights Hospitaller, Order of
the, grant of Templar property
Papal Bull (Pastoralis
Praeeminentiae), 94–5, 97, 98,
101, 104, 119, 130, 213

Papal Bull (*Vox in Excelso*), 97
Papal Inquisition, 95, 97, 99, 102, 119, 212
Parker, Martin, 71, 160–62, 184–5, 199, 222, 236
Parliament, 28, 49–51, 54, 61, 155, 156, 216
Pastoralis Praeeminentiae, see Papal Bull
Payens, Hugues de, 89
Peasants' Revolt, 41, 200
Percy Folio, 20, 154, 165–6, 176, 181
Percy, Bishop Thomas, 20, 165–6, 199, 226
Perth, Council of, 68
Philip II ('Augustus'), King of France, 34–5, 48
Philip IV ('le Bel'), King of France, 87, 89, 91, 92–3, 94, 96–8, 118
Piers Plowman, 25, 249
pilgrims and pilgrimages, 89, 91, 117, 128, 133, 164, 213
Plompton Park, 65, 207, 208, 249
Pontefract, 106, 107
posse comitatus, 114; *see also* Conservators of the Peace
Potter, the, 21, 73, 78, 81, 108, 164, 222
Potter, Robin Hood and the, see ballads about Robin Hood
preceptories, 101, 105, 119, 211–12, 214
Prince Edward, *see* Edward I '(Longshanks'), King of England
Prince John, *see* John I ('Lackland'), King of England
Puck, 142, 240; *see also* Green Man
Puritan interpretation of the Bible, 200
Pyle, Howard, 55, 103, 119, 170

quarterstaff, 73, 143, 229
Queen of May, *see* May Day Games

Rains, Claude, 171
Raleigh, Sir Walter, 156, 167
rangers, *see* foresters
Ranulf, Randolf, Randolph, Earl of Chester, 25, 39–40, 198, 202, 249
Rathbone, Basil, 171
Raven, William, 123
Red Roger, 178–9
Redesdale, Robin of, *see* Robin Hood, as an alias
Reliques of Ancient English Poetry, 199; *see also Percy Folio*
Reynold Greenleaf, 54, 56, 82
Richard at the Lee 'the poor knight', Sir, 21–3, 24, 44, 55, 56, 77–8, 80, 103, 108–10, 114, 118, 121, 122, 125–8, 131–3, 136, 146, 159, 162, 204, 208, 212–13, 216, 221, 224, 230, 235
Richard I 'the Lionheart', King of England, 12, 14, 25, 26, 28–9, 33–6, 38–9, 41–3, 44, 45–6, 47, 49, 67, 72, 106, 130, 136, 139, 144, 146, 159, 161–2, 165–6, 170–71, 184, 198–201, 203–4, 216, 224
Richard II 'of Bordeaux', King of England, 201
Richardson, Richard, 185
Ritson, Joseph, 15, 69, 187, 200, 226, 245
robbery, *see* Robin Hood, characteristics attributed to; *see also* criminal gangs
Robert I 'the Bruce', King of Scotland, 87–8
Robin et Marion, Le Jeu de, 144–145, 148–9
Robin Hood
    as an alias, 156, 204, 207
    as a criminal, 26–8, 45, 82, 83, 89, 128, 156, 203; *see also* Robin Hood, as an alias; Robin Hood, characteristics attributed to, robbery; violence and murder;

Robin Hood, as a surname and criminal label; king's felon assets of; *see* Merry Men, assets of
characteristics attributed to
courtesy, 17, 21, 23, 83–4, 128, 152, 155, 158, 195, 214
fellowship, 78, 80, 85, 103, 108, 112, 115, 122, 126, 130–33, 196, 205, 210–11, 237
generosity, 11, 22, 23, 24, 72, 118, 127, 162, 175, 195, 221
humour and comedy, 21, 27, 169
leadership, 12, 18, 21, 22–3, 29, 31, 72, 76, 78–81, 102–3, 152, 160, 196
loyalty, 11–12, 20, 23, 28, 53, 108, 166, 195, 215
piety, 18–19, 22–3, 28, 29, 52, 54, 84, 102, 108, 115, 119–22, 126–8, 134, 137, 144, 148–9, 152, 195, 210–11, 241
robbery, 19, 22, 28–9, 31–2, 36, 49, 52, 64, 83, 118, 126–9, 148, 155, 158, 162, 195, 203, 204, 205, 210
veneration of Mary Magdalene, *see* Mary Magdalene
veneration of the Virgin Mary, *see* Virgin Mary
violence and murder, 12, 20, 27–9, 31, 50, 52–4, 72, 82–3, 113, 121, 127, 129, 135, 170, 205
see also Merry Men, rules of conduct
in fiction
Ivanhoe, 140, 170, 199, 201
The Merry Adventures of Robin Hood, 55, 170
in film
Robin Hood and His Merry Men, 171
The Adventures of Robin Hood, 171

'gentrification', 144, 148–9, 157, 158–65; *see also* Robin Hood, as a historical figure; as a dux or duke; as an earl; as Earl of Huntingdon; Robin Hood, legend of, as Sir Robin of Locksley
as a historical figure
early references to, 17, 18, 20, 21, 25–9
among the 'disinherited', *see* 'disinherited' the; *see also* Godberd, Roger
death of, 23, 27, 37, 40, 144, 161–2, 175–9, 181, 184, 188, 204, 205, 212, 223, 247
as a dux or duke, 29, 36, 158, 160, 167
as an earl, 36–8, 71, 146–7, 158–9, 160, 162, 190, 197–9, as Earl of Huntingdon, 12, 38, 40, 146–7, 160–62, 183–6, 189–90, 196, 197–9, 234, 236–7
epitaphs, 183–6, 188–9, 247
grave, 37, 158, 174, 178–90, 212, 213
legend of, 11–13, 24–6, 32–3, 40–41, 115, 118–19, 135–7, 139, 144, 193–7, 199–201
as an ally of Richard 'the Lionheart', 12, 36, 38–9, 41–2, 44–6, 49, 67, 72, 130, 144, 146, 159, 161–2, 166, 170–71, 198–201, 216, 224
as an enemy of Prince John, 11–12, 41, 45, 72, 130, 136, 144, 146–7, 170–71, 194, 198–200; *see also* Fulk Fitzwarin
as a leader of peasants' revolt, 12, 45, 136, 149, 160, 170, 194–6, 202
Maid Marian, *see* Maid Marian; *see also* relationships with women

as Sir Robin of Locksley, 12,
149, 159–60, 162, 163, 165,
170–71, 244
to rob from the rich to give to
the poor, 24, 118, 131
as a Saxon, 11–12, 28, 32, 41,
74, 146, 149, 170–71, 196,
199–202
place names, 107, 173–4
plays
*Robin Hood and the
Knight/Sheriff*, 20, 137–9, 143,
240, 243
Robin Hood and the Friar,
137–8
see also Munday, Anthony
reasons for being outlawed, 11,
26–7, 36, 52, 54, 56–8, 64, 66–7,
69, 71–4, 83–5, 89, 102, 104,
109–10, 115, 119, 129–30,
146–7, 158–9, 162, 198–200,
204–6, 208, 210–11, 229
relationship with
the common folk, 12, 37, 45,
53–4, 136, 152, 160, 170, 180,
195, 205
the king, *see* Edward 'our
comely king'; *see also* as
an ally of Richard 'the
Lionheart'
Little John, 19–20, 27, 31, 43,
52, 54–5, 64, 66–7, 74–5,
80–82, 103, 108, 131, 177–8,
190, 233, 246
the Merry Men, *see* Merry
Men; *see also* Robin Hood,
characteristics attributed to,
fellowship
religious officials, 19, 22, 43,
84–5, 108, 115, 118, 120–22,
126–9, 133, 135, 137–41, 145,
148, 152, 162, 203–5, 210–11
the Sheriff of Nottingham, *see*
Sheriff of Nottingham
women, 29, 32, 119, 134, 149,

152, 158, 178, 210–11; *see also*
Maid Marian; Clorinda,
Queen of the Shepherds
skills attributed to
archery, 12, 19, 20, 22–3, 24,
25–26, 31, 36, 43, 54, 56–7,
77, 135–6, 143, 152–3, 154,
175, 178, 179, 181, 182, 183–4,
195, 210, 222, 226, 247
capable fighter and swordsman,
12, 20, 28–9, 31–2, 54, 56, 57,
58, 73, 77, 103, 121, 135–6,
138, 143, 147, 152, 164–6,
194–5, 210
military capability, 23, 55–7, 72,
77, 80, 102, 109, 119, 136, 147,
210–11
trickery and use of disguise,
20–21, 27, 82, 115, 128, 142,
147, 170, 204, 241
social status, *see* yeomen
rhymes, 11, 17–18, 25, 28, 33,
39–40, 54, 57, 65, 67, 74, 122,
139, 141, 151–2, 154, 166, 193,
206, 222, 226, 242
as a surname and criminal label,
48–9, 155–6, 203–4, 207
as a tourist attraction, 173–4
Rockingham Forest
Roger of Doncaster, or Donkesley,
176–7, 246; *see also* Red Roger
Rolle, Richard, 106, 235
roncin, *see* horses
Rutland, 40, 234
rymes, *see* Robin Hood, rhymes of

St Andrews, 68, 215
St Anne's Well, *see* Robin Hood,
place names
sacraments, 52, 121–2
Sad Shepherd, The, 148
Saladin, 34
Saladin Tithe, 35
sanctuary, right of, 129, 238–9
Saxon golden age, *see* Norman Yoke

Saxon green, *see* Lincoln green
Saylis, the, 106–7, 235
Scadlock, Scarlet, Scarlett,
  Scarlock, Scathelocke, *see* Will
  Scarlock
Scotichronicon, 26–8, 46, 51–3, 56,
  58, 66, 68, 74, 82, 113, 121–2,
  126, 141, 157, 169, 205–6, 213,
  243, 245
Scotland, 26–7, 29, 38, 46, 47,
  62–4, 68–9, 87–8, 94, 99, 143,
  157–8, 190, 199, 206, 238, 242
Scott, Sir Walter, 103, 140, 170,
  199–201
Scottish Wars of Independence, 88
*Sepulchral Monuments of Great
  Britain*, *see* Gough, Richard
Shakespeare, William, 167–8, 196
Shakespeare's Golden World,
  167–8, 194
Shakespeare's plays, 167–9
Sheriff of Nottingham, 12, 19–23,
  27–8, 41–3, 53, 56, 57, 77,
  82–3, 84, 88, 103, 112–15,
  120–22, 127, 128–9, 135, 137,
  165, 168, 171, 191, 194, 204–5,
  208–9, 226
Sheriff of Nottingham's cook, 22,
  73, 78, 82, 108, 113, 164
Sheriff of Nottingham's wife, 21
Sheriff, office of the, 42, 50–51, 88,
  113–15, 129–30, 208–9
Sheriffs, 28, 48, 52, 95–7, 105,
  112–15, 129, 212
Sherwood Forest, 12, 18, 20, 24,
  26, 32, 40, 44, 56, 65, 72, 104,
  106, 110, 113, 168, 191, 194, 196,
  202, 205, 215
Shooter's Hill, 152–3, 243
Skelbrooke, 107
Skell, River, 139
Sloane Manuscript, 38, 71,
  139, 141, 159–60, 162,
  181–2
society, *see* fraternity

South America, 45, 167
squires, 57, 78–80, 108, 126, 131,
  163–6
Stafford, Robert, *see* Friar Tuck, as
  an alias
Staynton, Elizabeth de, 181–2
Stirling Bridge, battle of, 63
Stow, John, 158
Stow, Percy, 171
Straw, Jack, 200
Stukeley, William, 38, 197

*Talkyng of the Munke and Robyn
  Hode*, *see* Monk, *Robin Hood
  and the*
Temple of Solomon, 90, 212
Tennyson, Alfred Lord, 173
Teutonic Knights, Order of, 92–3
Thierry, Jacques Nicholas
  Augustin, 170, 199
Thoresby, Ralph, 185–6, 189
Throsby, John, 187–8
Troyes, Council of, 90
turcoman, *see* horses
Tutbury, 155
Tyler, Wat, 156, 200

Urban II, Pope, 89–90
Urban IV, Pope, 50
usury in the Middle Ages, 91, 117,
  133

Vatican, 93, 95
Venables, Piers, 155
Vienne, Council of, 97
Virgin Mary, 19, 22, 23, 29, 108,
  119, 121–4, 127, 134, 142, 149,
  176, 198, 211, 236
*Vision of William Concerning
  Piers Plowman, The*, *see* Piers
  Plowman

Wakefield, Jolly Pinder of, 163,
  165–6
Wakefield, Robert Hood of, 208

Wales, 47, 61–2, 64, 143, 158, 211, 242

Wallace, William, 63–4, 69, 87, 196, 209, 215

Warwick, Sir Guy of, 163–4

Watling Street, 106–7

Watson, John, 189

Wemyss, Sir John of, 68

Wendenal, William de, Sheriff of Nottingham, 42

Wentbridge, 107, 235

Well, Robin Hood's, see Robin Hood, place names

West Riding, 105–6

Will Scarlock, 54–5, 73–4, 81–2, 102–3, 110, 132, 137, 141, 166, 171, 177, 191, 226, 239, 242, 244
grave, 191

Will Stutly, 170

William I 'the Conqueror', King of England, 41

William I 'the Lion', King of Scotland, 38, 199, 244

William IX, Count of Poitiers, son of Henry II 'Curtmantle', 33

William of Cloudesley, see Adam Bell

Windsor Forest, 43–4

Wrangbrook, 107

Wright, Thomas, 203, 220

Wyntoun, Andrew of, 26, 28–9, 33, 46, 49, 63–8, 85, 157, 197, 204, 206–7, 221, 228

Yardley, 40

yeomen, 17, 24, 36, 40, 43–4, 46, 56, 57, 71–3, 75–9, 81, 102, 108, 134, 138, 147, 151–2, 154, 156, 158, 161, 166, 173, 193, 195–7, 199, 201, 203, 205, 207–8, 210, 213, 240

Yeomen of the Crown, 19, 220, 227

Yeoman of the Forest, 76–7

yonge man, 75–6

York, 48, 105, 183–4, 187, 189, 212
abbey of St Mary's, 21–2, 122, 133
abbot of, 22, 121, 126–7, 131, 199
Archbishop of, 133
monk 'high cellarer' of, 22, 43, 108, 118, 122, 126–8, 162, 166, 204

Yorkshire, 20, 37, 104–8, 113, 115, 139, 151, 160, 162, 174, 176, 208–9, 211–14, 223, 234, 249